"I used to believe that life was the result of being either lucky, coincidental or earned through plain old-fashioned hard work.

Growing up in the small town of Sheboygan, Wisconsin, the author delves into his childhood, college years at the University of Wisconsin, and rise to affluence in his adult years. While the work certainly contains biographical elements, its crux revolves around the juxtaposition of the discovery of faith with a seemingly certain-death event.

With chapters divided into short sections, and scripture verses gracing many of the pages, the reading experience is seamless and easy. More importantly, the reader is left upon a cliffhanger, pondering the outcome of the author's encounter with the two-thousand-pound Cape buffalo that the African people nicknames "Black Death." Meanwhile, the reader learns about the writer's upbringing, from teaching skiing and the rowing prowess that resulted in a national championship to completing a ten-week Alpha course, which he compares to getting a diploma in Christian discipleship.

Interestingly, the author highlights what no one wants to hear: everyone has that Cape buffalo in their lives, the moment that brings them to the realization that they must walk in the steps of the Lord. Where a bow and arrow were moot, a small brown Bible was the difference between life and death for the author, an unquestionable turning point to faith and healing, both physical and spiritual. In the process of an extensive recovery, the author uses verses to provide lessons on the steps one can take to their own salvation and finding their own "heaven on earth." From his own experience, the author not only sheds light on faith but sparks a pertinent conversation on the dynamic between trophy hunting versus being a steward of wildlife. Overall, the memoir is engaging throughout and delivers a unique, refreshing spin on prototypical faith-based works."

—RECOMMENDED by the U.S. Review of Books

"Laurence W. Trotter II's brush with death anchors this inspirational memoir about God, miracles, and finding a greater purpose in life.

In 2012, adventure enthusiast Trotter found salvation during an African hunting expedition. Trotter was attacked by a Cape buffalo, an animal that hunting experts call the "Black Death." Miraculously, Trotter heard a voice during the attack guiding him to survival: "Stay on your back," the voice said. "Put your boots…between the horns and push away with your feet."

The African trackers and professional hunters who witnessed the attack agreed that "if [Trotter] hadn't done exactly what [he] did, [he] would have been killed." Though his mangled shoulder would require extensive surgeries and rehabilitation, Trotter walked away from the attack, attributing his survival to what he believes was God's voice, sparing his life for the greater purpose of sharing God's realness with others. Trotter's memoir is a well written, effortless read. Trotter gains momentum in Chapter 7, focusing on his message the rest of the way.

Trotter accomplished his goal of "God being the main character" in this book; the later chapters center on God's involvement in Trotter's spiritual and physical healing. While many memoirists fail to connect with readers, Trotter finds the common thread through his story and ours: He believes we all have Cape buffalo stories of miracles and divine intervention, reaffirming "that God is alive…real and proactive in all our lives today."

Trotter's testimony should inspire Christians to look for the hand of God guiding their lives and will likely be enthusiastically passed to others."

—BlueInk Review

"A man recounts his long road to spiritual maturity, a journey marked by a gruesome accident, in this memoir.

Trotter had all the worldly trappings of conventional success: wealth and its appurtenances, an accomplished career as an entrepreneur, and a happy family. But he experienced a tedious absence of complete fulfillment, a discontentment he could not comprehensively articulate. In the troubled wake of the author's divorce, that sense of dissatisfaction intensified, and finally he took the advice of his eldest daughter, Amy, to seek solace and guidance in his Christian faith. Trotter began to read the Bible regularly—he calls it a "central component of my life"—and started to frequent church as well. He even had a mystical experience during a religious retreat, a vision that left him "trembling in awe." Still, the culminating moment of his spiritual development came in 2012 while he was on a hunting expedition on the plains of South Africa. He was charged and gruesomely mauled by a Cape buffalo, a beast so dangerous it has earned the moniker Black Death. Abrie, the professional hunter leading the safari, subsequently said he saw the author bathed in a column of light and an angel overhead "boxing the horns of the beast."

In his heartfelt book, Trotter, with impressive candor and unabashed emotion, denotes this as his turning point, the event that finalized his utter devotion to God. This lucid story of spiritual enlightenment offers some rich and thought-provoking details that many Christians will find comforting. But ultimately, this is a familiar, even formulaic account of finding God in the detritus of catastrophe. Even the crucial lesson—openness and submission to God and the complete authority of the Bible—won't surprise believers or persuade skeptics. In addition, the author writes with a self-confidence that rules out philosophical circumspection: "Why can't we experience the Kingdom of Heaven on Earth as Jesus asked us to pray in the Lord's Prayer? The answer is, of course, we can."

A frank but familiar account of an extensive spiritual odyssey."

—Kirkus Reviews

"Seeing the Light Through Black Death is a fascinating religious memoir that draws lessons from a life-changing cape buffalo attack.

Laurence W. Trotter II's memoir *Seeing the Light Through Black Death* draws spiritual lessons from personal events, including a near fatal cape buffalo attack.

Trotter was born in 1954 on a Spokane Air Force base. From an early age, he spent much time outdoors with his father, skiing, hunting, and fishing; he became an accomplished rower through the Boy Scouts. His fascination with the outdoors continued into adulthood; in 2012, it led him to travel to South Africa for an exhilarating hunting trip. There, he was attacked by a buffalo.

The book prefaces the attack with explanations of cape buffalo themselves, covering their physical appearance, behavior, and predators; it discusses trophy hunting, including arguments for and those against the sport, with relevant statistics and references to organizations on both sides of the debate. This informative work results in a broad overview of the circumstances related to Trotter's attack; it is followed by striking details of the attack, including the speed of the charging bull, and the fact that one member of the hunting team scrambled for his gun in the course of it. Trotter's sense of fear and desperation during the incident is clear; the grueling, emotional process of treatment and healing that followed, which included multiple surgeries, is also covered.

The book's sections are thematic; they concentrate on gleaning lessons from Trotter's experiences, and their messages are easy to identify. For instance, while he's home and waiting for surgery, Trotter reflects on the three weeks that brought him to this point; he explains the period as a blessing in disguise, one that helped him to realize that there was a reason for his survival. Quotes from the Christian scriptures are shared, too; they are separated from the main text and support Trotter's takes on topics including love, purpose, compassion, and giving back.

Trotter moves from his own story toward encouraging others to recognize and find comfort in God's presence during the defining periods of their lives. All of its chapters return to this notion, helping to bind it together, from its reflections on a national championship win in rowing that is attributed to prayer, to Trotter's daughter's uplifting recovery from a life-threatening medical condition.

Seeing the Light Through Black Death is a fascinating religious memoir that draws lessons from a life-changing cape buffalo attack."

—Clarion Review

"Larry, I thoroughly enjoyed your testimony – my heart was warmed. I am the pastor at John's church in Mayville. Your near death experience and the miracles that you encountered throughout your life are certainly a worthy witness to share with others. I agree that we all have a Black Death story or two, although not always a near death experience, and that how we perceive God and our faith play a role in whether we see life as full of miracles and angels or just seemingly random events. In my faith journey, I believe that I see acts of God's love and grace in many people that I encounter – I often think of them as angels on earth that are building God's kingdom on earth. While I have not had similar experiences like you share with an angel guiding your movements and reactions, I truly believe that God works in our lives in different and miraculous ways. May God's blessings surround you."

—Steve DeLano

"Congratulations! I loved your book. Thanks for giving of your life to write it. I hope that it is read in church book clubs and that it ignites a spiritual revival. I'm so proud of you."

—The Rev. Arthur B. Hancock

SEEING THE LIGHT THROUGH BLACK DEATH
Salvation in the African Savanna

Laurence W. Trotter II

Papa's Cape Buffalo Attack - Ellianna Martha Malkowski, age three, 2012

Order this book online at www.trafford.com
or email orders@trafford.com

To order the actual live video of the Cape Buffalo Stalk and Attack, go to the
following website: www.SeeingtheLightThroughBlackDeath.com

Most Trafford titles are also available at major online book retailers.

Print information available on the last page.

ISBN: 978-1-6987-0213-1 (sc)
ISBN: 978-1-6987-0215-5 (hc)
ISBN: 978-1-6987-0214-8 (e)

Library of Congress Control Number: 2020912455

Trafford rev. 06/15/2021

 www.trafford.com

North America & international
toll-free: 844-688-6899 (USA & Canada)
fax: 812 355 4082

CONTENTS

ACKNOWLEDGMENTS

With the utmost honor and reverence, I fervently acknowledge the ever-presence of God and the workings of the Holy Spirit in my life and writing this book. Furthermore, with the greatest respect possible, I honor my four children, their spouses, and their children, my treasures, who have all contributed in significant ways to this witness of a lifetime of miracles. Bless you all, and thank you from your dad and papa.

From friends and teachers at US Grant grade school, Urban Junior High School, and North High School Sheboygan, Wisconsin, to the coaches, the boys in the boats of the University of Wisconsin rowing teams, and the Spirit of Henley 1973 to the professors and mentors of every endeavor I explored at Madison, I honor you all for teaching, leading, and sharing your best.

My special thank you is extended to Prof. James A. Graaskamp and Coach Doug Neil. Praise to thee our alma mater. For all the counselors, leaders, and fellow scouts who helped shape my spirit through the programs of the Boy Scouts of America in Wisconsin as well as the Philmont Scout Ranch, New Mexico, I salute you all with honor and thanksgiving.

For all the Professional Ski Instructors of America national demonstration team leaders, members, and education staff who mentored and trained me, my sincere thank you. To all my amazing friends, accountability partners, brothers, and sisters in Christ, all glory be to God, with special appreciation and brotherly love, more specifically honoring my beautiful bride, Diane; the Honorable Judge John R. Storck; Dr. Randall L. Zieth; the Vicar Emeritus Mark G. Huggenvik; the Reverend Stuart Brooks Keith III; Mr. Alan W. Comerer; and their wives. Thank you for creating in me a new heart, Alpha International, National Cursillo Movement and Episcopal Church of the USA, Monarch Cursillo Organization of Wisconsin, Colorado Episcopal Cursillo, and the Episcopal Church of the Transfiguration Vail, Colorado.

The twelve chapters are dedicated to God's messengers, the twelve apostles. *Seeing the Light through Black Death, Salvation in the African Savanna* is dedicated to God's clear message and command: "No more extreme pursuits. Focus on God and family the rest of your life." This includes my personal dedication to the ministry of sharing this message and witnesses experienced over my lifetime. As a paramount prayer in response to God's miracle and message, I lift my ultimate thankfulness and gratitude to God in the name of the Father, Son, and Holy Spirit, who saved my physical and spiritual life. All glory be to our awesome God.

Furthermore, this book is dedicated to my wife Diane's family and my family, both living on Earth now and living eternally in Heaven. To my two brothers and their extended families, our relatives, and especially Mom and Dad, I beseech thee to hear my thank you, good Lord. To our immediate family: Diane's three daughters—Emily and her husband, Tim, and their children Greta, Charlie, and Sammy; Jane and her husband, Luke, and baby Everleigh; and Maggie and her husband, Phillip and newborn George—my two daughters—Amy and her husband, Aaron, and their children Peyton and Chance; and Martha and her husband, David, and their children Ellianna, Preston, Gavin, and Gabriel—and my two sons Matthew, and Michael and his wife, Christina, and newborn Camden.

Finally, this book is dedicated to all the future additions to our family and all families all over the world with their own Cape buffalo stories.

All thanks be to God. Amen.

INTRODUCTION

*I am the vine; you are the branches. If you remain in me and I in
you, you will bear much fruit; apart from me you can do nothing.*
—John 15:5 (NIV)

The bull thought I was dead. He looked up from the shattered mess
he made of my bow and arrows and stared directly into my eyes.
His empty gaze pierced through me while he prepared to mount his
final charge. I knew my life was over. This was the day I was going
to die. Only a miracle could change that. As it turned out, that was
exactly what happened.

This is a true story. Not your typical outdoor exploits set in the
wilderness pitting good guys against bad but rather a metamorphosis
that would question virtually everything I knew about my life,—who
I was, what I needed to change, and how I was supposed to live.
It's a story about redemption and working out my salvation, a story
about how I seemingly had it all—a successful string of businesses,
a long-term marriage, four loving children, and more friends than I
could count. The only part of the equation missing was me,—my true
purpose for being on this planet and a deeper relationship with God.

Do Everything Without Grumbling

¹² Therefore, my dear friends, as you have always
obeyed—not only in my presence but now much more
in my absence—continue to work out your salvation...
Philippians 2:12 (NIV)

CHAPTER ONE: INTRODUCTION

Looking back from age sixty-six over the course of my first forty-eight years, I hoped I'd become a success. I had all the "stuff" to prove it: cars, homes, expensive sports equipment, and —all the manmade material possessions I thought I was supposed to own to live a full and meaningful life. Yet I still sensed something was missing. I couldn't put my finger on it, but I knew there was a void that desperately needed filling, and I'd never know peace until I found it. I pleaded to God, again and again, to send me an answer, to communicate with me in some manner. But God's time is different than ours.

Year after year, I pushed through life, convincing myself that I was doing the best I could with what I had to work with. And I was until 2002, when my eldest daughter, Amy, convinced me to open myself as a vessel to receive the Word of God. Without knowing exactly why, I was finally ready to receive direction from God about what I should be doing with my life. But it didn't come in the mail. It didn't magically pop up as a tweet on my smartphone. Instead, the ultimate message I'd been waiting for came barreling down on me ten years later in the form of a two-thousand-pound Cape buffalo. And the beast was intent on making sure I received it. Those twenty seconds turned my life upside down physically, emotionally, and spiritually. I've never been the same since.

Seeing the Light through Black Death – Salvation in the African Savanna is also a success story, how a little kid from Sheboygan, Wisconsin, grew up as an honor student and award-winning athlete, a successful businessman, and father of four. But that's not what made my life a success. It took an angel to finally deliver God's true purpose for me in the middle of a Cape buffalo attack: focus on God and family for the rest of your days here on Earth. It wasn't until after Black Death ("Black Death" is the descriptive name given to the African Buffalo) attacked me, that I learned that everyone has a Cape buffalo story. Some have more than one. But it's up to us to become willing to accept our destiny and walk with Christ.

This book is divided into twelve chapters as God's twelve messengers, the twelve apostles, beginning with this introduction, followed by "Chapter Two - All or Nothing at All," where I start down the road in pursuit of excellence, embracing the Boy Scouts of America while struggling to understand where spirituality fit into my life. The precedent to my team's spectacular victories at the 1973 Henley Royal Regatta, graduation from the University of Wisconsin, and my first success with understanding the Word of God. You couldn't create a more poignant story.

In "Chapter Three - Making God Laugh," I thought I was invincible. The world was my oyster. After discovering the thrill of successfully creating a new business, turning around bankruptcy, and the successful sale of the company with my dad at Colonial Container Corporation, I embarked on a career caring for and ministering to seniors, pioneering my own company, Senior American Housing, Incorporated. This led to an invitation to Washington, D.C., meeting with our district congressmen and being presented the "Entrepreneur of the Year" award by Pres. George W. Bush. It was also the time when I started to embrace one of my life's passions: teaching skiing in Vail, Colorado.

"Chapter Four - Challenges and Solutions for Modern Christians" recounts the most important turning points, or waypoints if you're a navigator, in my life: embracing the Bible and unconditionally accepting the Word of God. The little brown Bible I received from the Gideons International became my lifelong friend, accompanying me wherever I went—perched high in tree stands above the deer woods of Wisconsin, traveling on airplanes, to the fateful day in Africa. Reading the Bible daily triggered a period of time of metamorphosis when my faith began to mature exponentially while I simultaneously participated in Cursillo weekends and discovered ways to begin serving God here on Earth.

Even though I've tried to be a steward of wildlife and the environment, I understand that the world of hunting can be controversial, particularly the multimillion-dollar business of "Big Five" trophy hunting in Africa. So in "Chapter Five - Trophy Hunters versus Elmer Fudd," I thought it would be worth spending time discussing the hunting industry, the good and the bad. Even before Cecil, Zimbabwe's beloved twelve-year-old lion, was stalked and killed in 2015 by an American trophy hunter, hunting animals for sport has been controversial. At the same time, hunting in Africa infuses vital resources into local communities for building schools, hospitals, and water systems. I'm hoping anyone considering themselves a steward of our environment would contemplate the many complex aspects of this discussion. But this is a story about miracles, not a pro or con argument for or against hunting, even though an African venue became the location of the most dramatic miracle.

In 2012, I lived through the most meaningful experience in a series of metamorphoses. I was financially secure, recently divorced, and fully embracing my growing relationship with God. It was time to treat myself by checking an item off my bucket list: a monthlong hunting adventure in the savanna plains of Africa. "Chapter Six - Meet the Dagga Boys" sets the stage for encountering African Cape buffalo for my first time. Notoriously known as "Black Death," they're considered one of the most dangerous animals on the planet. Meeting a Dagga Boy was Satan's temptation enticing me to take on Black Death with a bow and arrow.

When purchasing my Hoyt compound bow over a decade before encountering Black Death, for hunting elk in Colorado and deer in Wisconsin, I never in my wildest imagination suspected it would be useless when attacked by a Cape buffalo on July 3, 2012. In "Chapter Seven - Four Men and a Bakkie," I share what it's like to come face-to-face with Black Death on its terms. After days leading up to the confrontation, it was over in a matter of seconds. Sprawled out on the ground, I was staring down death until a miracle happened: I was rescued by the hand of God and an intervening angel. Apparently, it was not yet my time to die.

As a healthy, resilient man, I didn't spend much time in hospitals. Staying in shape and avoiding predictable risks, I'd led a medically uncomplicated life until the day of the attack. Those twenty seconds made up for a lifetime of sound judgment and safe practices. In "Chapter Eight - The Little Brown Bible and a Cross," begins the long, grueling journey from the threshold of death to my full and miraculous recovery. The healing would include not one but three major surgeries and countless hours of physical and spiritual therapy. The entire process is a testament to the boundless support of medical professionals, spiritual advisors, friends, and family spread over two continents.

Stranded in South Africa after the first of three major surgeries, I finally had time to confront my predicament. In "Chapter Nine - Nothing Says Africa like a Zebra," I continued down my road to recovery and giving my utmost to my relationship with God as I attempted to salvage the remnants of an adventure gone wrong. Even with all I'd been through, I still managed to squeeze a modicum of appreciation out of the immensity of experiences South Africa had to offer. Then the nightmare took a turn for the worse. I was evacuated back to my home in Vail, Colorado, for the final leg of my long, arduous recovery.

Over the progression of my path of healing many spiritual questions were spinning in my mind: Do we really believe in angels? Or are they just ornaments we put on the top of Christmas trees once a year? Do we believe in miracles? Or are they just stories written in scripture by saints shortly after Jesus's time on Earth? There are hundreds of books written about both, so is there truth to them?

Have you ever contemplated the meaning of life? How about the meaning of Heaven? Most Christians spend their entire lives preparing for the afterlife. But what if we didn't have to wait until the end of our time on Earth to begin enjoying Heaven? In "Chapter Ten - On Earth as It Is in Heaven," I share with readers what I've learned since my Cape buffalo attack, how each and every one of us can influence the quality of our lives while still on Earth regardless of our phase in life or our physical age. I further share the key to enjoying Heaven on Earth. The key to enjoying Heaven on Earth lies in adopting a proper perspective. A perspective that includes making choices about how we can live our lives now, how we share space with our fellow man and choices that will ensure that we will see Jesus sitting at the right hand of our Father in Heaven for eternity.

When you think about it, time helps us separate events. Accordingly, between the time I was attacked by a Cape buffalo and my perceived urgency to share a true miracle, now seems the appropriate time to reveal my witness. In "Chapter Eleven - Why so Long?" I discovered there's a time and place for everything. After sharing my story with hundreds of fellow worshippers, friends, and family, I realized that God's message was worthy of a larger audience. But it took over seven years to understand the scope of God's message and how best to share it with others. Had I attempted to publish the story during my early recovery, I would have missed all the important lessons calling me to move beyond keeping the miracles written in this book to myself. Discernment takes time. Discernment involves listening to the One who sent the answer to decades of prayers.

In "Chapter Twelve - Epilogue," I pause to ponder all the amazing gifts God has bestowed upon me and what I can do to give back to others. That fateful day of the Cape buffalo attack, God delivered a strong message about how I needed to change my life. In no uncertain terms, God commanded me, "No more extreme pursuits. Focus on

God and family for the rest of your life." That's exactly what I've been doing since.

Since the attack by Black Death, I've learned that everyone has a Cape buffalo story. It might represent twenty seconds like mine or stretch out over a lifetime of challenges. It might happen to just you, or it might affect your entire family. Whatever the situation, the answer to all of our stories is the same.

This book is not intended to be my autobiography or a hunting story or an adventure one might read in *National Geographic* magazine. Instead, it's my opportunity to share with you the Word of God relating to miracles I've witnessed and how God can help you achieve Heaven on Earth and the peace of God, transcending all understanding. By opening the eyes of our hearts, allowing ourselves to become vessels of the Holy Spirit; trusting God, asking for God's forgiveness; surrendering to Jesus as He finishes His work on us by molding us into who we were designed to be is no easy task, but hopefully, for you, it won't require a Cape buffalo attack.

Laurence W. Trotter II

CHAPTER TWO

ALL OR NOTHING AT ALL

³ Children are a heritage from the Lord,
offspring a reward from him.
⁴ Like arrows in the hands of a warrior
are children born in one's youth.
⁵ Blessed is the man
whose quiver is full of them.
They will not be put to shame
when they contend with their opponents in court.
—Psalm 127:3–5 (NIV)

For as long as I can remember, I've always seemed to thrive in the face of new challenges, the opportunities to learn new skills and techniques, and expand my knowledge about additional facets of life and then doing them the best I can as I continue to improve. Whether it's skiing waist-deep powder in the back bowls of Vail, studying the New Testament, or learning how to be a better human being overall, I've been intrinsically motivated to pursue excellence. Inspired to a level where it's never been enough for me to simply learn a new skill or gain new knowledge. There's always been a need to feel deep in my heart that I'm taking my endeavors as far as I can go physically, mentally, and spiritually. All thanks be to God and my parents' influence.

Looking back, I have my parents to thank for a full spectrum of opportunities they provided. I was born on February 24, 1954, in Spokane, Washington, on a "Strategic Air Command" (SAC) air force base. After graduating from the University of Wisconsin, my mother, Elizabeth Alice Edwards, and my father, Laurence Whittemore

Trotter, were married on December 20, 1950. In those war days, life and timing were different. My father was drafted into the air force immediately following college in 1950 and received top-secret military orders to be stationed at Andersen Air Force Base in Guam for (4) four years of active duty. He was part of a top-secret squad of military police responsible for the security and transportation of twenty nuclear bombs from somewhere deep in New Mexico to the island in the South Pacific, in the event they'd be needed during the Korean War (1950-53). In my early years, my mother had her hands full keeping track of me; my younger brother, James Edwards Trotter; and my youngest brother, Robert Turner Trotter. One might say my dad liked to run a tight ship, inevitably the result of the military life he lived during those war years and living on a Strategic Air Command Base. His only brother, William, also served in the military as a career naval officer, while my grandfather was a salesman and the music director of their Episcopal Church. My great-grandfather was the Reverend William Ramsay Trotter, born on November 30, 1856, and the Episcopal priest at the Trinity Episcopal Church in Bristol, Rhode Island.

My mom was the glue that held our family together. My brother Rob always liked to label people with goofy names as a way to entertain us. My name was "Hogan," after the popular television series *Hogan's Heroes* because I was always making plans and organizing activities. His nickname for my mom was "Lucy," after Lucille Ball from the *I Love Lucy* series. That was eventually abbreviated to "Lu," so we liked to call my mom Lu the Glue.

Ours was a true University of Wisconsin family. My maternal grandfather earned his Juris Doctorate there and was a successful attorney in the Superior, Wisconsin, and Duluth, Minnesota, areas. During the great depression, he became a bankruptcy attorney and then a federal bankruptcy judge. Stricken with blindness from retinitis pigmentosa, he literally practiced law under the auspices of "blind justice." All three of my mother's brothers went there too, going on to become successful attorneys, followed by my dad and my mom, where she earned her degree in medical diagnosis. Ultimately, I followed in their footsteps, beginning as a freshman in the fall of 1972, with my brothers close behind. In summary, my family of clergy, attorneys, military, and loving members were all role models that laid the foundation for my personal spiritual journey.

After my dad was honorably discharged from the air force in the mid-1950s, he worked in sales with several different companies. Initially, he sold policies in the insurance business, and then in 1960, he switched to the paper and packaging business, first for the International Paper Company and then for Hoerner Waldorf, which eventually became the Jefferson Smurfit Corporation.

As a freshman in college, I had aspirations of becoming an orthopedic surgeon, so I declared myself premed. At the same time, I took a lot of business courses and triple majored in economics, business management, and real estate development. Ultimately, I ended up graduating from the University of Wisconsin School of Business.

Who could have predicted as a college boy that years later, I would fulfill my purpose in life by combining my interest in medicine with a real estate education to pioneer a new concept in assisted living for elderly in Wisconsin, a model design accomplished in concert with Gov. Tommy Thompson, Secretary of DHFS Joseph Leann, and the Wisconsin Housing and Economic Development Authority? This became my passion and ministry for over twenty-eight years.

> I believe that spot in time or waypoint was one of the most important acts of divine intervention I've experienced, being raised by the hand of God to more than I could be on my own. Even though I worked hard in school, at the time, I had no idea where I was headed or that I would ultimately be working with and ministering to the elderly, so I just pushed along. Ultimately, it would take a string of miracles to actualize this true calling. Had I been a more mature Christian at the time, I would have known that God had my back from the beginning.[11] *"For I know the plans I have for you," declares the Lord, "plans to prosper you and not to harm you, plans to give you hope and a future."*
> —Jeremiah 29:11 (NIV)

My parents each contributed uniquely to who I am today, but more notably taught me the foundational building blocks and preparation for a fascinating spiritual journey that would unfold. My dad taught me the "hard skills," beginning with skiing, hunting, fishing, shooting guns, archery, and a love of the great outdoors. He would, as I grew up, mentor me on connecting with people, building rapport, and long-term personal relationships and friendships that endure to this day. I learned the "soft skills" from my mom: love, family, and more intimate interpersonal relationships. Raised as a Presbyterian, she felt it was important for all us kids to be exposed to our own sense of spirituality beginning with Sunday school at St. Andrews Episcopal Church in Madison and, from 1960 through high school, Grace Episcopal Church in Sheboygan, Wisconsin. That's where you'd find us Sunday mornings as part of what we called at that point in my life as going to church.

I can remember my dad complaining about being "over churched" as a child, so he attended services less frequently—a scenario lots of kids our age seemed to share at the time. But even though he didn't participate in weekly services, he contributed in other ways by supporting the Episcopal Church behind the scenes. In the final years of his life, I was fortunate enough to bring him back into the fold at the Episcopal Church in Vail, where he attended services regularly on Sundays as well as Bible studies—all the activities he missed as an adult but enjoyed until he passed away on September 26, 2018.

Ironically, my real spiritual journey began when I was seven years old, starting in the Cub Scouts. When I turned eleven years old, I was eligible for the Boy Scouts, so I jumped at the opportunity to move up. My father had been in the Boy Scouts too, so he thought it would be good for us boys to experience the great outdoors classroom and its natural "cathedrals." He also contributed by being involved with the leadership of our troop.

Two of the first ideals you're introduced to in the Boy Scouts are the oath and the twelve points of the scout law:

- **A Scout is Trustworthy**. A Scout tells the truth. He is honest, and he keeps his promises. People can depend on him.
- **A Scout is Loyal**. A Scout is true to his family, friends, Scout leaders, school, and nation.
- **A Scout is Helpful**. A Scout cares about other people. He willingly volunteers to help others without expecting payment or reward.
- **A Scout is Friendly**. A Scout is a friend to all. He is a brother to other Scouts. He offers his friendship to people of all races

and nations and respects them even if their beliefs and customs are different from his own.

- **A Scout is Courteous**. A Scout is polite to everyone regardless of age or position. He knows that using good manners makes it easier for people to get along.
- **A Scout is Kind**. A Scout knows there is strength in being gentle. He treats others as he wants to be treated. *Without good reason, he does not harm or kill any living thing.*
- **A Scout is Obedient**. A Scout follows the rules of his family, school, and troop. He obeys the laws of his community and country. If he thinks these rules and laws are unfair, he tries to have them changed in an orderly manner rather than disobeying them.
- **A Scout is Cheerful**. A Scout looks for the bright side of life. He cheerfully does tasks that come his way. He tries to make others happy.
- **A Scout is Thrifty**. A Scout works to pay his own way and to help others. He saves for the future. He protects and conserves natural resources. He carefully uses time and property.
- **A Scout is Brave**. A Scout can face danger although he is afraid. He has the courage to stand for what he thinks is right even if others laugh at him or threaten him.
- **A Scout is Clean**. A Scout keeps his body and mind fit and clean. He chooses the company of those who live by high standards. He helps keep his home and community clean.
- **A Scout is Reverent**. A Scout is reverent toward God. He is faithful in his religious duties. He respects the beliefs of others.
- With the scout oath, we pledged,

On my honor, I will do my best
To do my duty to God and my country and to obey the Scout Law;
To help other people at all times;
To keep myself physically strong, mentally awake and morally straight.

Even though I was spiritually immature, the scouts helped plant some of the first seeds of my faith and spirituality that would continue to grow as an adult.

I took to Boy Scouts like a fish to water. I loved the opportunities of achieving goals, so by the time I completed the program, I'd earned the rank of Eagle Scout in as brief a time allowed by the organization. I started at age eleven, and a month before I turned thirteen in 1967, I'd already earned the rank of Eagle Scout. Twelve weeks later, I went through the Court of Awards and Honor for Eagle Scout. That was a big deal. As a young boy, it was huge. Less than 2 percent of all Boy Scouts earn that rank, I was blessed to earn the Eagle award. In retrospect, it turned out to be one of several momentous waypoints in my life.

Continuing to work my way through the scouting curriculum and earning bronze, gold, and silver palms enriched my motivation. Then further adding Scout Lifeguard, being elected to the Order of the Arrow and becoming a Brotherhood member—the service component of the Boy Scouts where we helped set up and take down the summer camps—as well as all the leadership roles available compiled to my burgeoning list of achievements.

Moving rapidly through the Boy Scout program and earning every possible award of achievement in as short a time possible built my confidence until at age fourteen when I finally ran up against a wall—an award called God and Country. Even though I didn't entirely understand what it entailed, I made it a point to add it to my list of scouting accomplishments. So I approached the first requirement by meeting with my spiritual advisor—in my case, an Episcopal priest. He told me, "Your first requirement is to start reading the Bible."

So enthusiastically, I dove into the book of Matthew in the New Testament. I got as far as the first few pages, struggling with an endless list of the thirty-three generations of man until I got stuck. No matter how many times I tried, I couldn't get through the words. It just didn't make any sense to me. So faced with my first taste of failure, I decided I'd have to leave that for another time. This failure was a moment in time where unknowingly, God was molding my character.

Throughout my life, I've always tried to improve. I've tried to become a better person in all components of my life, including my vocation and recreational interests. I often struggled, searching for ways to change myself into a better person, father, husband, brother, and friend. Many times we can't change on our own. We need a form of external help. In this particular case, it was my daughter Amy, who was my catalyst for an epic breakthrough. We prayed together, knocked on Heaven's door, and asked our Father in Heaven, Jesus, and the Holy Spirit to intervene in my life. After our communication with God, I started reading the Bible every day. I couldn't put it down.

Once again, I started reading the book of Matthew in the New Testament—the same wall I ran into so long ago. However, this time it was like connecting to the Internet. The Word of God began downloading with absolute clarity. This time the undertaking was different. As I became immersed in the scriptures, I felt Jesus speaking directly to me. Every time I picked up the Bible and started reading new scriptures, my thirst was insatiable. Reading the bible daily turned out to be one of the most significant waypoints of my life. From that point on, I never looked back.

Instead of simply looking for answers, I began reexamining other patterns in my life that had changed, many without me realizing the development. The first recollection that came to me was way back when my sixth-grade teacher called my mother and confessed to her that I wasn't doing well in school, in particular, taking tests. So my mother, coming from a family of highly educated attorneys (as well as her own accomplishments), took time to teach me how to study. Her tutoring was like an epiphany and turned out to be one of the major triumphs of my life. Overnight, I started excelling in school, all because, by that time, I was desperate for a solution, one that God would ultimately offer me. The answer had been right there all along, inside me during my young life. I just never took the time to understand it.

My first measurable success came in geography. When I was old enough to start taking tests, I went from doing very poorly to consistently scoring 100 percent. This performance continued to soar through the seventh grade when we started getting graded. Consistently earning straight As. Learning how to study properly, how to remember information, and score well on tests became sustainable. Impressive even to myself, I discovered that I was quite good at math. I loved its logic. Suddenly, it all made sense to me. From that point on, I consistently got straight As in math, biology, chemistry, physics, and all the other sciences.

At first, I struggled to find the answer to why I'd become so successful—literally overnight. Too young to recognize that God had always been working in my life, all I could come up with was "something just clicked." Nevertheless, I basked in the glory of achievement. The better I performed, the harder I worked.

Looking back, I have to acknowledge that it's human nature to be the best that we can be. Deep down inside, we all want to excel in the endeavors that are important to us. What stops many of us is the vehicle—or the lack of one. Oftentimes, we're so wrapped up in the problem we don't see the solution sitting right in front of us. But all good outcomes eventually arrive on time.

Even at that tender age, my math and science teachers encouraged me to start thinking about a career in medicine. Yet at the same time, I was still passionate about art. All my art teachers told me I should focus my efforts on my gifted artistic side of life. Still, others told me for doctors, the resolution lies in combining both because most successful practitioners combine math, science, and art in their practices. That's where I thought I was heading.

Once I started doing well in school, I was on a mission. Nothing in the world exceeded the thrill of doing well. Learning to surpass my own personal bests— would come in useful later when I was dropped into the pool of over thirty-seven thousand students at the University of Wisconsin who, like me, were graded on a curve. I was finally on my way.

During the 1960s and 1970s, Sheboygan, Wisconsin, was a close-knit community of about fifty-five thousand residents and a wonderful place to be a kid. Thriving in school, I even had time to compete in team sports and scout troop activities with my friends; some of which I've managed to maintain friendships with to this day. Spring sports like track and tennis were fun but didn't play football because I enjoyed being in the outdoors in the fall. I didn't play basketball because it would have competed with skiing in the winter, which has grown into a lifelong passion.

During the last day of our annual summer Boy Scout camp, we competed in a demanding event called the Around the Bay Relay on Cedar Lake, which started at the flagpole in front of the mess hall. The first runner was tasked with sprinting up a steep hill while carrying a baton. Once he reached the top, he handed it off to another runner, who had to cover a much longer distance, eventually arriving at the end of a point that jutted out into the lake. He handed the baton off to two people waiting in a rowboat—one person rowed, while the other was designated the coxswain —although looking back, he really didn't do much more than yell at the guy rowing.

The two had to row across the bay, and when they got to the other side, they handed the baton off to another person who ran it down to another point and then handed it off to two boys waiting in a canoe, who paddled it to the next leg of the race. When the canoe finally glided into the swimming area, they handed it off to a swimmer, who swam it to the beach and then ran it up to yet another runner who was waiting at the top of a set of stairs and back to the flagpole where the relay finished.

Originally, our troop assigned me to the canoe because I was the only one capable of paddling the canoe straight and fast. Once handed the baton, we'd blow past our competition. Then I rediscovered rowing at scout camp. Recalling fond memories of my cousin Pat Edwards teaching me how to row at age 10 at Uncle Rod's cabin (her dad) flashed into my mind's eye. Pat spotted me struggling with the oars in a small fishing boat and rescued me. At the time Pat was a summer camp counselor and shared her skills with me. Pat was my first rowing coach, then my second rowing coach was the waterfront director at scout camp.

About four years into scouting, I went for the Boy Scouts of America Lifeguard status, which entailed learning how to rescue someone from the water using both a canoe and a rowboat. That year, before the relay, they asked, "Who wants to take the rowboat?" Nobody wanted to row the small aluminum boat, so I said, "I'll give it a try." Little did I know that impulsive decision was going to become a life-changing event, affecting nearly every aspect of my physical and spiritual being for the rest of my life.

That year, we were poised in the rowboat, waiting for our runner to come up to us with the baton. All the other boats were long gone and already halfway across the lake. We waited and waited and waited. Finally, our runner came gasping up and thrust out the baton. I started rowing like a man with a mission rather than just a boy rowing a boat. The observers watching the race from the shore said it looked like we took off in a motorboat. We caught up with and blew past all the other boats, arriving on shore minutes before any of the other craft. From that year on, we never lost the relay—as long as I was in the rowboat.

The years rolled by, and I was accepted to the University of Wisconsin. One day before my freshman year, my mother reminded me of my success in the relays and said, "Maybe you should look into being on the rowing team." I didn't have a clue about the sport of real rowing. I'd never even seen their racing shells. But I knew enough to know it probably wasn't anything like heaving an aluminum craft across Cedar Lake in a relay race on the last day of summer camp. So I said, "OK. I'll look into it."

On our first day of college, my roommate and I were milling around Adams Hall right next to the university boathouse. He was one of the smaller guys in our high school, one of my best friends and my first college roommate. So we decided to walk down and take a look around. The boathouse was mysteriously exquisite and stood right on the shore of Lake Mendota. A beautiful deck stretched out in front, jutting into the lake where they put the rowing shells in the water. In our eyes, it looked like a country club.

We walked around the outside of the boathouse and past the window of the coach's office. When we peeked inside, Doug Neil, the freshman rowing coach, came out and said, "You guys look like you're interested in crew."

"Why's that?"

"Well, with your size, you look like an oarsman. And your friend here looks like a coxswain."

"Well, I guess we'd like to learn a little bit about it."

"Come on down tomorrow to practice, and you can try out for the rowing team."

Come to think of it, we didn't think we'd ever seen anyone actually row in a racing shell, so we had no idea what we were getting ourselves into. But I was young and inquisitive. I'd figure it out as I went along.

On the first day of rowing tryouts, we started in "the barge." The barge was a behemoth craft, eight feet wide by twenty-five feet long, and could accommodate twenty oarsmen at one time—ten on each side—as well as space for a coxswain in the back. There was a narrow plank in between the rowers, where the coach could walk back and forth, "coaching" us. It reminded me a little of the Egyptian slave ship Charleton Heston rowed in the movie *Ben-Hur*.

There must have been over one hundred freshmen trying out for the team that year. The coaches eliminated half of them during the first week. The second week, they weeded out more rowers until they had enough to man three shells: about twenty-five to thirty oarsmen and several coxswains. Then we started practicing in actual rowing shells. We also had an indoor rowing tank we could use during inclement weather.

Back in the fall of 1972, rowing shells were wafer-thin cedarwood works of art with thirteen-foot wooden oars with "tulip blades." The wooden equipment was tuned like a Stradivarius violin. I instantly fell in love with the sport. I loved everything about rowing because it required balance, physical strength, endurance, teamwork, and perseverance. Spiritual growth would come later.

After the coaches made their final cuts, the freshman team consisted of a first, second, and third boat. I was elated to make the first boat. Our crew would row as the freshman crew that year, and as we improved, we were occasionally allowed to train with the junior varsity and varsity teams.

As freshmen, we didn't have any formal races scheduled for the fall other than racing against ourselves, but nevertheless, our coach was amazing. He previously rowed for the crews of the legendary University of Washington—the source of the 2013 book *The Boys in the Boat*, about the crew team that won the national championship, going on to become the 1936 Olympic gold medal-winning champions for the United States, setting a new world's record in Berlin, Germany. I didn't realize it until a few years ago when I read the book, but everything he taught us originated from that award-winning team.

Years later, a few people from my church in Vail—including our vicar, Mark Huggenvik, the best man at my wedding—said you *have* to read that book. So he gave me a copy, and I inhaled the book in a couple of sittings. As freshmen, we didn't even know our coach had that distinction from the school that was such a dominant force in rowing. But there we were, at *the right place at the right time.*

Doug Neil trained us all winter to win, similar to the quote made famous by the Green Bay Packers coach Vince Lombardi: "Winning isn't everything. It's the only thing!"

We trained, and we trained, and we trained. By the time spring arrived, I was in the number 1 freshman boat, in the best physical condition of my life, along with my friend John Storck, who would later go on to be the Honorable Judge John R. Storck, Chair of the Chief Judges Committee for the State of Wisconsin, living in Mayville, Wisconsin, where he grew up.

We started rowing our first competitive races that spring season in 1973. The first races scheduled were the Midwestern championships. We went on to win every race at that regatta. All our Wisconsin crews eventually swept the entire field in all the races we entered. The regatta crews we were pitted against included Purdue, Kansas State, Notre Dame University, as well as others of the best crew teams in the Midwest.

At the time, we had no idea how good we really were, but our coach kept us motivated by reminding us, "You guys are capable of winning the national championship." That was constantly on his mind the entire season he trained us.

We competed in the Eastern Sprints at Lake Quinsigamond next to Worcester, Massachusetts, but never came in better than the top 3 positions simply because the eastern schools were so strong and way ahead of us in available water time. We couldn't train half the season when Lake Mendota was frozen solid. Later that year, we hosted a varsity race between Dartmouth, MIT, and the University of Wisconsin on Lake Mendota. After the race, they invited anyone who wanted to, to row along with the other teams.

Feeling very honored, I was invited to row with the MIT crew as an exchange member in their varsity boat. As a freshman, that was an experience I'll never forget—a chance to row in the boat with the big guys. Then we were off to the national championships on Lake Onondaga at the University of Syracuse, where we ended up making it into the final six regatta boats.

We were all confident we had a good team, but each of us was individually plagued by one fear: no one wanted to be the weak link in the chain. So individually I became willing to pull out all the stops, including talking to God. Even though I'd competed before, for some reason, I decided this time to pray to God that we'd be successful on that particular day. At that age, I was still spiritually immature, but I'd heard about Jesus saying, "If you knock at my Father's door in Heaven, He will be there for you." So for the first time, I could remember I asked God for help. In return, He delivered a message similar to Isaiah's:

^{10} *So do not fear, for I am with you; do not be dismayed, for I am your God. I will strengthen you and help you; I will uphold you with my righteous right hand.*

—Isaiah 41:10 (NIV)

We were poised at the start of the national championship race for the inter-collegiate rowing championships. They didn't start the races with guns. The judges in the official's yacht that followed behind the racing crews simply announced, "Are you ready? Ready all. Row," followed by dropping a flag.

We had an abysmal start. We were in last place and then started veering out of our lane. The official's boat came up behind us and said over an amplified loudspeaker, "Wisconsin, get back in your lane or you'll be disqualified." That got our attention. The coxswain steered us back into our lane, and we started to really row, eventually creeping up on the other five boats.

Just like in *The Boys in the Boat*, our coach taught us to row at a long strong, steady pace at a lower stroke rate. We slowly began creeping up on the rest of the boats. At the one-thousand-meter mark of the two-thousand-meter course, we pulled our famous "Wisconsin Power Twenty." After reading the book decades later, I learned that's exactly what *they* did: they would accelerate and move past their competition.

Our boat took off. We had what's known in rowing circles as "swing." Swing is when the entire team rows in perfect synchrony. On the "catch" phase—when the oars precisely dip into the water—our boat surged high on its keel, flying through the recovery. We rowed by all the other crews, except MIT, in less than twenty strokes. As we used to say, "We broke everybody's back."

We still had another one thousand meters to go, so we just kept rowing. We inched up, neck and neck against the first-place MIT team, and moved into the final five hundred meters and then ramped up the stroke rate. At the finish line, we passed them in a photo finish. We won the national championship, and we earned the first gold medal of our lives.

Together, with the other crews from the University of Wisconsin, we swept the national titles—one of the only teams in U.S. history to do so, besides Penn State back in those days. We won everything there was to win, including the Ten Eyck Award, the team that won the most points at the regatta.

Our dramatic winning "Sweep" generated a lot of activity within our alumni association. The association demanded, "They have to go to Henley!" The Henley Royal Regatta was established on March 26,

1839, and is a rowing event held annually on the River Thames by the town of Henley-on-Thames, England.

According to the *Encyclopedia Britannica*, "The Henley Royal Regatta is an annual four-day series of rowing races held the first week in July on the River Thames at Henley-on-Thames, Oxfordshire, England. The regatta was established in 1839 and in 1851 Prince Albert became its patron and gave the event its 'royal' prefix. The regulation distance for the races is 2,100 meters (1 mile, 550 yards). Probably the most significant of the traditional Henley races is the Grand Challenge Cup, the oldest (established in 1839), which usually attracts the world's finest eights (crews using eight oars), and the Diamond Challenge Sculls, one of the world's top single sculls events (one man, two oars). There are several other events, for various types of crews, most of which are open to entries from anywhere in the world."

The alumni association was tasked with raising enough money to send all three national champion crews to the race. At first, they limited their fundraising efforts exclusively to the varsity team. Then they raised enough to send the junior varsity crew as well. Undaunted, the dads of the freshmen crew members rallied and started working on raising enough money to send us.

My friend Ross Graves's father, Robert (Bob) was a Wisconsin national champion oarsman himself, so he spearheaded the fundraising efforts. John Storck's dad was a successful attorney, so he jumped on the bandwagon and started raising money. Our stroke oarsman, John Bauch, whose dad was a successful accountant got involved as well. My dad contacted our friend Herbert V. Kohler Jr., a member of the Kohler family of Wisconsin, CEO and Chairman of the Board of the Kohler Company, to help raise more funds. The Uihlein family, owners of the famous Schlitz Brewery, pitched in to help. Money started pouring in from everywhere, from a diversity of donors. We were blessed again. Collectively, they raised enough money to send all three of our crews to Henley that year.

When we flew to the UK, we carried our own thirteen-foot long oars through the airports and stowed them in the luggage compartment, along with our sixty-three-foot racing shells. We raced the same type of boat used by *The Boys in the Boat*, a George Yeoman Pocock handmade west coast cedar shell with Sitka spruce tulip bladed oars.

When we arrived, we stayed on the Oxford campus. Oxford and Cambridge were the first teams to row on an international level, eventually becoming the Henley Royal Regatta, attended by the Queen of England.

Our coaches wanted to get our crews into the Oxford races because there was a host of international crews coming to row at the brand-new Holm Pierpont Water Sports Center. The University of Washington sent its varsity, junior varsity, and freshman crews and represented the pacific contingent of the United States. They singled out our team by claiming that they, not us, were the reigning US national champions. Our varsity crew absolutely killed theirs. Then our freshman crew rowed in a race against Washington's freshman and junior varsity teams, and we beat both of them. Our JV crew beat Washington's JV crew as well. The newspapers read, "Wisconsin Sweeps Washington's Crews."

All our teams were doing better than anyone had imagined. Our freshman crew won everything we could win at Oxford. Then we moved on to the Henley Royal Regatta and won all our heats leading to the final. Our varsity crew did well, but they didn't win all their heats. The junior varsity crew won all their heats but the last one. In their semifinal race, they set a world's record.

Two members of our freshman crew got sick during the races, so we failed to win our final heat. We didn't win the Thames Cup, but we did set a world's record on July 6, 1973, in the semifinal race, so all in all, it was an experience that still feels like a dream. Lifetime bonds were formed, and we were the 1973 Boys in the Boats. That record still exists for wooden boats using wooden oars. John Storck and I have talked about filing a formal petition, with the Guinness Book of World Records, to establish a permanent world record for wooden boats with wooden oars, but we haven't followed through on that effort yet.

All this started with rowing as a Boy Scout and my mom asking me to think about rowing when I first went to college.

Earning my way into the varsity crew in the fall of my sophomore year was exciting, but it was never quite the same as our freshman boys in the boat. Competition for seats in the varsity crew was brutal because we had three national championship crews competing for seats in one boat. It was a character-building year as I'd be in the varsity boat for weeks, and then I was out. It was fame to failure. My name was on the varsity roster and an airline ticket with my name for the Head of the Charles race in Boston, but God had a different plan to shape me into who He intended me to be.

The emotional roller coaster was excruciatingly painful, to love rowing so much yet be bounced around with such intense competition among friends who had all become brothers during the Henley trip. In the spring of my sophomore year, I injured my back rowing on an ergometer. As a freshman, I had the highest ergo score of the boat, and then suddenly, I felt like a wounded duck. My feelings, heart, and soul were devastated. But all thanks be to God, I can still row my single scull at age sixty-six despite the injuries incurred over my life, especially those inflicted by Black Death. In my junior year, I rowed in the four-man varsity boat and won a bronze medal at the national championships. The year 1973 was the only Henley trip for the Wisconsin crews during my four years at Madison.

At one point, I entertained going on to train and try out for the US Olympic team, but it never worked out. By that time, the initial thrill of rowing became secondary to what was beginning to evolve into another entirely different phase of my life. But I continued to row—simply because I loved it. I still do. Overall, I didn't do as well as I hoped, yet I continued to row using my own single scull rowing shell, personal ergometer, and rowing on the Fox River at my house of thirty-five years in Wisconsin and later at my lake house. Finding ergometers at the Vail Racquet Club, the Boulder Recreation Center, and using my Silver Sneakers Medicare pass to access ergometers allows me to keep rowing into the sunset wherever I'm located. Even with my injured shoulder, I try to row six days a week year-round on my Concept2 ergo or on the water in my shell. But that's not the end of the rowing story.

My daughter Amy moved to Sacramento, California, with her husband Aaron, so when I started visiting her, I'd go down to the Sacramento Rowing Club. Their two-thousand-meter course is located on the American River and is the same course they use for the Pacific Twelve regattas, where Washington crews compete today. Initially, I had to get checked out by the staff to row, but after they reviewed my background and watched me row, they allowed me to use one of their rental single sculls whenever I liked.

One evening I saw a group of "older" people milling about, getting ready to row in an eight-man shell. So I walked up to them and asked, "What are you guys doing?"

"We're training for the master's races." I'd heard about the master's racing program, so I asked them,

"Do you ever have any room for someone to row with you?"

"Yeah, actually, we do. Do you want to row with us?"

"Yes!"

"What's your background? Have you ever rowed before?" So I told them, and they pleaded, "Will you row with us?"

"Love to, but it looks like you already have a full boat."

"We'll take somebody out of the boat. Welcome to the team."

On May 9, 2015, I rowed in the master's regatta with the Sacramento Rowing Club master's team on the PAC 12 championship course. We practiced together a couple of weeks leading up to the race but not exclusively the final race crew. On race day, the stroke oarsman, whom I'd not met or rowed with before, approached me and said, "I heard you're rowing with our crew in the race. Do you think you'll be able to keep up with us?"

One of the guys I had been practicing with in the masters training program at the boathouse said, "Don't worry about him. He rowed the Henley after winning the national championship."

"Well, we're probably going to row at thirty-four strokes per minute. Can you handle that?"

"Fine. That should be no problem."

"Where did you row?"

"University of Wisconsin."

"Oh! OK. You're in."

We managed to slip in twenty minutes of practice right before the race and focused on our starts. We had a couple of poor attempts, followed by one phenomenal start. Our shell took off in balance with swing and acceleration. I thought, *Déjà vu . . . Feels like 1973. If we can do that again, we'll do really well.*

Minutes later we were lining up in our starting lane for the race, preparing to be poised at the starting line and ready along with the other five boats. When the race started, I felt like I was right back at the Henley Royal Regatta. It wasn't a bad start like we had at the 1973 national championships. It was better than anything we had done in our practices. We took off. We were ahead of everyone by a considerable margin, with the other five boats trailing far behind us. We just kept rowing at thirty-four strokes per minute and pulled way ahead.

We had a young gal as a coxswain with limited experience. When we got down to the last one hundred meters, we were for all intents and purposes already the winner. At the same time, I was waiting for the coxswain to start calling up the stroke rate. With my previous experience, even if you're ahead, we always accelerated during the last two hundred meters. Yet we kept rowing at a steady thirty-four strokes/minute. I said, "Let's go, let's go, let's go. Let's take up the stroke."

The guys said, "We can't row any harder."

"C'mon, guys. We gotta go."

But they kept to their original pace. During the final one hundred meters, a master's team from San Francisco surged ahead and took first place. As our Kevlar shell with carbon hatchet oars glided to a stop, the stroke oar exclaimed, "Hey Wisconsin, I could feel you in the boat...that's fastest we've ever raced". I was frustrated but ecstatic to be competing at sixty-one years old, with a broken shoulder, like a nineteen-year-old again. Later we learned that the winning San Francisco crew was in their 40's, while our crew was in their 60's. I have to say, I still had plenty in the tank and was ready to take the stroke up to thirty-six plus!

Reflecting back forty-seven years upon the national championship regatta of the 1973 season as a Wisconsin Badger, I felt like I had a real connection with God. When we rowed in the national championship final race, I was engulfed by an out-of-body experience. I remember during the final two-hundred-meter sprint feeling like I had literally left my own body. Energy enveloped me. I experienced a supernatural surge of strength as the boat raced with acceleration. Our crew of nineteen-year-old boys was flying with swing and harmony. When that happened, there was an adrenaline, mental, and inspirational rush that came over the entire crew. The boat felt like the keel was skimming over the surface of the water and had become lighter than air. Recounting the micro details of every moment I witnessed as we crossed the finish line, is as clear in my mind's eye today as it was that historic day. It's my conviction that God answered my prayers and raised me to be more than I could be on my own. It wouldn't be the last experience I witnessed like that over the next forty-six years or the last prayers answered. All glory be to God.

> [13] *No temptation has overtaken you except what is common to mankind. And God is faithful; he will not let you be tempted beyond what you can bear. But when you are tempted, he will also provide a way out so that you can endure it.*
> —1 Corinthians 10:13 (NIV)

The final sprint of that national championship race convinced me that it was truly a God thing, this out-of-body experience. It felt like it wasn't even me rowing. I had a similar thing happen years later when I thought I was dead when I thought the Cape buffalo had crushed me to death when I heard and felt bones crunching and shattering. It was like I wasn't even in my own body. Then accompanied by all the light, I thought, *This is what you always read about with near-death experiences.*

But of course, I was still there.

Recalling life as an eleven-year-old scout, I was trying to be reverent, along with trustworthy, loyal, helpful, friendly, courteous, kind, obedient, cheerful, thrifty, brave, and clean. I would frequently visit the chapel at Boy Scout camp. I believed there was a creator. I just knew somebody had to have created it all. As I studied astronomy, geology, ecology, soil and water conservation, and the universe as part of earning various merit badges, I was convinced there wasn't any way all this could have been created by accident. I have always believed it was more than improbable but rather impossible that creation happened by accident.

I never believed solely in Darwin's theory of evolution either— that we just evolved from one form of matter to another, without a supreme architect of the universe. At the same time, I do believe in concepts such as plant succession and evolutionary periods of time related to life and geology on earth. But who designed evolution? Who designed the essence of creation, regardless of how small we break down tissue into cells to biochemistry, from chemistry to elements and atoms, atoms down to quarks and preons theorized by the study of quantum physics? It's always been my belief that there has to be a supreme creator. Our native Americans believe in a Creator as well as most religions. I was always searching for an answer. The truth.

I remember while taking biochemistry, we learned that the molecular structures of hemoglobin and chlorophyll were essentially the same as our professor diagrammed them on the blackboard. The difference is that hemoglobin is built around iron, whereas chlorophyll is built around magnesium.

The primary function of hemoglobin is to transport oxygen from the lungs to many parts of the body, so our cells can burn the carbohydrates we eat, providing energy for our cellular functions. Hemoglobin is composed of five elements: carbon, hydrogen, oxygen, and nitrogen plus iron. Four elements are organized around iron. Chlorophyll is found in virtually all photosynthetic organisms, including trees, green plants, and algae. Chlorophyll absorbs energy from the sun's light. This energy is used to convert carbon dioxide, brought in from the atmosphere, into carbohydrates. Who could have come up with a design like that other than our Creator, aka God? One molecular structure, hemoglobin, delivers oxygen to burn carbohydrates that powers our bodies and produces CO_2 that we exhale, while the other uses the sun's energy to produce carbohydrates from the sap of the plant, CO_2 and, the conversion reaction of chlorophyll produces oxygen we breathe. I believe the truth of this biochemical cycle of life could not have happened by accident or some mystical evolution. This realization was a significant proof for me, at that waypoint of my life as a student of biochemistry.

Continually looking for the truth in every aspect of my life gave me the relentless motivation to continue studying and learning. Beginning in the Boy Scouts, I believed the proof of the existence of God was becoming apparent to me. As I got older, I participated in six of the seven sacraments of the church: the holy baptism, the holy eucharist, confirmation, reconciliation of a penitent, holy matrimony, and unction as a layperson. Nineteen Seventy-Eight, Nancy and I were married and we witnessed our four children being born and baptized. Back then, I learned a little about the Bible as I continued to live my life, but I would honestly have to call myself a nominal Christian during that phase of my life, attending church on Christmas, Easter, and a few other Sunday services believing in God and creation but was still spiritually immature.

All the while, life events were happening that caused me to pause and think, *How did I do that?* I started to accept that I wasn't accomplishing my goals entirely on my own, even rowing a boat across a lake. There was some higher power guiding my success.

While studying in college, I would shift into miraculous modes of understanding, where absorbing new concepts and terms were effortless. With a visual learning capability, some might call photographic memory I could remember complicated biochemistry like the Krebs Cycle, but certainly far from genius. Communicating more and more with God, I was witnessing states of mind and achievements that were far beyond my inherent abilities.

Always trying to learn more, I found myself on a continuum quest for knowledge and truth. Pushing through life, I became a successful businessman and, together with my wife, raised four beautiful children. It wasn't until later with maturity that I realized I wasn't on my own, and *"pushing"* wasn't the answer. While I wasn't particularly bad or behaving inappropriately, there were times when I just wasn't as good a father as I could have been or as good a husband as I should have been. But I felt at the time that I did the best I could without really understanding my spiritual immaturity.

So going back to when I was forty-eight years old again, as previously mentioned, Amy urged me to start reading the Bible. She saw in me the potential to become a better person. She had already started down her own path of becoming a devoted Christian. My other daughter, Martha, was also well along on her spiritual journey. Yes, children teaching their father was true. My daughters were more spiritually mature than I was. Opening my spirit to listening and learning from my children was a breakthrough experience. It dawned on me that pushing through life was not the same as pulling on an oar. Pushing was not the answer. Another waypoint on my journey.

Once I got started, I couldn't stop. I was given a little brown Bible on my birthday, February 24, 2002, and started carrying it with me all the time. When I started reading the Word, it's as if I went online and started downloading information from Heaven with incredible clarity. Consuming reams of information was amazing. God was sending the Word straight to me.

Suddenly, the issues I had struggled with were making sense to me. I felt, *Wow. So there's the answer to this question. That's the answer to that question. Here's how this issue ties to that way of living. A definite wow experience!*

Of course, I loved economics and anatomy, so I was always fascinated with the way the components of a whole economy or the anatomy of a body interrelated with one another. I'd heard bits and pieces of scripture from a wide variety of spiritual people, including my daughters, who had become involved with reading the Bible at St. John's Catholic School, where we chose to enroll our four kids, even though we weren't Roman Catholic. Then my breakthrough was studying the interrelationships between the different books of the bible, old and new testament, psalms, and proverbs.

By the time I reached fifty years old, I'd read the Bible from cover to cover. I meditated over the entire New Testament and tried to integrate its meaning into my life. Just like I tried to do when I was fourteen years old, I read all the books within the Bible in order. I loved the book of John and was overwhelmed with the energy of the Holy Spirit, by Saint John's clarity and expression of the crucifixion and proof of the resurrection. Doubting Thomas was a powerful confirmation that Jesus broke the bonds of death and is alive for eternity. He is alive today, as I've witnessed directly.

The bible became a central component of my life. The word of God helped me look back at the way life worked out and how life was supposed to be:

> *Now Thomas (also known as Didymus), one of the Twelve, was not with the disciples when Jesus came. So the other disciples told him, "We have seen the Lord!" But he said to them, "Unless I see the nail marks in his hands and put my finger where the nails were, and put my hand into his side, I will not believe." A week later his disciples were in the house again, and Thomas was with them. Though the doors were locked, Jesus came and stood among them and said, "Peace be with you!" Then he said to Thomas, "Put your finger here; see my hands. Reach out your hand and put it into my side.*

*Stop doubting and believe." Thomas said to him, "My Lord
and my God!" Then Jesus told him, "Because you have seen
me, you have believed; blessed are those who have not seen
and yet have believed."*

—John 20:24–31 (NIV)

Around the same time, I started attending church regularly. Then
in January 2002, the elders of the St. Peter's Episcopal Church in
Ripon, Wisconsin, asked me to be on the board of directors, called
the vestry. The priest said, "We're doing this thing called Alpha.
Our church puts it on in conjunction with the international leader
Nicky Gumbel out of the UK. It's for the entire Global Anglican
Community and Episcopal Church of the United States. Would you
like to participate?" Of course, I was all in.

Alpha lasted ten weeks and addressed the fundamental components
of Christianity on a weekly basis. There was a dinner at the church
in the evening, followed by a short message delivered by the priest
or a recorded message by Nicky Gumbel. After that, we'd break into
smaller groups and discuss what we'd heard and what it meant to us.
Alpha was awesome and inspiring.

Weeks later in the Alpha schedule, we conducted a "Holy Spirit
Weekend" at a small retreat center at nearby Green Lake—the same
lake where my brother in Christ, Randy Zieth, and I had been
waterskiing for decades. We conducted a Friday night and Saturday
session. I remember how passionate I was learning about the Word
of God. I couldn't learn enough. I wanted to understand more and
more about our creator, Jesus, the truth about Him, and reconcile the
confusion in my mind—it was truly a transformational waypoint in
my life.

There were more books to read like *A Case for Christ* by Lee
Strobel. Strobel was a former investigative journalist and forensics
expert at the *Chicago Tribune* who started as an atheist and then ended
up becoming an American Christian author. He completed a forensics
study trying to prove to the world that Christ isn't for real, but by the
end of the book, he'd become a minister.

On Saturday of the holy spirit retreat, there were a dozen of us
holding hands in a circle, which included members of the vestry,
members of our parish, and people from our local community. We
reached a particular point after studying about the Holy Spirit in the

Old and New Testaments when Father Guy began to pray out loud. He lapsed into speaking in tongues and called upon the Holy Spirit to come into us. A huge wave of energy entered the entire room. He told us to continue praying with our eyes closed and holding each other's hands as we stood in the circle. I kept repeating to myself, *Let go . . . Just let go. Surrender. Let go and surrender to Jesus. Holy Spirit, come into me and take over.*

As my spirit surrendered to Jesus, a brilliant purple vision came into my mind's eye, beginning as a small circle and started to glow. It grew bigger and bigger until it filled my mind's eye. All the while, I continued to say to myself, *Let go and surrender to Jesus. Holy Spirit, come into me!*

The purple glow shifted to a black-and-white image of Jesus looking straight into my eyes. Jesus and I were face-to-face. I'd never witnessed a vision like it before, although I have since, but not as graphically stunning. My whole being was trembling in awe...another magnificent waypoint.

By that time, the other participants had already let go of my hands as I continued to stand there alone in a trance. I couldn't let go of the image. Eventually, people started to drift away, and the image vanished. I thought *I don't think my life is going to be the same anymore.*

Since Alpha and the Holy Spirit weekend, my understanding is that we are all part of a broken world. Everyone is flawed. The realization, *people don't go to church because they're perfect*, emerged. They go because they need repair, recovery, and a loving community to help them understand a better way of life. We are all flawed and most likely we don't know what to do about it. The church is like a hospital for our spirits and souls. My daughter recognized that I was just another one of those flawed individuals, and she wanted me to see the way and live a better life.

As a young athlete, I hadn't yet realized that there was a good and bad side of having an intense focus on a goal, committing yourself from start to finish, no matter what it took. But that's what it took to row two thousand meters and win. There was no time to think about it, just do it. There was no time to have a committee meeting. It was *"All or nothing at all."*

So I lived my life like that and probably drove my family crazy. My perspective was that every minute counts. Every day is a gift and an opportunity to get better at whatever we choose to do. We shouldn't waste a second of our time here on Earth. Life was like a race.

There were times when I wasn't a very good example of a Christian. I was always in a hurry, pushing myself and the people around me. Always late because I tried to do too much in too little time. Rude, actually. If goals weren't accomplished, I'd get upset. My negative behavior spilled over onto other people, even those I loved.

That's where Amy helped. She showed me the way to become a better person without losing my relationships with God and the people in my life. I needed to learn how to become a better father, brother, and husband. I learned that life is a balance of mind, body, and spirit. We can't have one without the other. It all seemed so simple and obvious, but changing a mindset is not so easy.

At times, I regretted that I hadn't learned how to read the Bible earlier in my life. I wish I'd read the Bible before I got married and became a father, a leader in business, an entrepreneur, the CEO, and chairman of the board of my own company. I wish I knew then what I know now about how to live a Christian life on Earth.

If anyone sins and treats other people poorly, the Bible tells us clearly how to reconcile it:

Dealing with a Sinning Brother

   15 Moreover if your brother sins against you, go and tell him his fault between you and him alone. If he hears you, you have gained your brother. 16 But if he will not hear, take with you one or two more, that "by the mouth of two or three witnesses every word may be established." 17 And if he refuses to hear them, tell it to the church. But if he refuses even to hear the church, let him be to you like a heathen and a tax collector.
   18 Assuredly, I say to you, whatever you bind on earth will be bound in heaven, and whatever you loose on earth will be loosed in heaven.
   19 "Again I say to you that if two of you agree on earth concerning anything that they ask, it will be done for them by My Father in heaven. 20 For where two or three are gathered together in My name, I am there in the midst of them.
   The Parable of the Unforgiving Servant

> [21] *Then Peter came to Him and said, "Lord, how often shall my brother sin against me, and I forgive him? Up to seven times?"*
>
> [22] *Jesus said to him, "I do not say to you, up to seven times, but up to seventy times seven."*
>
> —Matthew 18:15–22 (NKJV)

If we struggle in any part of our life, the answers are all at our fingertips. Heaven and Earth are tied together, but we have to be willing to surrender and open ourselves to God's Word. Jesus came to Earth as the Word to teach us about His Father's Kingdom of Heaven as our example of how the world can be. All we have to do is open the floodgates so the information can pour into us. Opening the floodgates from Heaven requires regularly reading the Bible. We won't get much from occasionally reading it—most certainly shorting ourselves.

Ironically, we can read a passage once and receive one message. Later in our life, we can reread the same passage and come away with a completely different message depending on our more recent experiences. Why doesn't the same reflection happen each time we reread God's Word? Because as finite beings on Earth, it's impossible for us to fully comprehend God's wisdom in a single sitting. I believe it takes a lifetime to understand what Jesus is trying to teach us and only until we actually see God's Kingdom in Heaven firsthand and feel peace beyond our comprehension, will we have the most complete understanding.

God is talking to us all the time. That's the point of this book. God is not only for real, but God's also alive and constantly in our lives if we allow God in. God's talking to us all the time if we recognize it. God is constantly performing miracles—the events people take for granted and interpret as "just being lucky." Are people lucky or blessed?

All the milestones and waypoints I've described here have been breakthroughs in my life. Alpha was the equivalent of getting a high school diploma in Christianity. Waypoints in navigation have both distance/time and direction components or a vector to plot your way to the waypoint. Understanding that God is the waymaker and his Will and plan is the course, became more and more apparent. This waypoint, where having experienced the vision of Jesus face-to-face, convinced me that my life was never going to be the same again. Early on, I was afraid to share my experiences with very many people for fear of what they might think about me. Father Guy asked me about my Holy Spirit weekend experience, and after explaining my vision he said, "Whoa. That's a goose bumper vision. But that's what happens."

Many very spiritual people I met during my first years of studying the Word of God, including clergy, shared with me that the closer we get to Christ, we will experience difficulties in conflict with the way of life of discipleship. Satan is constantly trying to destroy our progress. Additional spiritually mature people I've known, over the last decades, have further shared the same experience. I now accept my metamorphosis delivered by Alpha as a stage, a step, akin to an academic degree.

At that point in my life, as a committed member of the vestry, the other members suggested that I continue my metamorphosis by participating in a Cursillo weekend. My first reaction was "What in the world is that? Do you mean there's more?"

Completing the Alpha ten-week program definitely catapulted me into a discipleship mode, where I was trying to become more Christlike. That's what Christianity really means, trying to become more like and walk in the ways of Christ. Even though I'd tried many times in the past to follow Him, I kept failing over and over. But the splendor of the goal of striving to become more like Christ is accepting that no one's perfect, including ourselves.

If we fall or experience failure in some aspect of our lives (or come face-to-face with a life-changing event like I did), it's never too late to pick up and start again. Whether we're at the beginning of our life or farther down the road, the most important concept to remember is that life is a journey, a walk with the very best possible friend, the waymaker—Jesus.

Sometimes the journey appears to be simple and relatively straightforward. Other times, it's convoluted and hard to understand what direction God wants us to take. Paramount is perceiving and understanding the effects on ourselves as we listen to God's will while we continue our walk with Jesus on our pathway of life.

CHAPTER THREE

MAKING GOD LAUGH

Trust in the Lord with all your heart and lean not on your own understanding; in all your ways submit to him, and he will make your paths straight.

—Proverbs 3:5–6 (NIV)

L ike most energetic young students about to embark on their college education, I had no idea where I was heading. I thought I did, but as time played out, I discovered there was much more to life than simply making plans.

At the time, I was vacillating between premed and pursuing a degree in business administration. I prayed to God, asking for guidance and what direction I should take. With my success in advanced placement courses, I would have been accepted into almost any course of study. But for some reason, I limited my options to just those two.

Eventually, I started leaning more and more toward the business side that included economics and real estate development. Undoubtedly, my relatives on my mother's side of the family who were all attorneys and real estate developers played a subliminal part in my decision.

While studying at the University of Wisconsin, I found and pursued the renowned James A. Graaskamp real estate program. In my junior and senior years, continuing a focus in the school of business, I completed my degree in business administration with a triple major in economics, management, and real estate. The future looked rosy.

Throughout my school years, economics, entrepreneurship, and learning how to start and run your own business were constant subjects of conversation at the dinner table. I loved the idea of entrepreneurship: being the captain of my own ship and learning how to navigate my own business. During his career in sales, my dad also entertained similar ideas. So in the summer of 1975, he struck out on his own and started a small packaging company called the Colonial Container Corporation. I was his first employee.

Even though I hadn't graduated yet, I was eager to join him. My dad was a fabulous salesperson and understood the intricacies of sales and marketing a successful business. During the second semester of my senior year, I was already on the road selling for our new company while managing to squeeze in time to study until I earned my degree in May of 1976.

The world was my oyster once again. I felt God behind me giving me the ability and energy to be more than I thought I could be. It was the common thread that ran through my early life in the Boy Scouts and then later while rowing and studying at college. It was obvious to me that I must have had help. There's no way I could have accomplished the ambitions I had all by myself.

Woody Allen once said, "If you want to make God laugh, tell Him your plans." In retrospect, I think that's true; man makes plans, and God laughs. As young adults, we set out in a direction to set the world on fire. It never occurs to us that situations could go wrong and shove us off our path. So we press forward, full steam ahead.

In my early years right out of school, I felt that if I wanted to attain a goal, it was entirely up to me to get it done. That's the entrepreneurial mindset. But as I grew older, I realized that no goals were accomplished without the hand of God. God's fingerprints are indelibly etched all over my life, from beginning to now.

As the decades marched on and my spirituality grew, more and more frequently I asked for God's will instead of mine. Beginning to understand that I was part of God's creation and plan, I truly believed that there was a purpose behind outcomes that occurred and why people take positive action in their lives.

Over the years, I've read hundreds of books seeking the truth: the Bible, Lee Strobel's, *The Case for Christ,* Oswald Chambers, *My Utmost for His Highest,* Sarah Young, *Jesus Calling*: Enjoying Peace in His Presence, and Rick Warren's *The Purpose Driven Life,* to name just a few. In Warren's book, he talks about the five purposes of life—or, as I like to call them, the five SHIPS: worship, fellowship, discipleship, stewardship, and apostleship. I truly believe in them. They're easy to remember, and I always share them with people, whenever the topic of "What on earth are we here for?" comes up. That question is the central question of Pastor Rick Warren's must-read book.

As my spirituality matured, it was uncanny how my empathy helped people I met, who were struggling with their own spirituality. They'd lost their spiritual base because of significant losses they encountered in their lives; spouses who had died, injuries, diseases, family issues, and other life crises. Fortunately, there were times when I could be there for those people and help them grow closer to Christ. Once they realized it was Jesus they needed in the center of their lives and nothing else helped them grieve their losses, their perspective and perception shifted. The closest example to me was my father. Mom passed away at ninety years old, and he was devastated. In the end, after a life void of the church, he grew closer to Christ before he finally passed away at ninety years old on September 26, 2018.

My eulogy at his celebration of life service was specifically about him growing closer to Christ. It wasn't about his life, so much as it was about him finding his way to Christ in his final years on earth, encouraged by the loving-kindness of our Christian community of sisters and brothers forming the body of our church. He loved Father Brooks and started attending worship services and Bible studies regularly during his last stage of life. He loved the sermons, and he grew spiritually, at an accelerated rate, until his final day. I'm totally convinced he passed to Heaven and rejoined Mom for eternity. I literally felt his spirit with a Holy Spirit visit me the moment he passed from his physical body one hundred miles away, as confirmed by my brother Rob, who was at his deathbed.

During college, I gained confidence by accomplishing so many new objectives. Feeling invincible, I also had to remember why I was capable of such accomplishments. Knowing there was more than me involved. Understanding that I wasn't accomplishing my ambitious goals on my own was the tether or anchoring line that's always brought me back to Jesus, our anchor, in times of doubt and confusion.

Looking back, I was unconsciously out of focus from a clear paradigm of how much better life could be. I hadn't read the entire Bible before or even after college. Not until twenty-eight years after I graduated from college did I finish reading it for the first time. As you recall, I attempted to read the Bible when I was fourteen but got stuck in Matthew, the first book of the New Testament.

In the next decade, from twenty-two to thirty-two, I was not a regular Bible reader. The most I'd read were the readings during church services. We'd have to go to church services every Sunday for at least three straight years before we would read the majority of the Bible. The necessary motivation, dedication of time and spiritual maturity level weren't present yet.

From thirty-two to forty-two, I wasn't living a fully optimal life as an individual, a husband, or a father of four. I had more flaws than I could accept. Then between forty-two and fifty-two, my spiritual growth miraculously started to bloom. To this day, I know absolutely that my spiritual health and soul blossomed as I began exercising my spirit, not just my mind and body, searching for answers in the Bible.

If there's one single point I've learned in my lifetime, for me, it's the importance of reading the Bible, the most significant book I have ever read and studied. Imagine a world of peace, joy, and love instead of watching the news and observing displays of the seven deadly sins.

As Jesus said, "Ours is a broken world." Who can disagree when there's sin everywhere? There are people who have turned their backs on spirituality. When you get right down to it, my daughter Amy was right. My daughter Martha was also in the same place as Amy spiritually. Both my daughters are beautiful Christians. They've chosen spiritual paths that include studying the Bible, going to Bible studies, and sharing with other Christians. They're strong, independent women guiding their children through the complexities of life while at the same time, sharing beautiful relationships with the families of their siblings and friends. They're maturing rapidly, and they're only in their late thirties and early forties. They're way ahead of where I was—way ahead.

During the ensuing years following college, my dad and I grew our company together. I started in sales and then became vice president of sales. But it wasn't always a bed of roses. We faced bankruptcy twice: the first time was in 1976, after being in business for less than two years. My dad had a partner that didn't work out. But live, learn, and let die.

Whether we want to call them miracles or God simply raising us to reach beyond what we thought we were capable, we ended up turning the company around again, a second time in the eighties.

With the help of my mother's brother, Rodney James Edwards, an accomplished attorney winning cases at U.S. Supreme Court, not only did he negotiate plans with major suppliers and creditors, but he also restructured the company and infused it with cash. In turn, we gave him 10 percent of the company's stock.

Instead of going through bankruptcy court, uncle Rod handled the legal matters. Rod reorganized the company and made my dad chairman of the board and me president of the company. "I'm counting on you to turn the company around," my uncle Rod said to me. Quite a challenge at twenty-nine years old.

He named my mom vice president and treasurer, so she controlled the purse strings. My brother Jim was made the vice president of research and development and manufacturing. We literally picked ourselves up by our bootstraps. We couldn't have done it without the hand of God.

God's fingerprints are all over Colonial Container Corporation too. We came out of the bankruptcy successfully, built it back up, and I paid my uncle back 100 percent, so he tendered his 10 percent stock ownership back to me. In 1989, we successfully sold the company. I used the 10 percent of the sales proceeds that I received from the dissolution of my stock to start Senior American Housing, Incorporated in January 1990. I learned more about people and business in the fourteen years at Colonial Container Corporation than if I'd stayed at the University of Wisconsin and studied for another ten years.

During my initial years in the real world and business, I learned there are people from all walks of life. Some good, some not so good but most needing some form of help. If we look at our Father in Heaven as a beacon of light, God's always sending, always reaching out to us. Whether we decide to receive God's messages is up to us. It's always been apparent who embraces God versus those who choose to live life on their own.

Owning, operating, and eventually selling our own company was an amazing learning experience. It was like getting a Ph.D. in business, especially understanding relationships with the different people pools involved: customers, employees, suppliers, community, and stockholders.

When we decided to sell the company, my dad asked me if I thought it was a good idea. I said, "Yeah, let's do it." Menasha

Corporation, one of the top 5 corporations in Wisconsin, made us an offer we couldn't refuse. As part of the sale, I agreed to stay on for another year as the general manager, learning even more from the transition. A good friend of mine once said, "The only thing worse than working for yourself is working for someone else." I couldn't agree more. While I thought it was interesting working for a big corporation, I felt trapped like a worker bee in a hive, so I was ready to leave after a year.

While I was president of Colonial Container Corporation, I was elected to the Green Lake County Board and learned about the public sector. Upon being sworn into office, I was appointed to the Finance, Law Enforcement and (Strategic and Economic Planning) committees. Part of my effort was to help establish the Green Lake County Economic Development Corporation as well as being appointed its first president. We were trying to make a positive impact on our little county in the center of Wisconsin.

Returning to the first words of my Boy Scout oath: "On my honor, I will do my best to do my duty to God and my country", reinforced my focus. Being in business, one can't help but notice the political climate of our country and the effects it has on our economy. My education and experience taught me it is easier to understand the whole of the interrelated components of a business entity or public organization or government at any level, from city and county to state and federal, as if it was alive. So I thought I should try to do my duty and contribute as a public leader. After all, people asked me to share my leadership, and I was duly elected by the people of the county. Offering myself at that time to some type of service in the public sector seemed appropriate. There certainly was no money involved. I simply thought it would be the right meaningful contribution to give and help provide leadership for our county.

The first action I conducted was to develop a county vision, mission statement, and plan. As the president of the Green Lake Economic Development Corporation, I developed an overall economic development plan called the OEDP and asked professionals to come in as resources for our efforts. All this was happening at the ripe old age of thirty-five.

We developed an encompassing plan. One of the facts we learned was that we had a disproportionate number of seniors in our county's population. We had two nursing homes, but we didn't have any way to take care of the elderly needing assisted living. There was an element missing to adequately take care of our seniors.

We lived in a system of small rural communities, like the city of Princeton, which at the time only had 1,400 residents. The biggest city in Green Lake County was Berlin, with 5,500. Then there was the city of Green Lake that was even smaller than Princeton with under 1,000 residents. Most of the population lived on lakes, streams, and farms.

We were trying to come up with a more efficient way to serve the small communities that were having trouble sustaining themselves. We looked at the full gamut of issues from law enforcement to the economics of scale of economy. We asked ourselves, what were our economic strengths and opportunities as well as weaknesses and challenges? The centers of these small towns were like ghost towns. There were vacant buildings everywhere, but they were in beautiful historic communities. There had to be a way to work together to make our small rural communities thrive.

We needed a vision: to take care of the needs of people and help the county grow economically. Many of the empty buildings were located in the central downtown area, so we began designating them historic districts. Then there was discussion that we find developers to come in and renovate the beautiful vacant buildings into useful projects that would benefit the community—possibly housing for seniors.

It was my vision that there was a wonderful opportunity to combine the two. The other members of the board agreed and suggested that we attract developers to rehabilitate some of these buildings.

After months of futilely engaging with developers, we discovered that most of them weren't particularly interested in improving a rural part of Wisconsin. They didn't believe our county was the economic expansion center of the country. In fact, it was just the opposite.

Then I thought, *Hey. That's what I studied at the University of Wisconsin.* So I began to develop a feasibility analysis document to raise downtown properties to higher and better use. I found that we already had designations within the Department of Health and Family Services existing care system for providing care to the elderly. There were two: one was a skilled nursing facility or SNF, and the other was a community-based residential facility or CBRF. Our county had a few smaller existing developments designated as senior apartments as well as the traditional nursing homes already mentioned. But we didn't have any providers in between. What we needed was a CBRF.

Initiating a study on the old buildings with the intent of making them historic projects, I focused on developing a select site into a state-of-the-art CBRF that would act as an assisted-living facility for taking care of seniors who didn't need a skilled nursing home. An assisted living facility for people who just needed assistance with activities of daily living but not an SNF. I put together a model and took it to the Wisconsin Housing and Economic Development Authority (WHEDA) in Madison and met with their underwriters. They knew all about my background from studying under Prof. James A. Graaskamp and his real estate development program at the school of business from my résumé, right down to my history of being an Eagle Scout.

The Development Authority asked me to come up with a business plan for my purpose built proposed idea. The next moment I learned underwriting was putting together a loan package for me. At that spot in time, I was just finishing the end of my term as a Green Lake County Board member, so I resigned during my last month in office and chose not to run for reelection. I didn't want any issues relating to conflicts of interest. Then I established a new company with John Storck as my corporate counsel.

We started a corporation called Senior American Housing, Incorporated in January 1990. It was spawned from my love for medicine and business and ended up becoming a ministry to the elderly. As my spirituality grew and evolved, my focus became less on the business side and more on the ministry of providing care and solutions for seniors. I pioneered a new model for the state. Throughout 1990, we incorporated the new corporation and secured a low-interest nonrecourse loan for $1.4 million from WHEDA. We started construction, and by the end of the year, we had an occupancy permit for our first facility. We were on time and under budget.

Ironically, it ended up not actually being in Green Lake County. We looked at doing a project in Berlin and were also investigating launching it in Princeton, where I lived. We listened to God and built it in Ripon, Wisconsin. If we would have gone forward with the project in Princeton, it would have most likely failed. It reminded me of Garth Brook's song, "Unanswered Prayers." All this took place the year after selling Colonial Container Corporation.

When I opened the American House of Ripon at the beginning of 1991, Gov. Tommy Thompson came to the grand opening in June to officiate. There was a seamless transition from exiting my previously owned business to starting a completely different type of business, in a radically different direction, all in just over one year. I can truthfully say that it was not possible without help from John Storck representing me as my attorney and the hand of God. It was solely a leap of faith on my part, without any guidance or financial help from my family.

In 1995, I wrote a letter to Governor Thompson, suggesting that we redesign long-term care for the elderly and use my model for assisted living as a new concept, transitioning away from traditional nursing homes and CBRFs. He got involved and helped create the Assisted Living Initiative in 1997. It promulgated into law with specific rules and regulations in 1998. A new designation resulted called a CALF or certified assisted-living facility rather than a CBRF.

At the time, it was a revolutionary change in the way we cared for the elderly. We collaborated between the private and public sectors and redesigned long-term care in Wisconsin. The residents lived in their own independent apartments rather than cubicles like in nursing homes. That was the real estate part of the equation. On the medical side of the model design, we employed registered nurses as health-care coordinators who oversaw medication management, care plans, and the monitoring of residents' health.

My whole model was about moving away from an institutional setting to a household concept, a central community, homelike living space with an interactive kitchen at the center of activity spaces. The model was the first in the state to provide seniors with their own apartments with fully functional kitchens and a full array of care—a concept I coined "Aging in Place." The staff provided personal care for the residents in their own space while respecting their privacy and dignity. We made the central dining room and living spaces as homey as possible instead of the sterile environment people usually came to expect at previously designed care facilities.

Unfortunately, politicians got involved and started scheduling an endless list of hearings. Bureaucrats wanting more control and regulators started to get involved. They drafted more regulations and changed the name from CALF to RCAC—residential care apartment complex. Before the name changed, we had the number 1 and 2 CALFs in the state. Officially, I was presented with several awards from the Wisconsin legislature and governor for our breakthrough developments in caring for seniors. During September 2001—the year of the catastrophic 9/11 attacks—Pres. George W. Bush bestowed on me the Entrepreneur of the Year award for the work I accomplished with Senior American Housing. I flew to Washington, D.C., from elk hunting in Colorado on Friday, September 28.

When I arrived in Washington, I met Tom Petrie, who was the congressman for our district in Wisconsin. He arranged high-level clearance for me so that I could experience special tours like the underground tunnel system, a view typical visitors never get to see.

Walking on foot from Arlington National Cemetery to every one of the national monuments: the Lincoln Memorial, Jefferson Memorial, Franklin Delano Roosevelt Memorial, Korean War Veterans Memorial, Vietnam Veterans Memorial, Martin Luther King, Jr. Memorial, and the Washington Monument, I truly felt a pure sense of patriotism and allegiance to our flag and the scout oath, "On my honor, I will do my duty, to God and my country…".

Actually, I read every word on those memorials as well as the cornerstone on the inside wall of the Washington Monument near the elevator, where the Masons secured it on July 4, 1848. George Washington was a Mason, as were thirteen of the other inscribers of the Declaration of Independence. After touring all the memorials, I continued to the White House, where it was surrounded by two rows of fences for several weeks following 9/11.

Being there for October first, with the anniversary of the Berlin Wall coming down, I was invited to lunch with a group of German dignitaries and congressmen, including Petrie, on that special day of reverence and celebration. Throughout my visit to Washington DC, I had an extraordinary opportunity to experience the principles our founding forefathers built this great nation on. There's a big difference between googling or standing in front of the memorials reliving our country's historic struggles and brilliant words of wisdom.

On October 2, I was presented with the Entrepreneur of the Year award by George W. Bush. While I was there, senators and congressmen were working on redesigning health care, so I was asked to participate and experience a wonderful opportunity to add my views with others in high places. They liked my assisted living household concept that cut the cost of long-term care in half or in other words took care of twice as many elderly for the same cost as SNF's. They understood our country's aging population was rapidly expanding with the front wave of baby boomers approaching. Feeling a sense of fulfillment, realizing that I was actually contributing to our society, I left Washington DC truly appreciating our God and Country and experienced a feeling of deep peace, though only weeks before we all had lived through the 911 nightmare. God bless America.

Along this life journey, I passed many milestones or waypoints, from simple to miraculous, where God lifted me and helped me accomplish His will. The assisted-living model I began formalizing in 1988 while I was researching the idea began to materialize and become reality in 1990. It was a long road after twenty-eight years of giving it my best. I ended up selling the first assisted-living business in 2010 and the last facilities in 2016.

There is no way I could have accomplished any of the development and operating processes entirely on my own. It took sacrifices from my wife and kids as well as God answering my endless prayers. It took friends like John Storck, employees buying into our mission of ministering to seniors, and many other people pools to make our mission of "Developing better living for seniors" a sustainable endeavor. I couldn't have done it without my experience at the University of Wisconsin. All the pieces of the puzzle fit together in harmony over the long run, though initially, it appeared that the obstacles I encountered were impassable. The dots eventually connected as we combined a medical model with a real estate plan. As it turned out, it was almost unbelievable how this viable outcome, originating in school studying premed, economics, business management, and real estate development, occurred. I had no inkling, even when I was in the packaging business after college, that my journey would evolve so seamlessly until I surrendered to God's will, fully trusted in God, and God showed me the way. Without question, God transformed me into becoming more than I was capable of by myself.

By that spot in time, I was immersed in prayer and Bible study, learning more about God and thinking less about me. But at the same time, I was still far from being the man God designed me to be. Evidently, I was a reasonably good father because all four of our kids turned out to be well-adjusted, successful contributing citizens in a not-so-perfect world, producing seven healthy children of their own. I couldn't have asked for them to be any better. The fingerprints of God are all over them, whether they realize it. I know my daughters are aware of their spiritual base, and my sons are farther along their spiritual journey than I was at their age. Everyone's on their own personal path. None of us are alike. The only constant is that God is always with all of us all the time. All the time, God is good.

Looking back, it was never about Larry Trotter. It was always about giving the glory to God as He kept giving me the gift of a unique type of vision, a perception that allowed me to be able to look at buildings and turn them into both historic monuments and assisted-living projects. It was a miracle that brought together the best people for the best type of project. God gave me those visions. He brought all those people together which developed into personal and business-related relationships that continue to this day. It was a glorious unfolding over time.

I have to admit that I prayed. I prayed endlessly for positive visions to become reality. This is another point that I've learned. If we pray about an idea we've imagined positively long enough and it fits with God's will, it's as if God shifts the universe to make it happen. The infinite pieces and movements of the universe certainly do not shift because of my will. They occur because of God's will.

> *For still the vision awaits its appointed time; it hastens to the end—it will not lie. If it seems slow, wait for it; it will surely come; it will not delay.*
> —Habakkuk 2:3 (ESV)

Today what impresses me most is how many opportunities came to me. Fortunately, they were recognizable, but more importantly, is to recognize all the amazing people who helped me along the way. People helping, over and over, was obvious during my lifetime. On the other hand, look at what *wouldn't* have happened if my mother had never suggested I go and check out the rowing team. If I never made the team, chances are, I probably would have never met, John Storck. What if I had gone on to study medicine? I might have become a doctor, but I would have never been in the position to help so many people as I did through Senior American Housing. Of course, there are so many companies bigger than mine, but we lead the charge for senior care and housing solutions in Wisconsin. Those treasures will always have a place in Heaven, while the material stuff on Earth crumbles away. This is another perspective of how our life journey unfolds.

From age (fourteen - fifteen) I sheared Christmas Trees for G.R. Kirk Tree Co. at $1.60/hour until promoted to Supervisor where I earned $2.00/hour from (sixteen-eighteen) for a summer job. My first construction job was in the Vail Valley during the summer of 1974 while trying to help finance my way through college. There weren't many opportunities in Wisconsin that year, but in Vail, Colorado, I'd heard about their construction job opportunities galore. I didn't work a summer job in the summer of 1973 at age 19, because we trained after the National Championship victory for the Henley. My parents met and worked with Dave Cole back in the late 1960s and early 1970s during our family ski vacations. Dave was their broker when they bought a parcel to build a duplex on a few years down the road. He was also the first president of the Vail Board of Realtors. So in the summer of 1974 at age 20, I called Dave, and he said, "Come on out and I'll help you get started. You can stay with me for a while until you can figure out what you'd like to do."

The day after I arrived, I started applying for jobs. The job I had my eye on was a chainsaw operator on Vail Pass. I worked another construction job for a while until the logging company invited me in for an interview. They immediately saw a guy standing six feet four inches, a motivated strapping athlete in peak condition, experienced in chainsaw operation, looking for work. They said *I'll bet this guy can really cut trees.* So they hired me at $7.50/hour. That was my primary job that summer, sawing the cut line over Vail Pass for the new I-70 highway. The Eisenhower Tunnel was already open, but the Johnson Tunnel hadn't been drilled or cut yet. They were tasked with getting four lanes open by the fall of 1979. It was an incredible job, felling enormous trees, watching huge D9 Cats pulling logs away with choker chains like they were toothpicks.

Even though I always considered myself a man of prayer, a hard worker, and a person who gets tasks done, I believe it was ultimately

God's hand responsible for whatever I decided to do. It felt like I was an instrument of God's will simply because I was open enough to ask what God's plans were for me. In the summer of 1974, I thought, *Someday I am going to move permanently to Vail. I'm going to live there, ski, and sell real estate.* After all, my real estate studies at the university had already started the wheels in motion—or at least I thought they had.

God just laughed. The real plan was for me to work with my family and be an entrepreneur with them in the protective and graphics packaging business. Then I met my wife, Nancy, the daughter of a local family business owner in the area. That most certainly changed my life, and I felt like I was really getting good at "Making God Laugh." We fell in love, got married, and had four beautiful children. I was married to Nancy for thirty-five years.

While I didn't end up moving to Vail to develop and sell real estate, I did continue to ski there over the years. The whole ski story is quite an evolutionary tale as they usually are. Throngs of people who went to Vail during the 1960s, planning on staying for just a few days, weeks, or a single ski season, ended up living there for the rest of their lives.

My father was the original skier in the family. We would ski Vail as a family from 1965 on for one to two weeks annually. Closer to home, we skied little hills like Skyline near Friendship, Wisconsin. It couldn't have been more than three hundred vertical feet, and its only lift was a rope tow made from a long line slung over the rear wheel of a running tractor wheel.

We also skied at a little ski area called Hidden Valley, owned by an Austrian ski racer and instructor named Hans Froehlich. He brought over the Austrian technique, which was the original method taught at the time. My dad was interested in finding an inexpensive way for the family to ski, along with performing a valuable service, so he decided to look into ski patrolling. One day he asked Froehlich if he needed any ski patrolmen. He said, "We do, yes sir. Do you want to be the ski patrol *director*?" So my dad started the ski patrol at Hidden Valley with two other guys, the smallest ski patrol staff at the world's smallest ski hill.

In those days, we lived in Sheboygan, Wisconsin, where my dad was working for the International Paper Company. Coincidentally, he met the Testwuide family that owned Schreiber Malt, a company that provided malt for the breweries in Milwaukee, Wisconsin.

They told my dad, "You've got to go to Vail, Colorado because our son Paul is out there skiing at this brand-new, fabulous ski area." He was the fifth ski patrol director at Vail and eventually evolved into being one of the top vice presidents of the corporation. As ski patrol director, he developed industry-changing procedures for lift and gondola evacuations, avalanche routes, handling explosives, setting up on-mountain communications, and devising medical protocols that are still in use today. He ultimately became the senior vice president and chief operating officer for Vail and Beaver Creek and helped develop the two resorts.

Paul Testwuide became a family friend and was at my dad's ninetieth birthday party and his funeral. When we were kids, we always wanted to go ski with Paul. At six feet five inches, he was a mountain of a man. He even made me look small. But in 1965, I was just a little kid following Paul, down powder runs like "Cow's Face," with snow up to our chests. We kids were terrible skiers. We didn't have a clue how to ski that stuff. We were falling and flailing, just trying to survive.

Vail was my favorite destination for skiing and was always in the back of my mind. But for better or worse, skiing was purely my avocation, never my vocation. Nevertheless, I learned how to ski fairly well over the years from Paul Testwuide in Vail and Hans Froehlich at Hidden Valley, who, incidentally, went on to become one of the first certified ski instructors in the country.

All this was at the very beginning of PSIA, the Professional Ski Instructors of America, the professional association that oversees professional ski instructor training and certification all over the country. Today there are more than thirty-three thousand members in eight divisions.

When our family started skiing Vail, none of us could ski powder worth a hoot. But our skiing skills skyrocketed because now we were skiing a real mountain with real snow. We learned how to do parallel turns in deep powder back then, yet I've always worked on improving my technique. When I went to the University of Wisconsin, I wanted to keep skiing (which seemed like it cost a phenomenal amount of money in those days), so I thought, *Why don't I do the ski patrol gig like my dad?*

So I went through ski patrol training in the Madison area. When I went for my Basic National Ski Patrol certification, they asked me, "Where'd you learn how to ski?" I told them I'd skied several little hills around Wisconsin, but I really learned how to ski in Vail, Colorado. They were impressed as I zipped through all the training and testing without any issues, including toboggan handling. I already had first aid training as a Boy Scout and lifeguard, so I just needed to update it through the American Red Cross. With my focus on pre-med in college, the plan was making sense and fitting together nicely.

Near college, I skied on the ski patrol at a little area by the Wisconsin River near Spring Green called Wintergreen—Wintergreen in Spring Green. That was also the town where Ross Graves grew up, who was one of the boys in our boat, along with John Storck and me. So together with John Bauch, John Mercier, Joe Knight, Karl Newman—all seven of us rowing guys, the majority of the boat—we skied there during the winter, even though our rowing coach frowned on it. He didn't want any of us to break our legs. We convinced him it was balance training for the boat.

Then I went through the National Ski Patrol Senior Certification training and testing, and once again, they asked me where I learned how to ski. So I told them Vail. They said, "We like how you ski. Is there any way you could help teach the ski patrollers how to ski better?"

"Well, sure. What do you want me to do?"

"You can be the training advisor for the National Ski Patrol in the southwestern region of Wisconsin here in the Madison area." That was how I started teaching skiing: teaching skiing improvement to ski patrollers at twenty years old.

When I graduated from Madison in May 1976, I found that I enjoyed teaching skiing more than picking up broken bodies on the hill. I thought maybe I should start teaching skiing instead. Teaching people how to ski safely seemed more proactive than rescuing someone who'd already injured themselves. Of course, both are noble endeavors, but ultimately, I ended up choosing what I thought was the more proactive approach, where I continue today, sharing my passion for skiing with people from all over the world.

The year I graduated from college, before becoming more involved with ski instructing, I moved up to the cottage that my mom bought by Wautoma, near a brand-new little ski area by Mount Morris, called Nordic Mountain. It was a cute little hill, and it did have a chairlift, so it was big time for Wisconsin in those days. I talked to Bill Kramer, the owner of the ski area, and he said, "Yeah, we need ski patrolman here. Do you want to be the ski patrol director?" So just like my dad, I started ski patrolling. We had two ski patrol directors in one family. It must have been the Paul Testwuide influence on a microscale.

In 1974, while I was still in college, my dad and my brother Jim—along with Jerry Berg, another instructor I'd teach with later in Vail—passed their PSIA associate certifications together. They were teaching skiing at a tiny ski area named Sunburst. Shortly after I started as ski patrol director during the 1976–1977 ski season, my dad came over to Nordic Mountain where I was and asked them if they needed a ski instructor. He eventually ended up becoming their ski school director. So there were the two Trotters: directors of the ski school and ski patrol.

While I patrolled, I started getting involved more and more with PSIA and went through their training programs. At the same time, while I was teaching skiing and ski patrolling at Nordic Mountain, I applied to take the ski instructor certification examination. I went up to the Indian Head ski area in Upper Michigan for my first certification in March 1977 and passed the associate certification with flying colors. The next year, I went to take my full certification and passed. I had the hardest examiner one could draw. Just to yank my chain, he wrote a big "F" across the top of my scorecard on the third and final day, making sure I saw him mark it in bold. I saw a glimpse of the "F" and was crestfallen. I thought I flunked. In those days, they didn't tell us immediately if we passed or not. When it came time to find out whether we did, they called out "Larry Trotter, full certification." The F meant "full," not "flunk."

Following the presentation event, the PSIA examiners asked me where I learned how to ski. So once again, I told them Vail. They said, "Why don't you come back for the examiner tryouts in the fall of 1978?" So I did. There were over one hundred people who tried out at a little ski area called Wild Mountain near Taylors Falls, Wisconsin. I was the first one in the parking lot early the first morning. The second one was Jerry Sorenson. We started talking and went through the tryouts together for the entire four-day weekend. We were the only two who made the cut and passed to become PSIA certification examiners. Jerry still teaches at Vail out of Lionshead. So there's another example of how God puts people together. I was the first candidate in the parking lot. Jerry was the second.

Jerry Sorenson and I became examiners in the fall of 1978 and level III examiners the following year. I was an examiner for about fifteen years; Jerry was an examiner for more than twenty-six. Jerry and I still share a lot of time skiing together and enjoying water sports together back in the Midwest during the summer. Additionally, I attended PSIA academies in 1981 and 1983 and participated in an examiner exchange in 1981 with Austria, where I skied for a week with Karl Spann, the head certification examiner of Austria. He was our host, and he had been at Sun Valley, Idaho, teaching instructors how to ski as well as the renowned skier Corky Fowler, found on the cover of *SKI Magazine* and other media back in the seventies. We enjoyed our time together. While there, I met a wonderful instructor from Vail named Jean Weiss, who was the first woman on the PSIA National Demonstration Team and participated in the 1968 Interski at Aspen, Colorado. She had met Karl Spann previously in Sun Valley, where he visited her at their ranch. Talk about a small world and how God brings people together. Eventually, when I transferred from Beaver Creek and started teaching as a member of the Vail Village Ski School, she was there. She still remembered me from Austria, and our friendship continues today. In 1982, I went through the French certification process and have continued for decades to try and ski with the best in ski teaching. I was always the big guy, built for rowing but not exactly for skiing. Skiing continues to be my lifelong learning sport, and it makes me "younger next year." Oftentimes in life, there is never a finish line.

Embracing ski teaching like I did all of my endeavors, from skiing, teaching methodology to movement analysis, I was like a sponge, totally immersed in the art and science of teaching skiing, attempting to do it at the best skill level I could. Just like in business, God's fingerprints were all over my skiing career while I discovered one of my true passions in life.

> [31] *So whether you eat or drink or whatever you do, do it all for the glory of God.*
>
> —1 Corinthians 10:31 (NIV)

Even today, I find it interesting how often we can meet people in a location thousands of miles from home and re-engage in relationships with them years later in our own backyard, under completely different circumstances. Jerry Sorenson, Jerry Berg, and Jean Weiss are just a few skier standout examples. God had a hand in guiding each of us through our pursuit of excellence.

Still involved with Colonial Container Corporation I traveled to Vail to train and teach skiing part-time. Skiing was my passion sport, and I loved sharing it with other people. When creating Senior American Housing as well as two more projects, I continued teaching for Vail Resorts. Wherever I went, whatever I did, skiing was always on my mind.

Continuing to go out to Vail in the 1980s as a PSIA level III examiner I enjoyed skiing with the ski school directors and supervisors: Mike Porter, Chris Ryman, Jens Husted, Dee Byrne, John Boles, Jerry Berg, and many others. In the spring of 1986, Dee Byrne and John Boles said, "You know, Larry, you come out here for training every year, and we know you live in Wisconsin, but when you come out next year, we want you to wear blue," meaning I was actually going to start *teaching* skiing at the Vail/Beaver Creek Ski and Snowsports School with the best skiers and the best ski school in the world.

So beginning in December 1987, I started teaching part-time at the Beaver Creek destination ski resort. That increased from fifteen days to thirty-plus days. Teaching out of Beaver Creek for twenty-five years, followed by another eight with the Vail Village Ski School, I continue teaching skiing because I love it. I love to share my passion with others. I love the entire learning process involved with it as well as the growth and skill development. I'm now in my thirty-third year of teaching skiing for Vail Resorts and forty-five years of teaching skiing from when I first started teaching ski patrollers at age twenty.

Every single day, with each and every client, I have the privilege to share my overwhelming gratitude for living in an environment where skiing on top of a snow-covered mountain, marveling at the spectacular 360 degree views are consistently delightful to the soul. This stirring of the soul is a visual and spiritual stimulation response to such a grand landscape only God could have created.

Since the Cape buffalo attack, I've also become a mountaintop minister at Two Elk, the restaurant located on the top and east side of Vail Mountain, overlooking the legendary back bowls. I've always felt that my journey to Vail was a spiritual one. It's been like an annual seasonal pilgrimage. I've never experienced any sight quite like skiing on the top of Vail Mountain, with the Holy Cross Wilderness looming in the background. When we gaze at the 3,000-vertical-foot cross made out of rock and snow carved into the peak of the 14,005-foot-high Mount of the Holy Cross, we have to ask, *How did that happen? By accident?* Believe me, there's no way any of this could have happened by accident.

> [3] *Commit to the Lord whatever you do, and he will establish your plans.*
>
> —Proverbs 16:3 (NIV)

When looking at the view while riding Gondola One out of Vail Village, the grandeur of the Gore Range is breathtaking as well. It's easy to understand what's drawn all of us here for so many years.

Before I became an official resident of Colorado in 2010, three years earlier, I spoke to Fred Rumford. Fred was the ski school director at Beaver Creek at the time and I asked him about coming out to teach full time—he hired me to teach more than sixty days a year.

Teaching full time at Beaver Creek for those three winter seasons convinced me to move my residency from Wisconsin to Colorado. I would come out and live in the mountains during the ski season and commute to Beaver Creek each day. Fred moved to Keystone to be the director of skiing and then director of Crested Butte, followed by returning to Keystone, ultimately being promoted to senior director of guest services and ski school for all of Vail. Coincidentally, I met my new bride while she worked for Fred.

Diane was working part-time in special operations guest services. Our first date was skiing all day. After that, we discovered we were made for each other. Everything she loves, I love. Everything I love, she loves. We believe it's a match made in Heaven.

Once again, I paused to ponder what would have happened if I'd moved to Vail right after graduating from college. If I had, I would have missed the opportunity to work with my family. I'd have missed the opportunity to be a pioneer in the assisted-living business. I would have missed the opportunity to be awarded the Entrepreneur of the Year by Pres. George W. Bush. But most importantly, I might not have married when I did and had four beautiful children. But that would have been my plan, most certainly not God's.

Truly, I do regret that I didn't read the Bible earlier in life. I wish I would have continued reading it back in my Boy Scout days and not caved in as easily as I did. But I didn't. It was the direction of the pathway taken at the time. I do believe that God shapes us through all the milestones and waypoints we experience. God is constantly molding us into the person He designed us to be. Sometimes I could be stubborn and didn't always follow God's will, but overall, when I've prayed and followed God's path, incredible results happened that I couldn't have accomplished on my own.

If there's one facet of my life that I felt was a sad failure, it was my marriage to Nancy. But I can honestly admit that I did try. I did pray. I asked priests to be involved, and we went through seven years of marriage counseling. I was convinced that God was involved, but I didn't understand how or what God's plan might be. Even though I was absolutely set against divorce, I kept wondering what God's will was for us after praying for so many years.

After three years of engaging in legal action with our county judge, he said we had to bring our relationship to some kind of conclusion one way or the other. So on October 26, 2010, at nine o'clock in the morning, we went before him again.

Our priest was there, and when we prayed, it felt like God took over.

The result was that we were officially divorced before noon that day.

Looking back over my life, I've experienced many miracles with my family, friends, and business ventures. But I asked myself, "Were they answers to my prayers? What could I have done to make life better for everyone?"

Once my divorce was final, I started asking God, "What would you like me to do with the rest of my life? Can you just send me a sign, some kind of message?" After twelve years of intense praying, the message was delivered by over two thousand pounds of Black Death. The ultimate message was simple and short, so obvious when we think about it: to not focus on extreme pursuits anymore but to focus on God and family for the rest of my life. That was God's answer to my prayers.

While waiting for them to roll me into the Steadman Clinic operating room for the second of three surgeries, Father Brooks told me on the phone, "Larry, you're a big guy living a big life. It would have taken a lot more than an e-mail for God to get your attention, so he sent you an African Cape buffalo."

It worked.

CHAPTER FOUR

CHALLENGES AND SOLUTIONS FOR MODERN CHRISTIANS

Then Jesus declared, "I am the bread of life. Whoever comes to me will never go hungry, and whoever believes in me will never be thirsty."

—John 6:35 (NIV)

Long before I was staring eyes to eyes with an African Cape buffalo, I was grappling with a list of struggles that to me seemed just as life-threatening. I'd survived not one but two bankruptcies, a failed marriage, and wasn't ecstatic about my life in general. Of course, anyone looking at me from the outside saw an entirely different image. I managed to pull off a long list of successes and accomplishments long before I'd even hit midlife—more than most people experience in their entire lives. But on the inside, I was still a mess. I just couldn't put my finger on what it was.

Remember, it was back in 2002 when Amy caught me during a particularly vulnerable moment and first convinced me to start reading the Bible daily. Together, let's unpack what became the most crucial milestone and waypoint of my life a bit more. Reading the Word of God was working so well in Amy's life, she was anxious to share the good news with me. But it wasn't going to be easy. Ever since my failure at attempting to read the scriptures when I was a Boy Scout, I avoided contact with the Bible. At that point in time, the occasional readings at church services seemed like plenty. How could there possibly be enough time in my life to read another book? Stopping the hustle and bustle of life, pushing to get stuff done, just to read another book with the title Bible?

Fundamentally I wasn't afraid of the Bible, so I opened the doors of my assisted-living facilities to the people from Gideons International February of 2002, inadvertently not realizing it was my birthday. The Gideons came into our facilities and gave each of the residents copies of their Bibles. They had a variety of different sizes and colors and I was personally interested in a handy brown miniature-size copy, so they gave me one for my birthday. I call it my little brown Bible and still read it today. At the time, I remember thinking, *I can take this with me anywhere.*

There are more than sixty versions of the Bible, divided into word-for-word, meaning-to-meaning, and paraphrased versions. The most popular is the King James Version and makes up 55 percent of all the Bibles sold. That's followed by the New International Version (19 percent) and the New Revised Standard Version (7 percent). But they all deliver the Word of God and are wonderful resources. My little brown Bible was of the New King James Version.

All Bibles are divided into two major sections: the thirty-nine books of the Old Testament followed by the twenty-seven books of the New Testament—sixty-six books in all. The Old Testament is considered the foundation of the Bible and establishes many principles, prophecies, and the history of the people, tribes at the time and describes the wrath of God against sin. The New Testament builds on the foundation of the Old Testament and describes the revelations of God, focusing on the Son of Man, Jesus, His teachings, healing miracles and describes the grace of God with sinners. God's apostles wrote in detail how Jesus, the son of our Father in Heaven was born into this world as a man and is indeed the Word of God. The apostles further detail Jesus's death, for all of us to understand that we are essentially washed with Jesus's own blood and cleansed of all our sins of the past, present, and future.

One of the complaints I'm sure we've all heard from nonreaders is how difficult the Bible is to understand. For many, that may be true. Take any book written two thousand years ago and we're likely to run into challenges with the way authors wrote back then. Oftentimes, the writers of the various books of the Bible wrote in parables or simple stories designed to convey their message to the poor, uneducated masses. Fortunately, it does get easier.

Today many active Christians faced with challenges recommend going to the Bible for answers. They say, "All the answers to our problems are in there." But for those who don't read the Bible regularly, it can be a daunting experience. Of course, with the Internet, it's become infinitely easier. All the versions of the Bible are now online. We can find anything we desire about the subject of "pain" as an example by simply running a Google search or by using Bible Gateway:

Suffering for Being a Christian

> *¹² Dear friends, do not be surprised at the fiery ordeal that has come on you to test you, as though something strange were happening to you. ¹³ But rejoice inasmuch as you participate in the sufferings of Christ, so that you may be overjoyed when his glory is revealed. ¹⁴ If you are insulted because of the name of Christ, you are blessed, for the Spirit of glory and of God rests on you.*
>
> —1 Peter 4:12–14 (NIV)

If we don't have access to the internet, Gideon's Bibles have handy indices and contents that will point us in the right direction. Most established churches sponsor weekly Bible study classes, where we can learn how to get the most out of the Bible and interact with others interested in learning about the Word of God.

By the time I got to the book of John, I felt like I was literally downloading the Word of God straight from Heaven. There were times while sitting alone in a tree stand, I'd have to wait hours to see a whitetail deer. During those moments, it's beautiful to simply watch all the outdoor activities of animals and the leaves falling from the treetops. I carried that little brown Bible in my backpack and, in between gazing at wildlife, read it for hours.

When I traveled on business, I'd carry my little brown Bible in the pocket of my sport coat. This time, I finally made it past the thirty-three generations in the book of Matthew. After that, I was hooked. I couldn't stop reading it. I read each book of the New Testament from beginning to end.

Essentially I started reading the Word on my forty-eighth birthday and before turning fifty years old finished reading the entire New Testament, meditating on every word, line, and paragraph. I read King David's five books of 150 Psalms as well as King Solomon's thirty-one chapters of Proverbs. There are highlighted sections in my Bible left over from the first several times I read it. Some are underlined in pen, some yellow highlighting, while others are marked by golden aspen leaves at the place where I left off while hunting elk in the mountains with a bow and arrow.

Peacefully I was in total harmony with all the birds, deer, elk, mountain lions, bears, pine martens, coyotes, porcupines, and bighorn sheep. How long I read depended if I was in a meditative mode or not. It could be fifteen minutes or fifteen hours. Much of my reading time was while enjoying the surroundings of wilderness and observing wildlife as my spirit was immersed in the little brown Bible. I always brought still and video cameras along with me, even when I was hunting. I'd video more animals in a single season than most people have seen in their lifetime.

When I shared the videos with people, they'd ask, "Why didn't you shoot them?" They didn't get it, for I was purely out there to be close to nature and wildlife, to observe them and enjoy the beauty of it all, the best of creation.

Ironically, it was also a time of immense conflict in my life. Nancy and I were two years into what would turn out to be seven years of marriage counseling in an attempt to save our marriage. I discovered that no matter who we have relationships with—whether it's our siblings or other family members, business partners, and associates, or skiing buddies—eventually, there's going to be conflict in our life because no two people are the same. It's not a matter of *if* it's going to happen but when and *how* we're going to resolve it. I found many of the answers to my questions in the book of Matthew 18:15–22, where Jesus spoke directly about how to resolve conflicts:

Dealing with a Sinning Brother

15 Moreover if your brother sins against you, go and tell him his fault between you and him alone. If he hears you, you have gained your brother. 16 But if he will not hear, take with you one or two more, that "by the mouth of two or three *witnesses every word may be established." ¹⁷ And if he refuses to hear them, tell it to the church. But if he refuses even to hear the church, let him be to you like a heathen and a tax collector.*

¹⁸ Assuredly, I say to you, whatever you bind on earth will be bound in heaven, and whatever you loose on earth will be loosed in heaven.

¹⁹ Again I say to you that if two of you agree on earth concerning anything that they ask, it will be done for them by My Father in heaven. ²⁰ For where two or three are gathered together in My name, I am there in the midst of them.

The Parable of the Unforgiving Servant

²¹ Then Peter came to Him and said, "Lord, how often shall my brother sin against me, and I forgive him? Up to seven times?"

*²² Jesus said to him, "I do not say to you, up to seven times, but **up to seventy times seven**."*

—Matthew 18:15–22 (NKJV)

At that spot in time, I also attended several seminars about conflict resolution, including Stephen Covey's "The 7 Habits of Highly Effective People":

- **Be proactive**. You have a natural need to wield influence on the world around you so don't spend your time just reacting to external events and circumstances. Take charge and assume responsibility for your life.
- **Begin with an end in mind**. Don't spend your life working aimlessly, tackling whatever job is at hand. Have a vision for the future and align your actions accordingly to make it into a reality.
- **Put first things first**. To prioritize your work, focus on what's important, meaning the things that bring you closer to your vision of the future. Don't get distracted by urgent but unimportant tasks.
- **Think win-win**. When negotiating with others, don't try to get the biggest slice of the cake, but rather find a division that is acceptable to all parties. You will still get your fair share and build strong positive relationships in the process.

- **Seek first to understand, then to be understood**. When someone presents us with a problem, we often jump right to giving a solution. This is a mistake. We should first take time to really listen to the other person and only then make recommendations.
- **Synergize**. Adopt the guiding principle that in a group, the contributions of many will far exceed those of any individual. This will help you achieve goals you could never have reached on your own.
- **Sharpen the saw**. Don't work yourself to death. Strive for a sustainable lifestyle that affords you time to recuperate, recharge, and be effective in the long-term.

A common thread began repeating itself: if only I'd fulfilled the requirements for God and country with the Boy Scouts and read the Bible then, how much richer my marriage would have been. How much richer being a parent would have been. How much more I could have given to the church by being involved, giving time as well as knowledge, talent, and treasure.

Reading the Word of God has certainly been one of the most momentous changes I've made in my life. But I realized that I couldn't expect to see differences by merely secluding myself in a corner reading the Bible. Change would really depend on reaching out and extending myself into the community, interacting and exchanging with other Christians.

People who gather in church are far from perfect. They'll be the first to admit that. They're merely together with the rest of the broken world on a path of discovery and recovery, trying to figure out how they can learn to live better. When we start sharing the solutions we've learned along our spiritual journey, what we've learned to do (and sometimes what not to do), we begin to enjoy the meaning of living a fully engaged Christian life.

All the new understanding conveyed by the Word led to bonding with individuals—mentors, if you will—particularly when I went through my Cursillo weekend. The Cursillo movement was started by the Roman Catholic Church who granted permission to use their program to the Anglican-English church and the Episcopal Church of the United States. The first Cursillo pilgrimage numbered over 70,000 young people walking "The Way of St James" to St James Roman

Catholic Cathedral, Spain (Santiago de Compostela), in 1948. It is the site of the burial grounds of the remains of St James. People have been making the pilgrimages since St James was buried and there's a wonderful movie called, The Way, starring Martin Sheen worth watching. Methodists, Lutherans, and Presbyterians have a similar program.

The weekends typically began on a Thursday evening and end on Sunday night. Over the course of the simulated pilgrimage "three-day weekend," a team of clergy and laypeople present a series of fifteen talks to the new candidates, delivered in a specific order, meant to call on the Holy Spirit to offer guidance and enlightenment.

The candidates live as a small Christian community and learn how others received the same presentations. Topics include the following and more:

- The layperson's role in the church
- The meaning of grace and the sacraments
- The importance of prayer
- The role of Christian leadership in the community
- How our calling can help bring Christ to the environments in which we live
- The importance of supporting one another in an effort to live a Christian life

Everyone participating in Cursillo has the common goal of becoming a better person and ultimately becoming the person God has designed them to be. When we put together that kind of collective motivation for an entire weekend, with open and engaging minds, it's hard to put the outcome into words. Metamorphosis isn't a big enough term to describe it. Transformation isn't enough. It's simply life-altering.

Participation in Cursillo begins with sponsorship from a member of the church who has already gone through Cursillo, followed by an endorsement from their clergy. The application requires that the prospective participants be somewhere along the path of a spiritual journey.

During the Cursillo weekend, messages come in—often e-mailed—in the form of beautifully designed pages from Cursillo chapters all over the world. They're received by the worship director of the "Palanca Chapel." The messages are called Palanca which are essentially prayers of leverage for the candidates with the collective prayer power of the entire Global Christian community magnified by praying corporately and simultaneously for the candidates who are living through the 3-day pilgrimage experience.

At the conclusion of the weekend, each participant (now called a Cursillista) receives a simple cross made of metal and yarn. While it may only be worth a few cents in literal value, the crosses are priceless to the people receiving them. On the back of my cross, it says, "Jesus is counting on you."

After completing the initial Cursillo weekend, Cursillistas can sustain their relationships by meeting with other Cursillistas in their individual geographical locations—usually near the church they attend.

Cursillistas get together regularly through "fourth-day" meetings called grouping. There's a prayer format, followed by a discussion when members meet to share where they are on their individual and community spiritual *journey* or *camino* or our *way* of discipleship. Discipleship means to take up the discipline of walking the pathway of Jesus or following *the way* of Jesus.

Cursillo weekends are **not** like a clique and don't carry any special designation. Instead, they're opportunities for people who have gone through this transformational process to willingly meet in a communal Christian atmosphere and assist new candidates with the completion of their transformational weekend. There are larger gatherings hosted by the diocese. At the diocese level, they conduct an Ultreya (or reunion in Spanish), where Cursillistas meet regularly in their regional geographic area—sometimes even at the state level. Once a Cursillista, the bond between brothers and sisters is more than one would expect, and it is lifelong.

I enjoyed my Cursillo weekend so much I went on to be a presenter for future weekends; usually giving "Rollos" or the short talks that addressed one of the fifteen different topics of Christianity or serving in the Palanca Chapel. Examples of topics I presented have been on our environment, where we live and work and how we interrelate with others, as well as laity and piety. In all, I've participated in over eight Cursillo weekends, several in Colorado, and many more in Wisconsin. Some of the best people I know are on those teams, both clergy, and laity.

Cursillo weekends do shape and change the lives of good Christians and help form them into amazing brothers and sisters. They become more involved in every aspect of living the great commandment to love one another as Jesus loves us, to love our neighbors as ourselves, every aspect of living more and more like Jesus and acting proactively as a Christian.

Listening to hundreds of testimonies by presenters at Cursillo weekends who have lived through all kinds of addictions and struggles, unbelievable difficulties, from fighting in the Vietnam War to losing close family members—every kind of catastrophe we can think of and how they lived through it, is truly a treasure to hear, understand and comprehend.

When we start sharing these stories, we find out that everyone has difficulties and struggles. I've shared my Cape buffalo story with thousands of people. The most common thread that runs through sharing is everyone does indeed have a Cape buffalo story in their life. It may not be Black Death in Africa. It could be cancer or dealing with an addiction of a family member or their own personal struggles. But together, by sharing, we can grow stronger.

Margaret Millar once said, "Life is something that happens to you while you're making other plans." We think we're developing an intricate plan for life, but in reality, God's already been working on it. And God's way ahead of us.

I learned there are all sorts of venues for practicing a Christian life if we're open to them and willing to engage with other people, venues that help us share our struggles and challenges as we live our lives.

In 1998, I was on the Bay Lakes Council Executive Board of the BSA when my eldest son, Matthew, signed up to go to the PhilMont Scout Ranch. The ranch is located near the town of Cimmaron, New Mexico, and covers more than 219 square miles of wilderness in the Sangre de Cristo Mountains. It was donated in 1938 by Waite Phillips, the original pioneer owner of Phillips Petroleum, and is now owned and operated by the Boy Scouts of America. Between the first week of June and the end of August each year, more than twenty-two thousand scouts and their adult leaders backpack through the ranch's wilderness on a series of spiritual treks.

We could not afford the Philmont trip when I was a scout, so I signed up and joined Matt as one of the six adult leaders for thirty scouts. We trekked through some of the most beautiful wilderness of New Mexico all together as three crews of 10 scouts.

The boys led and took care of themselves during the ten-day trek, over one hundred miles on foot, carrying all their gear for sleeping, eating, and surviving in the wilderness. In addition to the scouts and adult leaders, the trek also included at least one chaplain. While the scouts were hiking on foot, the chaplain drove ahead to our destination in a four-wheel-drive vehicle and set up a beautiful outdoor service. We sang all kinds of songs, including the "Philmont Hymn," which includes words from the scriptures. Another song we sang was "On Eagles Wings" written by Michael Joncas in 1977:

> *You who dwell in the shelter of the Lord*
> *Who abide in His shadow for life*
> *Say to the Lord, "My Refuge*
> *My Rock in Whom I trust."*
> *And He will raise you up on eagle's wings*
> *Bear you on the breath of dawn*
> *Make you to shine like the sun*
> *And hold you in the palm of His Hand . . .*

Every night, the crew of ten Boy Scouts and two adult advisors would participate in a sharing communication called Thorns and Roses. A scout would begin by sharing a thorn: what was the worst episode that happened to him that day? It could have been something that challenged him on the trek, a relationship with someone in the crew, or even a negative thought he had. After going around the circle, the same scout would describe one of his roses: what was the best experience that happened to him that day? Until everyone had a chance to contribute, including the adult advisers. It was a fabulous way to resolve conflicts and end the day with a positive mindset. It kept that crew of boys in about as much harmony as we could expect for a group of young men of ages ranging from fourteen to twenty.

The concept many people grapple with is not only asking God for help during hard times but more importantly asking for help during good times when all seems well. The truth is, God is already aware of our situation long before we appeal to Him. God is always present and proactive. Regardless of what we're going through, God's miles ahead of us, already working on a solution, or God's plan was made long ago. But we need to allow God to work in our lives. We need to be open. We can't expect serenity if we only knock on God's door when we need help. Rather, we need to be close to Jesus all the time. We need to have a continuous, loving relationship, especially when we're going through insurmountable life and deadly challenges, like near-death experiences, a subject that would become near and dear to my heart.

There's a remarkable book called *The Shack* that presents Christianity in a whole different light. It was also made into a stunning movie. In the story, God is an African American woman named Papa. She's a beautiful lady and presents a different way of experiencing Christianity. Every time I finish watching it, I want to watch it again.

Another book worth reading that was made into a movie is *Heaven Is for Real*. It's a true story about a small boy who died on an operating table and had an out-of-body experience. He looked down at his mother in one room and his father sitting in another. The boy went to Heaven and was with Jesus until he was given the blessing to come back to life on earth. After he returned, his parents asked him questions and showed him pictures as he clung to his story that he saw Jesus Christ. Mysteriously, Akiane Kramarik painted a picture of Jesus called *Prince of Peace* at age eight from dreams, and the boy confirmed that's exactly what Jesus looks like, with green eyes, sitting atop a beautiful white horse. It certainly wasn't the image they taught us in Sunday school.

The difference between those experiences and mine with Black Death is that mine is the only near-death experience we know of that's been confirmed by ten other objective observers. When the newspaper article about my attack came out in August 2012, dozens of my ski instructor and realtor friends like Ed said, "I read about your near-death experience, but nobody has ever witnessed anything like your story. Yours was the first."

Living a Christian life is not just in spirit. Jesus's way of life includes mind, body, and spirit—our collective being. I've always believed that we can't have mental and spiritual growth without having a physically fit body, as we promised in the Scout Oath.

However, we need to be mindful of individual physical and mental medical conditions, age, special situations and disabilities. Each of us, in concert with our personal physicians must personalize a fitness plan that is appropriate for our individual possiblies. We have to exercise all the intricate facets of our lives. On the other hand, we can't just exercise our body and hope that it will result in spiritual growth. We have to take care of our entire being to positively contribute to our whole health.

One of the best books I've read on the subject of comprehensive health is titled *Younger Next Year* by (Harry) Henry S. Lodge, MD, and Chris Crowley, JD. In the book, they describe the four simple lifestyle disciplines we must include in our lives if we're going to feel and look like we're fifty when we're eighty-five or more years old: (1) regular exercise, (2) eating well, (3) having a close-knit family structure, and (4) finding and participating in a venture we're passionate about. Health is a matter of mind, body, and spirit.

I also enjoy participating in yoga, Pilates, and meditation. Back in my rowing days, we learned how to meditate. We trained ourselves on how to use our minds to dissociate from bodily pain so that we could row through increased thresholds of discomfort and pain, then keep pulling, no matter what we were faced with. We learned that pain is just a feeling we create in our minds. People can tolerate more pain than they realize.

We've all heard about people who can tolerate unbelievable amounts of pain. Holocaust survivors are good examples of that. Louie Zamperini in the book *Unbroken* by Laura Hillebrand is another. The minuscule Italian went from competing in the 1936 Olympic Games in Berlin to being shot down in his B24 bomber, stranded in the Pacific Ocean, and then tortured in a Japanese concentration camp before being rescued.

Another movie I can recommend is *God's Not Dead: A Light in Darkness*, with the song "God's Not Dead (Like a Lion)" sung by the popular Christian music group the Newsboys:

> *Let love explode and bring the dead to life*
> *A love so bold to see a revolution somehow . . .*
> *Now I'm lost in Your freedom*
> *And this world I'll overcome*
> *My God's not dead, He's surely alive*

He's living on the inside, roaring like a lion . . .

Help is out there in many different formats, reminding us of the breadth and depth of God's realm and popularity, including Christian music. When I lived in Wisconsin near Green Lake, we were close to Oshkosh, which some people know as the city that hosts the Experimental Aircraft Association fly-in week. They also sponsor a huge Christian music festival called Lifest. It's bigger than Woodstock and held during the second week of July every year, with over one hundred acts on seven stages, while all the audience raises their hands in the air, singing and praising God.

I remember standing twenty feet away, face-to-face with Chris Tomlin, one of the best American contemporary Christian music artists, worship leader, and songwriter in the world. He's a true conduit of the Holy Spirit. Looking eye to eye with him, singing out to the glory of God was an unforgettable waypoint and inspirational spot in time.

The night my dad died, I played Michael W. Smith's recordings all night long—another one of my very favorite channels to the Kingdom of Heaven. One of my bride's and my best friends, Barbie Huggenvik, shares her story when she stumbled onto Michael W. Smith playing the piano in the Beaver Creek Chapel. Barbie and her husband, our Vicar, Mark Huggenvik, were caretakers of the Beaver Creek Chapel. She heard somebody playing the piano in the chapel, so she thought, *I'd better go down and see who on earth is playing the piano. They're not supposed to be there playing.* Seated at the piano was Michael W. Smith. She said, "Normally, we don't let people play the piano unless during a service, but please continue playing." She was in tears. It became a private worship service in direct connection with the Kingdom of Heaven on the mountainside at Beaver Creek, Colorado.

After Michael left the valley, he sent the Huggenviks his entire collection of some of the best Christian music on the planet. These are all the little God winks and fingerprints that are everywhere if we're aware and open to receive them. You've probably noticed I have not mentioned the TV.

I used to believe that life was the result of being either lucky, coincidental or earned through plain old-fashioned hard work. But after six and a half decades, I discovered there's a lot more to life if we believe in the power of God and are willing to accept God's direction.

Nothing is an accident, not even being attacked by a two-thousand-pound Cape buffalo.

The first step, I believe, is to become an open vessel. One of the most remarkable quotes I've ever heard was an interview with Jimmy Page, the lead guitarist of Led Zeppelin. He was discussing their album *Led Zeppelin IV* when Page said, "We are all vessels of the Holy Spirit." Even with more obvious titles, did we realize there was a spiritual foundation in their music such as "Stairway to Heaven," one of the most popular rock songs of all time? Sometimes subliminal messages are present that we can notice or may not notice. Sometimes God's presence is obvious in the reflections of people's faces, like at a candlelight vigil service during Easter worship or chapel service at a Cursillo weekend.

Blaise Pascal said, "There is a God-shaped vacuum in the heart of each man which cannot be satisfied by any created thing but only by God the Creator, made known through Jesus Christ." Of course, Saint Paul the Apostle wrote similar language in his letter to the Ephesians 3:16–19 (NIV). When this concept becomes an understanding, one's perspective changes.

> *16 I pray that out of his glorious riches he may strengthen you with power through his Spirit in your inner being, 17 so that Christ may dwell in your hearts through faith. And I pray that you, being rooted and established in love, 18 may have power, together with all the Lord's holy people, to grasp how wide and long and high and deep is the love of Christ, 19 and to know this love that surpasses knowledge—that you may be filled to the measure of all the fullness of God.*
> —Ephesians 3:16–19 (NIV)

That's the first step I believe: experiencing an awareness. We have to open the vessel before we can receive. People do that by sharing their Cape buffalo stories with others. God is present more than we realize. God's proactive and so far ahead of us. It isn't until decades later that we may realize, "So *that's* why that happened." We just have to realize that God's plans are constantly in motion. Even today. Every day.

A question many people ponder is, where are we going to be for eternity? Eternity is a longer time than we can comprehend, especially when we're focused on this planet during our finite life, although I truly believe that we can have Heaven on Earth if we're open vessels. We can let God into our lives now. We can have the peace that surpasses all understanding now on Earth. We don't have to wait for Heaven.

There's a constant battle between the world today and the Kingdom of God. But the most repeated prayer Jesus taught us—the Lord's Prayer—confirms how we should pray:

> *8 Therefore do not be like them. For your Father knows the things you have need of before you ask Him. 9 In this manner, therefore, pray:*
> *Our Father in heaven,*
> *Hallowed be Your name.*
> *10 Your kingdom come.*
> *Your will be done*
> *On earth as it is in heaven.*
> *11 Give us this day our daily bread.*
> *12 And forgive us our debts,*
> *As we forgive our debtors.*
> *13 And do not lead us into temptation,*
> *But deliver us from the evil one.*
> *For Yours is the kingdom and the power and the glory forever.*
> *Amen.*
>
> —Matthew 6:8–13 (NKJV)

God wants life on Earth to be as it is in Heaven. If we think that way and we want our life on Earth to be as it is in Heaven, that means we want the Kingdom to be here now rather than to wait for it. I believe we already have the power to do that.

My understanding of revelation is that once the battle is over and Satan plunges into the abyss, there is Heavenly peace everywhere forevermore.

Stewardship and giving back to God's purpose and will has always been a significant concept to me. I believe we should give back to God a portion of ourselves for the purpose of assisting the hands and feet of Jesus here on Earth, to help deliver the ways of the Kingdom of Heaven to Earth. Living a life of value to our fellow man normally produces incomes, harvests, earnings, cash flow or other additional forms of compensation. I've always believed that if we're of value to our fellow man, then we'll be appropriately compensated. The more God given talents, gifts and value we are blessed with here on Earth, the larger the portion of our compensation can be given back to the Kingdom coming with God's will to Earth. Compensation we earn making our living or daily bread here on Earth is not bad, it's good. It's the stewardship of our earnings that matters.

There are many ways we can give back to God. We can give back our time, talent, and treasure. Some people have more treasure than time. Some people have more time and talent than treasure. Whatever the situation is, we can always give something back. Some people aren't financially in a position to give very much. Others give millions of dollars but may not be recognized for it because they prefer it that way. But everyone has the opportunity to give something back.

Can you imagine what our world would be like if everyone gave back just 10 percent of their time, talent, and treasure? This is what Jesus taught as tithing. Tithes were given by the patriarchs Abraham (Genesis 14:20 [NIV]) and Jacob (Genesis 28:22 [NIV]). A system of tithing or giving a tenth of what God provides us back to God is found under "tithe" twenty-nine times in the NIV of the Bible.

> ¹⁰ *"Bring the whole tithe into the storehouse, that there may be food in my house. Test me in this," says the Lord Almighty, "and see if I will not throw open the floodgates of heaven and pour out so much blessing that there will not be room enough to store it. ¹¹ I will prevent pests from devouring your crops, and the vines in your fields will not drop their fruit before it is ripe," says the Lord Almighty.*
> —Malachi 3:10–11 (NIV)

We've all read about people who have given substantially, with huge foundations, charitable entities, and trusts. Then there's the story of "The Widow's Offering" in Mark 12:41–44 (NIV), who only had a couple of alms left but still gave them all to Jesus:

> *Jesus sat down opposite the place where the offerings were put and watched the crowd putting their money into the temple treasury. Many rich people threw in large amounts.*

But a poor widow came and put in two very small
copper coins, worth only a few cents.
Calling his disciples to him, Jesus said, "Truly I tell you, this poor
widow has put more into the treasury than all the others.
They all gave out of their wealth; but she, out of her
poverty, put in everything—all she had to live on."

It often surprises Christians when they discover just how much the Bible talks about money. There are more than 2,300 verses related to money, wealth, and possessions. Jesus spoke about money roughly 15 percent of His preaching and eleven out of thirty-nine parables. It was one of His most sensitive and difficult subjects:

> *Do not store up for yourselves treasures on earth, where moths and vermin destroy, and where thieves break in and steal. But store up for yourselves treasures in heaven, where moths and vermin do not destroy, and where thieves do not break in and steal. For where your treasure is, there your heart will be also.*
> —Matthew 6:19–21 (NIV)

Jesus spoke about money not because he was obsessed with it or because he thought it was important to have lots of it, but because he knew that money was one of the most likely reasons someone either gave up following Him or chose to stay. Jesus presented us with a clear choice:

> *No one can serve two masters. Either you will hate the one and love the other, or you will be devoted to the one and despise the other. You cannot serve both* God *and money.*
> —Matthew 6:24 (NIV)

> *[23] Then Jesus said to his disciples, "Truly I tell you, it is hard for someone who is rich to enter the kingdom of heaven. [24] Again I tell you, it is easier for a camel to go through the eye of a needle than for someone who is rich to enter the kingdom of God."*
> —Matthew 19:23–24 (NIV)

I believe this doesn't mean, if we're of great value to mankind and we're being compensated accordingly, we can't get to Heaven if we accumulate significant earnings. However, if it seems difficult to give a portion of our wealth to God's charity, then our worship focus may be misdirected. Rather, it's an opportunity to give meaningfully and generously to charitable causes. Nothing material prevents anyone from being an open vessel for the Holy Spirit and allowing Christ to fill the void unless they fill themselves with worldly, material possessions and worship them as false gods.

My college buddy John Storck told me a story about his wife, Paula, while giving a presentation to their church. She held up a jar filled with multicolored marbles. On the outside, lying all by itself, was one white marble that represented God. There simply wasn't room for it. She said that's exactly how it can often be with our life. If we fill our life with everything until it's full, there will be no room for the white marble: God. But if we put the white marble in first, it will always be there, followed by all our other priorities.

After all those years of struggling, praying, and asking God to give me direction, he used Black Death to deliver my message. Apparently, my vessel was too full too much of the time. I was making progress in other areas by making room for God but only on the surface and at the top of the jar, where it was easy to trade another marble temporarily with the white marble. Simply put, the white marble didn't occupy a permanent position. God needed Black Death, a voice from Heaven, and an angel from the Kingdom, to get my attention. After my life was saved, while I was sitting in the dirt, overwhelmed with thankfulness and gratitude, I realized God answered my prayers by delivering the message I'd been waiting for. That message was, of course, to put the white marble in the jar first.

The voice verbally delivered two messages to save my *physical* life from Black Death. The third message was about saving my *spiritual* life, my soul. I did not argue with the voice on the day of the Cape buffalo attack, and I haven't argued with the message since. I have been focusing on God and giving back all of me that I have to give.

On the day of the attack, the voice said, "Focus on God and family," so I have been balancing my life with God and family. It's been a truly beautiful way of life filled with an abundance of love, joy, and peace. All glory be to God.

For five years following the attack, I was a mountaintop minister on top of Vail Mountain. I shared the weekly readings of the Old and New Testaments as well as the Gospel during our services. I shared my story. We sang songs like "Open the Eyes of My Heart" with Michael W. Smith singing the lead from my cell phone.

Open the eyes of my heart, Lord
Open the eyes of my heart
I want to see You, I want to see You . . .
To see You high and lifted up
Shinin' in the light of Your glory
Pour out Your power and love
As we sing holy, holy, holy . . .

I became more active with our church and have been an elected vestry board member for the maximum number of terms allowed by the church. I'll continue to be on the finance committee until they no longer need me. I treasure contributing to the worship services in every way I can, including being a chalice bearer. The role is my honor and privilege to serve actively and participate in the sacrament of communion with clergy and the members of our church. To me, it's a preview of the great banquet awaiting us with Jesus at His house in the Kingdom of Heaven, a glimpse of eternity with all our family members who have already passed.

Our church in the Vail Valley serves approximately 1,500 people at Christmastime. At our Christmas services, I've truly enjoyed working with Father Brooks and Vicar Mark Huggenvik and Vicar Emily Lukanich. Between Christmas Eve and Christmas Day, we conduct services at the Vail Chapel, at the Beaver Creek Chapel, and the Edwards Chapel. We have three physical locations devoted to our interfaith system here in the Vail Valley.

On Christmas Eve, I've been devoting my life evening and night from the four-thirty services in Beaver Creek to Vail and back to Beaver Creek again at ten o'clock. My wife, Diane, also serves as a chalice bearer, and it is truly a blessed Christmas serving Vail Valley.

We alternate between sharing Christmas in December with the body of Christ (our church family) and Diane's three daughters and their families. We celebrate Christmas with my two daughters, two sons, and their families in July. All thanks be to God.

I've thoroughly enjoyed being elected to and serving on the governing board of Cursillo, called the secretariat, for the Diocese of Colorado. At this point, witnessing God's message in this book *Seeing the Light through Black Death, Salvation in the African Savanna* has become my ministry and hope that we'll be able to share these witnesses among the brothers and sisters of the Cursillo movement, the branches of Jesus's vine, the body of Christ.

My wife and I have been trying to give back to God in every way we can. Jesus rose and ascended to Heaven. We truly believe He is risen indeed. But we are here now in the present to be His hands and feet today. We have the opportunity of doing His work here now. We can provide the handshakes and hugs and take people under our wings in times of need here on Earth currently, just as Jesus ministered when He first came.

On an annual basis, my wife's ministry is traveling on mission trips all over the world. She's the hands of Jesus on surgery tables as a retired surgical registered nurse. Recently, it's been in Zambia, Africa.

Since recovering from the attack in 2012, I've been designing my annual calendar around my family, being in the right places at the right time of the year. In the wintertime, we host them here in Vail. In the summer, we're at the lake in Wisconsin. Between the winter holidays, we travel to Dallas and stay with my daughter Martha, her husband, and four children. We spend as much time together as possible as a family as well as a Christian community.

We're growing together and learning from one another. I've learned more from my kids than I've learned from many other acquaintances combined. My eldest daughter lives in California, so we spent several weeks visiting her every year at the end of the ski season. We go from the beach to the mountains, wine country, and Yosemite. You name it. They're amazing places to share faith with my grandchildren, in some of the best classrooms of creation, out in God's country, standing under two-thousand-year-old sequoia, pointing out the upper and lower Yosemite Falls, Half Dome, and El Capitan.

All the lessons I learned in the outdoor classrooms as a Boy Scout, I now have the obligation, duty, and joy of sharing with my grandsons and granddaughters. They want to learn about creation and God. They're anxious to learn how to catch and release fish. They want to know how to shoot guns and bows and arrows and snow and water ski. They're getting out there and learning how to enjoy all those pursuits along their journey while learning and realizing life's a transformational process.

I believe that kids should be involved with all those types of exposures from an early age. I believe kids need the church, school, scouting, and athletics to understand how to enjoy a balanced life. It teaches them the value of recognizing the positive aspects of their life. If we can help our children develop an open heart, how to be an open vessel, filling it with Jesus and the Word of God, they're going to grow into healthy adults, well-rounded contributors to society, living the way Jesus taught us over two thousand years ago as written in the scriptures.

Like many kids at a young age, I was a terrible Sunday school student. I was a disrupter, busy bouncing off the walls. While my parents gave me every opportunity to embrace the Word of God, they learned that just dropping kids off in classrooms doesn't mean God's messages will stick. It has to happen daily—just as my daughter taught me. As parents and grandparents, we need to be living examples of the Christian life. Even today, I struggle with the example I was for my children. They saw me exhibiting poor behavior at times, certainly not always the best example or witness for a father of four. So when I tried to get better, they were naturally skeptical.

Filled with the right intentions, we do get better with time. People notice other people evolve and become kinder, gentler, living life with more self-control and patience. People witness our positive and negative attributes. That's where it's good to have "accountability partners" like my friend Randy Zieth. He and I have been accountability partners for decades. So is my college buddy, John Storck. We help one another, although I'm certain that they help me more than I help them. They'll call you out when you're stepping over the line. My wife is my closest partner in so many ways and a perceptive counselor. What a blessing to have friends and family as supportive compassionate sisters and brothers in Christ, all connected to the same source.

²¹ Would not God have discovered it, since he knows the secrets of the heart?

—Psalm 44:21 (NIV)

If our words or intonations aren't appropriate, our accountability partner will let us know. If we have a partner who is truly a friend, as well as a brother or sister in Christ, we can talk with them about anything. We can continue to learn and grow. Even after six and a half decades, I look forward to learning more about becoming a better man, father, grandfather, and brother.

Going back to my early childhood, I've always believed no matter what our endeavor, we want to surround ourselves with the best there is. If we want to be a better skier, we need to ski with the best skiers on the mountain. If you want to be a better wing shooter, stick with the best shooters. If you want to grow spiritually, align yourself with the best spiritual warriors you can find. That's what we get when we actively participate and engage with a Christian community in fellowship and worship services, regardless of the church of our choice. That's what happens when you go through Alpha, Cursillo, and stay connected to the vine.

Everyone needs a spiritual mentor. Clergy—including deacons, priests, and bishops— have spiritual partners they meet with regularly in both times of need and time of joy and peace. Whoever your spiritual advisor is, talk to them frequently. Sit down with them. Pour out your problems to them. What's not right in your life? What's not settled in your soul? Why you're not at peace?

Make no mistake; it's not easy to live a Christian life, but most people experience a metamorphosis while practicing Christian living, surrounded by friends and fellow believers. But when the chips are down and nobody's watching, we realize that God is *always* present, sending messages to us, reminding us that He's right there by our side.

Life can be so good, yet sometimes it's not. When I'm contemplating a situation, I imagine all the generations of my relatives who have already passed from this Earth, watching me from above. It realigns my perspective.

I feel that it's also important to give ourselves and other people credit for what and when we're living right. We live in a society of social media and are overwhelmed with electronic gadgets and an endless stream of bad news. Unfortunately, sensationalism still seems to sell. As a result, people don't give themselves enough credit when they're reaping the rewards of living a sound, balanced, healthy life. There's a wonderful quote from retired Admiral William McCraven's book *Make Your Bed: Little Things That Can Change Your Life . . . and Maybe the World*:

Changing the world can happen anywhere, and anyone can do it.

I've always believed that if we can go to bed at night recalling that we took at least one positive step to improve our life or the lives of other people mentally, physically, or spiritually, we've had a successful day.

One of the disciplines I got into the habit of a long time ago was praying at night before falling asleep. More recently, bedtime praying leads to a positive conversation with my wife, where we mutually share our daily stories of thorns and roses in a current and present manner. The two-way exchange naturally leads to mutually shared praying, where we both pray out loud together, alternating leadership. We have an open verbal three-way conversation every night, with Jesus in the center. No one is left out, and everyone hears each other's thoughts and prayer process. We start with our blessings and give thanks and praise to God. In hindsight, I sometimes wonder what would have happened if I'd done just that decades ago. God only knows where the path may have led, but God led me the way He did for His purpose and will, not my notions.

We may not always have the best day. But if we turn our lives over to God, reflecting on thankfulness with affirmations of gratitude and pray together in harmony, it's amazing how the end of our day will conclude, with an abundance of love, joy, hope, and peace, just as Jesus promised in scripture.

Yes, life can bring both, "Challenges and Solutions for Modern Christians", yet the simplest theme to remember is opening yourself to receive the Word of God as I witness to you right now, it will provide more freedom and peace than you could have ever imagine. It feels to easy sometimes to recognize Jesus's teachings for what they actually are, teachings that provide us how to live in harmony with truly loving relationships as marriages, parents, grandparents, brothers, sisters, friends, business partners, employers, employees, citizens, participating members of our communities, and so many more. It's ridiculous to think that Christian living only leads to a sequestered life in a monastery. We can still enjoy participating in all the passion activities we love, including experiencing the joyous gift of the great outdoors.

In 2012, I was at a time in my life when I wanted to spread my wings and experience more of God's creation and people. One of the adventures I'd always dreamed of doing was going on an African hunting safari and observing big game face-to-face, perhaps bringing home a zebra rug, photographing exotic animals, and interacting with the African culture. For once in my life, I had the money, the time, and the interest, so I thought it was worth exploring.

While I understand that hunting isn't for everyone, it's been an important part of my life since I was a child and, ultimately, the vehicle that brought me face-to-face with death, a metamorphic apex, and an understanding of God's design for my future. My walk with Jesus has helped me understand there's a diversity of people in the world and the importance of sharing different perspectives in thought, word, and deed, so I thought it was worth taking time to look into the hunting industry —its strengths, fallibilities, and what it contributes to humanity. It turned out to be much more complex than I thought.

CHAPTER FIVE

TROPHY HUNTERS VERSUS ELMER FUDD

It contained all kinds of four-footed animals, as well as reptiles and birds. Then a voice told him, "Get up, Peter. Kill and eat." "Surely not, Lord!" Peter replied. "I have never eaten anything impure or unclean." The voice spoke to him a second time, "Do not call anything impure that God has made clean."

—Acts of the Apostles 10:12–15 (NIV)

From as far back as 650 BC, the Assyrians hunted lions and other wild game—not necessarily for sustenance but as a rite of passage—a practice that's still passed down from generation to generation in all corners of the world, from the smallest Midwestern farms in the United States to international hunters. It was the same for me, but my father taught us, "Do not shoot anything unless you plan on eating it." My family enjoyed eating wild game and honored the harvest with painstaking details to present the fare elegantly. Nothing was wasted.

Both my parents loved the outdoors. My mother grew up accompanying her family to their cabin in Douglas County, Wisconsin, on the Upper St. Croix Lake. As a young boy, my father taught me about the great outdoors, the wildlife, and the awesome beauty the wilderness had to offer. He loved outdoor activities and took me everywhere with him. I fell in love with all aspects of being outside and learned how to immerse myself in the best of God's creations. Whether it was a canoe, camping, or a fishing trip, I was always all in.

By law, I wasn't allowed to hunt until I turned twelve, so he started me out shooting shotguns, bow, and arrows, and .22-caliber rifles at immovable targets and eventually moving targets. When I was finally old enough, I learned how to hunt using both guns and bows and catch and release trout with a fly rod. In 1963, my mom bought a cabin on a lake in the middle of Wisconsin that we cherished for the rest of our young lives. She knew how important lake life was as a factor in developing and maintaining family bonding from her childhood. It was there that I started bowhunting white-tailed deer. Eventually, I acquired my own lake cabin in the vicinity of where my mother's original family cabin was, sharing the same values and bonding with my family.

My mom was always concerned about me wandering into the woods during the deer gun-hunting season. Our cabin was surrounded by other gun-carrying characters. Nevertheless, my dad gave me a Remington 12-gauge shotgun when I graduated from high school. After I earned my degree from the University of Wisconsin School of Business, he presented me with a beautiful .270 deer hunting rifle and scope that I still own today. His parents gave him a Remington shotgun when he finished high school, and I own that gun as well. Like my dad, I'm passing those guns on to my sons when I move on to the great wilderness in the sky. The tradition completes the circle of life.

I enjoyed all types of hunting, but I went rifle hunting for white-tailed deer primarily for the social aspects of traipsing around the great outdoors with my friends and family. But to me, it always seemed like the woods were filled with more dangerous people toting guns during the deer gun-hunting season, than bows and arrows during the archery season. The famous Wisconsin white-tail gun-hunting season begins on the weekend before Thanksgiving and runs for nine consecutive days. Everyone hunts, even people who have no business lurking around the woods carrying lethal weapons. Companies shut down to let their employees run amok in the forest wearing their bright orange vests, chasing deer.

While initially, it was fun, I quickly outgrew it. There were just too many beer-guzzling Elmer Fudds running around with loaded weapons, asking, "Which way did that silly wabbit (in this case, deer) go?" Many of them didn't have a clue what they were doing, and people were inevitably maimed or killed by indiscriminate gunshot wounds. The deer ran for their lives. More were shot by accident than by design, and after opening day, we rarely saw any because they had escaped high-tailed deep into the thickest woods and swamps.

Conversely, when hunting with a bow and arrow, the deer move naturally, and a hunter has to be a skilled woodsman and learn intricate details about the animal's routines, habitat, and behavior. For me, it's always been a more sophisticated endeavor than aiming a rifle, pulling the trigger, and hoping for the best.

Being a guy who truly enjoyed studying deer and wildlife, as typical with all of my passion ventures, my approach was to explore all aspects of archery hunting to the nth degree. Known for a reputation for being one of the most disciplined and enduring hunters around, I spent as much time as possible in the woods. I just loved being out in the wild, observing nature, even when the hunting season was closed and throughout all four seasons. When I did decide to harvest one, I tried to make it the most humane harvest I could.

It's my belief archery hunting is more ethical and kinder to animals because it's a surgical procedure. We use razor-sharp surgical blades when we hunt. When harvesting a deer, the animal doesn't even know what happened. They start hemorrhaging and expire within a short peaceful time. By contrast, shooting an animal with a gun smashes bones, tears tissue, and the loud gunfire forces them to run away, probably suffering in pain, if not strategically shot with precision. I used the same precision archery approach later with the Cape buffalo, only it was more like he was hunting me than the other way around.

Today hunting wild animals in Africa conjures up graphic images of trophy hunters on the prowl for big game. The most blatant example occurred on the night of July 1, 2015, when the media covered a hunter who stalked and killed Cecil, Zimbabwe's beloved twelve-year-old lion, with a bow and arrow in Hwange National Park. Two years later, Cecil's son, Xanda, was shot and killed by other trophy hunters, leaving behind several young cubs.

This example of hunting certainly gave hunting a bad reputation, even though we learned firsthand that technically, the hunting was legal and within the park's perimeter hunting zone. After my wife's surgical mission trip to Zambia in September 2019, we spent four days in Hwange National Park, Zimbabwe, with professional guides on a photo safari. Not only did the safari offer fabulous viewing of virtually the majority of animals one would hope to observe, we also saw Cecile's widow, Ceca; two of his sons; and many grandchildren. We took adorable photos of the cubs and all the pride. Of course, I asked about the hunting incident. We learned that the parks have perimeter zones to try and contain the animals, so they don't wander out onto private and community land where residents farm and live. They don't want the animals roaming free and killing livestock or humans. So the perimeter buffer zone is a hunting zone with concessions operated by professional hunters legally under Zimbabwe laws, with the intent of scaring the animals back into the park refuge.

At the time Cecil was shot, he had been kicked out of the pride and was living solo in the hunting zone. We learned that it was legal to shoot a lion with a collar if they were in the hunting zone. Personally, I don't understand why anyone would want to shoot a lion, but I don't know why anyone would want to shoot an elephant or any of the big five animals either except maybe a Cape buffalo, whose population has been unthreatened. We thoroughly enjoyed watching the lions in their natural habitat, albeit a park. All thanks be to God that Theodore Roosevelt initiated our U.S. Parks system and the concept was further adopted in Africa, where reserves and parks were created there as well.

Remember my dad's quote: "Do not shoot anything unless you plan on eating it." I was in total alignment with his hunting creed then just as I am today. For the benefit of people who don't follow trophy hunting, I thought I'd take a moment to share some objective statistics, along with research we conducted ourselves.

Trophy hunting is big business. The Humane Society International estimates that more than $132 million or 0.03 percent of South and Eastern Africa's gross domestic product originates from 18,000 annual trophy hunters. The International Council for Game and Wildlife Conservation in partnership with the Food and Agriculture Organization calculates that over $183 million USD ($167 million EUR) was generated by hunting in 2008.

While trophy hunting is popular all over the world, the 540,000 square miles of private reserves of twenty-three African countries have long been considered a mecca for hunters. More than 18,000 sport tourists hunt elephants, rhinos, plains game, including buffalo, and export 126,000 trophies back to their homes, leaving behind more than $200 million for the local economies.

For the uninitiated, trophy hunting is defined as the practice of hunting wild game for sport and recreation according to *one perspective*. Trophies or parts of animals like their paws, antlers, horns, skin, and heads are removed from the animals, sent to taxidermists for preservation, and then shipped back to the hunter's home, where they occupy a position of prominence in their "game rooms."

The most popular game hunted by trophy hunters are members of the "Big Five": elephant, lion, leopard, rhino, and Cape buffalo, all of whom are strictly regulated, requiring government licenses to hunt. A smaller segment of trophy hunting is "canned hunting"—animals bred and held captive on high fenced private ranches—easy targets for trophy hunters.

Trophy hunting was famously originated and publicized in 1910 by Theodore Roosevelt, after leaving office as the twenty-sixth president of the United States. He spent nearly a year shooting and collecting thousands of African trophy specimens for the Smithsonian Museum of Natural History in Washington, D.C. Even today, it remains the most comprehensive collection of natural history in the world.

Roosevelt said, "There is no danger that the elephant will become extinct because large elephant reserves have been established; and furthermore, wise regulations have been adopted and are enforced; such as prohibiting the sale of tusks below a certain size, the shooting of females except for museums."

In 1934, a group of white hunters established the East African Professional Hunters Association, with headquarters in the Norfolk Hotel in Nairobi, Kenya. Their mission was to create and promote laws and regulations for hunting and a total ban on killing female animals, shooting from vehicles, and at watering holes. Even though their efforts were well-intentioned, they ultimately ended up eliminating thousands of big game animals from the African continent.

A total of one hundred years after Teddy Roosevelt visited Africa, many of the animal species he boasted would live forever are in danger of extinction. Conservationists fear that over half of today's endangered species will be wiped from the face of the earth by the end of the next century.

At the turn of the last century, when Africa settlers introduced domestic sheep and cattle, they were in much higher demand than wild animals until they were wiped out by rinderpest—a German word meaning "cattle plague." The pestilence killed 90 percent of cattle, buffalo, antelope, deer, giraffes, wildebeests, and warthogs until Arnold Theiler developed a vaccine that curbed the epidemic. Eventually, the wild animal populations returned, leading to the flourishing industry it is today.

So the battle over trophy hunting continues. Most of its bad press began when early European settlers indiscriminately slaughtered game. What remains are those who either support or stand defiantly against it.

The Battle over Big Game Trophy Hunting

There are a number of organizations for and against trophy hunting. Conservation Organizations include the following:

- Izaak Walton League
- Sierra Club
- National Wildlife Federation
- Wilderness Society
- National Audubon Society
- John Muir Society

Those against trophy hunting include the following:

- Humane Society of the United States
- Defenders of Wildlife
- People for the Ethical Treatment of Animals (PETA)
- Center for Biological Diversity
- Fund for Animals and American Society for the Prevention of Cruelty to Animals (ASPCA)
- Friends of Animals

Those who support hunting include, but not limited to, the following:

- Safari Club International
- Boone and Crockett Club
- Pope and Young Club
- Wild Sheep Foundation
- National Wild Turkey Federation
- Ruffed Grouse Society
- Ducks Unlimited
- Pheasants Forever
- Mule Deer Unlimited
- Whitetails Unlimited
- Quality Deer Management Association
- Rocky Mountain Elk Foundation
- Aldo Leopold Society
- Theodore Roosevelt Society
- Wisconsin Waterfowl Association
- Delta Waterfowl Association

To truly appreciate the peril of African big game hunting, it's important to understand the different threat levels defined by the International Union for Conservation of Nature (IUCN) Red List:

- Extinct (EX) – beyond a reasonable doubt that the species is no longer extant.
- Extinct in the wild (EW) – survives only in captivity, cultivation, and/or outside the native range, as presumed after exhaustive surveys.
- Critically endangered (CR) – in a particular and extreme critical state.
- Endangered (EN) – very high risk of extinction in the wild, meets any of the criteria for Endangered.
- Vulnerable (VU) – meets one of the five red list criteria and thus considered to be at high risk of unnatural (human-caused) extinction without further human intervention.
- Near threatened (NT) – close to being at high risk of extinction in the near future.
- Least concern (LC) – unlikely to become extinct in the near future.

- Data deficient (DD)
- Not evaluated (NE)

Personally, though I feel hunting ethically is a God-given right overall, I'm not high on some aspects of the commercial hunting industry—in Africa as well as other countries. I believe what my dad said, "If you're going to do it, do it right or don't do it at all". Shooting animals from the back of a moving Land Cruiser is not my idea of sport or good sportsmanship. I've always enjoyed hunting on my own using natural approaches in concert with God's intentions, leaving no footprints behind and low to zero environmental impact. It should not be about **only taking**, but giving back as exemplified by the many service organizations that contribute to soil, water, wildlife, and environmental conservation. Just as we learned in Boy Scouts. Some of my favorite conservationists are Aldo Leopold and his writings like *Sand County Almanac* and *Game Management* and John Muir with a plethora of writings like *Meditations of John Muir, Our National Parks, The Yosemite, Wilderness Essays, Story of My Boyhood and Youth, The writings of John Muir, Nature Writings* and much more.

My dad's hunting creed taught me: never shoot a single living species of our planet's fauna that you're not prepared to eat. Furthermore, he taught us the same principle applies to flora, that we should all be stewards of the environment, and he would explain how renewable resources like forests can be grown for paper and lumber. I continue to firmly agree with his conservation practices. Wildlife regulators are now starting to get stricter about the utilization of game. Here is an example, where hunters only use the breasts on birds and throw away the remainder of the meat on the carcass, such as the thighs and legs. This underuse of game is considered an act of waste labeled wanton waste by most state and province departments of parks and wildlife in North America. The worst act of wanton waste is killing wildlife and leaving them lay to rot or dumping them after shooting and collecting them. Animals should be cared for and harvested in the most humane way possible and completely utilized, prepared as a protein food source, and never shot to be dumped on an outfitter to dispose of the carcasses. In certain areas of the world, it is very appropriate for outfitters to legally sell or give the meat to local communities in need of food. There are also food bank programs that provide the hunter's harvests to needy people for no cost. These are ways of *giving back*. Thank you to the truly ethical outfitters around the world who practice, "Doing it right." I've thoroughly enjoyed hunting with their outfits. Two of my favorite and best outfitter examples are, Chris Widrig of Widrig Outfitters in the Yukon and Grant Abrahamson of East Cape Outfitters in South Africa.

But, how honorable and ethical are hunters that embrace slogans like "Hammer Time," "Slaughter Fest," "If it's brown it's down," "Wack'em and Stack'em"? Jesus said, "Get up, Peter. Kill and eat" (Acts 10:13 [NIV])—basically, the short version of my dad's creed. To me, that means treat the animal with respect, harvest them humanely, use a trained dog (preserve game, use a trained dog) for retrieving game, care for the proper preparation of the meat, including extracting the maximum meat from the carcass, cooking, and dining with friends and family. If the process is executed effectively, I believe wild game is healthier than high-production processed domestic animals. So I say, "If you're not going to eat it, don't shoot it." If you just want to shoot, go to a shooting range and shoot targets.

When I hunt, I like being immersed in nature and living in concert with the animals. I relish observing their behavior, how they live, where they go for water, and how they feed. I authentically enjoy the entire outdoor experience and not just shooting animals. Over the course of my life, I could have harvested many more animals than I did, but instead, I chose to shoot them with cameras instead of rifles or bows. I was recording wildlife and nature long before the practice was popularized via hunting television channels. Most of the hunting shows are very ethical and educate viewers about topics we've been discussing in this chapter. My salute to the many positive leaders in the hunting industry, thank you for sharing the best of hunting.

Hunters in Africa are required by law to hire a professional outfitter and at least one professional hunter and two trackers per hunter. It's similar in Canada and Alaska, where we're required to hire a licensed outfitter and hunt with the supervision of a licensed professional guide when hunting big game. They are there not only to find game but also to teach proper stewardship to visiting hunters unfamiliar with the wilderness, animal species, and their unique characteristics. In Africa, once an animal is harvested, trackers are at your side to take care of the meat as well. They transport it back to camp, where they have walk-in coolers and sophisticated cleaning facilities. They use the meat themselves in the camp, or they sell it to local restaurants and hotels. None of the meat is allowed to leave the country.

In the early days of African hunting safaris, hunters would literally walk ten to fifteen miles per day stalking animals with mobile bush camps carried by native Africans. It was true wilderness then, and hunters had to be highly skilled, rugged individuals to negotiate the terrain and raw environs. It was a costly affair to hire everything required to go on safari. Nowadays, most concessions drive hunters through the terrain in motorized vehicles. With private reserves, the property is fenced, so hunters rarely have to travel further than a few miles to take as many trophies as they can in the shortest amount of time. Today a hunter can still hunt on foot. But when they do, they put themselves at risk and on a more level playing field with wildlife that is not afraid of hunting the hunter.

Even with walking photo safaris, it's necessary to get around in Land Cruisers simply because there are so many dangerous animals like elephants, leopards, hippos, crocodiles, black mamba snakes, spiders, lions, Cape buffalo, and other deadly wildlife, dispersed over a wide area of topography. When hunting on a "glass or spot and stalk" (technique with binoculars on foot) safari, hunters are side by side with they're professional hunter, and they have two trackers spotting for wildlife.

For many hunters, taking trophies is part of the African experience. I know people who have homes they've expanded with additions specifically to house full body-mount trophies. It's a bit over the top for me but to each their own, and it is legal.

Again to me, hunting isn't just about shooting the animal. If someone does harvest an animal and would like to respect and honor the animal, the experience and memorialize the story, one can have a taxidermist mount and preserve them for display. Some people build elaborate display areas. Again for me, it's about harvesting ethically, humanely, and using 100 percent of the animal. If you're going to use their hides for clothing or rugs or other conversions, all the better. Only an elephant needs ivory, so thankfully, ivory is illegal, but the problem is poachers.

Arguments against Trophy Hunting

Opponents of trophy hunting are first in line to claim that it harms all species, not just members of the Big Five. Arguably, the most sought-after game are lions. Cape buffalo come in a close second and are the only one of the five that have been listed as LC by the IUCN.

One of the chief arguments against trophy hunting has been created by modern man. Hunters' approach to stalking animals has evolved from the slow-paced, once-sacred "thrill of the experience" mindset to a "hurry up, shoot as much as one can in the shortest amount of time" approach. Hunters would rather find easier, more rapid ways of shooting their targeted animals even if it means spending more money. Many private ranches charge between $10,000 to $15,000 USD for a single mature buffalo. Hunting Cape buffalo near Kruger National Park will typically set hunters back more than $30,000 per head.

Where a hunter might have once harvested a few animals over a week on foot, today's trophy hunters understandably demand more for their money. One commercial hunting outfit guarantees their guests will take twenty-one kills in a week with a money-back guarantee if they don't. They're able to do that by herding game and shooting from the back of vehicles.

While pro-hunting groups claim that a limited amount of hunting does not harm the animal populations, it appears that the opposite may be true. Every year, approximately six hundred lions are killed during trophy hunts. While that may not seem like a large number, it's enough to destabilize the lion's pride (the equivalent of their family structure), leading to even more deaths as outside male lions compete for dominance of the pride.

Trophy hunting is an expensive endeavor. It used to be practiced exclusively on foot, requiring a certain type of rugged individual who was not averse to spending a few weeks at a time roughing it in the bush, like our Rough Rider Teddy in 1910. Today many trophy hunters are more sedentary and less skilled. Like a strategically guided cruise missile, they're flown into remote locations by private charters, where hospitality staff cater to their every need. At the end of each hunting day, luxury accommodations, fine dining, wine, and amenities, including massages, are only minutes away from hunting grounds. Not exactly roughing it in the wilderness and experiencing the great outdoors.

There's also the risk that even with the best intentions, trophy hunting can be associated with poaching. While most outfitters are lawful and well-intentioned, they're constantly at risk. According to the report "The Myth of Trophy Hunting" by Save African Animals, "Opening up even a limited legal trade creates a smokescreen for poachers which is almost impossible to police."

In sub-Saharan Africa, there are more than 1.2 million square miles of hunting reserves-twenty-two percent more than all national parks of the region. Monitoring the area and enforcing hunting laws is an impossible proposition. Oftentimes, inaccurate reporting leads to misinformation that results in even more financial benefits for the unscrupulous few. Dr. Naomi Rose, a marine biologist who writes for the Humane Society of the United States blog, says, "Sport hunters' fees put economic pressure on managers to inflate hunting quotas beyond sustainable levels damaging natural ecosystems."

Those who oppose trophy hunting argue against hunting on at least two levels. First, it is ethically unjust to kill any animal for sport. If you aren't killing them for food or self-defense, there is no justification for taking an animal's life. Second, the revenue collected from trophy hunting is vastly overstated. The entire industry is threatened by corruption when it comes to managing money targeted for local businesses and indigenous populations. They argue by the time the hunters' fees are collected and distributed to booking agencies, outfitters, professional hunters, air charters, caterers, and camp managers, there's little, if anything, left for the local economy.

A study, authored by Economists at Large—commissioned by the International Fund for Animal Welfare, Humane Society of the United States, Humane Society International, and Born Free USA/ Born Free Foundation—concluded that "The suggestion that trophy hunting plays a significant role in African economic development is misguided." Economist Rod Campbell, the lead author of the study, said, "Revenues constitute only a fraction of a percent of GDP and almost none of that ever reaches rural communities."

Those supporting the U.S. Endangered Species Act claim listing the African lion and other animals targeted by trophy hunters as endangered species would prohibit the import of and commercial trade of animal body parts (animal trophies) and would reduce the number of animals killed each year.

Adam Roberts, executive vice president of Born Free USA, says, "The U.S. government has a serious responsibility to act promptly and try to prevent American hunters from killing wild lions, especially when the latest evidence shows that hunting is not economically beneficial. Listing the African lion under the Endangered Species Act will help lions at almost no cost to African communities. Government inaction could doom an already imperiled species to extinction through much of its range."

Arguments in Favor of Trophy Hunting

For better or worse, taking another animal's life has always reflected the laws of survival in the wild natural world. Carnivorous wildlife is at the top of the food chain. Man becomes the center of controversy when he shoots and kills without cause. Those in favor of trophy hunting may be better served by redefining trophy hunting.

A trophy to one person might represent a completely different paradigm to another. For a father-son or mother-daughter first time hunting experience, a young person harvesting their first duck or pheasant is a trophy. Most states and provinces across North America promote Youth Hunts as a way for young people to experience their first hunting adventure with family and friends, escorting them and providing an educational opportunity. Hunter safety education programs are also available on a state-by-state-wide basis. The young participants must pass tests to receive their certification for gun or archery safety, environmental, and wildlife stewardship. I believe that if everyone handling or owning a gun had to possess a hunter safety certification certificate, we wouldn't have gun control issues. If someone wants to own and use guns and not hunt, then a gun safety certification should be required by law in addition to enforcing existing gun acquisition and ownership license laws. If someone has mental issues, then the certification process should help screen students in the process of completing certification courses.

The United States and Canada already have programs in place, where third party verification is required to confirm mental stability, including requirements to confirm mental stability by the applicant's local police department where an applicate resides. In Canada, the license is called a "Possession and Acquisition License". We can't drive a car without taking a driver's education course and passing tests to obtain a driver's license. Why should anyone be allowed to purchase, own, or use a gun without a certification or license? Of course, outlaws can still break our laws as with anything, hence the slogan, "When guns are outlawed, only outlaws will have guns."

Here are other examples of definitions of trophy hunting:

- The first deer for a young person
- The first big game animal or small game animal
- 100 percent retrieval waterfowl hunt
- Best use of wild game
- Best dog work on an upland bird hunt
- One-shot big or small game hunt
- Best stewardship of the environment
- Quality Deer Management
- Quality game management on private land
- Harvest mature animals at the end of their life cycle
- Best sportsmanship, legal and ethical hunting examples

If the definition of trophy hunting is exercising poor sportsmanship, like shooting an animal and leaving it lie and rot because it's not big enough, then the trophy focus takes on a whole new meaning. Another negative connotation would be shooting ducks without a dog when hunters can't retrieve them effectively, resulting in the negative outcome of shooting and killing more than the regulated limit. Or willfully shooting over the legal game limit. Or shooting only the highest-scoring animals until the herd genetics decline. Or doing whatever it takes to shoot the biggest lion.

Normally, if a hunter is not a resident of the host country where they're hunting, a licensed commercial outfitter is required. So when examining African hunting, unless you are a native hunting for food or protecting yourself or property, we should call that **commercial hunting** and ensure that we don't include it in the definition of trophy hunting. In Wisconsin, if you are on a self-guided deer hunt with friends and family, that's not commercial hunting. But if you want to hunt deer or other big game in Canada as an example, then you're required to hire a professional outfitter who is trained and licensed as a commercial hunting concession. In other words, trophy hunting is not synonymous with commercial hunting. "Trophy Hunters versus Elmer Fudd", might be quite a confrontation, if Elmer only wants his first silly deer and shoots the biggest buck in the woods.

Supporters of commercial hunting claim that host countries benefit from millions of dollars of revenue left behind by hunting tourists. Those against it fear the extinction of species and irreparable harm to the environment. As it turns out, they're both right.

There are several arguments in favor of controlled hunting in Africa, specifically commercial hunting. Supporters claim that diseases introduced by domestic visitors and animals like cattle and dogs threaten indigenous African animal populations. They allege hunters are performing a crucial role in limiting the spread of diseased animals by culling out the weakest animals of the group. A good example is the old-age Cape buffalo.

Toward the end of their natural lives, old, sick, and diseased Cape buffalo wander to the periphery of the herd, where they are more accessible for hunters. Hunters perform a valuable service to the herd by taking out older bulls well beyond breeding age, whose presence may actually be a determent to the herd's propagation.

Another key to managing species like Cape buffalo is to limit hunting to males who have already contributed to breeding groups and to target no more than two percent of the total population. The pro-hunting blog *I Trophy Hunt* supports this point of view by suggesting that well-regulated hunts can effectively compensate for excess populations.

One success story is that of the white rhino in South Africa, whose numbers have been gradually increasing, thanks to well-managed commercial hunting programs in protected areas. This shines in the face of other countries like Kenya, where commercial hunting has been banned since 1977. Wildlife of all types has declined by more than 60 percent because of poorly managed conservation programs.

Operators of legitimate hunting reserves claim they are protecting wild animals by competing head-to-head with poachers. On the rise in many areas of Africa, poachers indiscriminately ambush wild animals using wire traps that snare, maim, and kill animals that fall victim to their inscrutable actions. But by hosting animals on private hunting reserves, visiting hunters are more apt to experience a more authentic adventure using their skills to overcome the savanna and ethically harvest wildlife—like Teddy Roosevelt did back in 1910.

The strongest and most popular arguments in favor of commercial hunting in Africa are conservation and support for economic growth. But does the industry really contribute effectively to the local economies? Therein lies the rub.

Dr. Rose argues, "Regarding the statement that trophy hunters do a lot for conservation, it's true that some portion of some hunters' fees goes to conservation in some countries, but it's rarely the major source of conservation funding. Usually middlemen—commercial outfitters—take the lion's share of sport hunting proceeds and local communities and conservation and management agencies get the dregs." The IUCN states, "Legal, well-regulated trophy hunting programs can, and do, play an important role in delivering benefits for both wildlife conservation and the livelihoods and well-being of indigenous and local communities living with wildlife."

Think about the limited approaches Africa has for generating conservation funding. The closest comparable activity to hunting is wildlife sightseeing. The revenue generated by sightseeing doesn't come close to the amount of money spent by commercial hunters. It also significantly impacts the ecosystem, requiring a larger footprint (sightseeing vehicles), carbon emissions, and infrastructure requirements.

One point opponents don't properly address is the economic differences between paying hunters' fees and the impact they can make on local communities. One trophy impala might cost a hunter $400. Kudo—a type of African antelope—could cost a hunter as much as $2,500 to harvest, while a Cape buffalo can often run more than $15,000 apiece. With the present currency exchange, that seemingly modest amount goes a long way in African communities.

Proponents claim that the revenue from commercial hunting helps fund important contributions to the community like health clinics, schools, water wells, and assistance against wildlife poaching. They are quick to point out that by paying African outfitters the fees for the game they harvest, they're making substantial contributions to the continent in the form of habitat protection.

The question of whether commercial hunting is ethically justifiable is a separate issue. While animal suffering can be minimized with sound hunting practices, the moral case for or against commercial hunting is a choice we must make as a society and as individuals.

There are also several less tangible benefits of commercial hunting. The Nambia-based company Kalahari Trophy Hunting suggests that commercial hunting can be an important educational experience for young people that emphasizes courage, generosity, humility, and fortitude. Helen Smith, an American forensic psychologist who works with children with propensities for violence, claims, "The Columbine High School shooting in 1999 never would have happened if those boys (Dylan Klebold and Eric Harris) had been properly mentored in hunting and shooting."

From what I've seen and learned during direct conversations with professional guides and hunters in Africa, the African commercial hunting industry is doing a good job of managing wildlife. Many herd sizes have actually increased in recent times. That's why Theodore Roosevelt kept fastidious records of his hunts. He started the Boone and Crockett Club, named after the famous North American outdoorsmen, Daniel Boone and Davey Crockett. Their purpose is to measure the animals: the actual dimensions of horns and antlers, the date of harvest, and other characteristics. Since the beginning of these records, many North America animal numbers, such as white-tailed deer as an example, have increased as well as becoming a healthier population and living to more mature age classes.

The Safari Club International is performing the same documentation. The result is hunters have contributed to increasingly larger herd sizes. Hunters, hunting fees, and private landowners have all contributed to both the growth of herd sizes and the quality of many species.

Over the years, I've been a donor and a sponsor of many wildlife conservation and hunting-related organizations, including Ducks Unlimited, Mule Deer Unlimited, Quality Deer Management, Whitetails Unlimited, Wisconsin Waterfowl Association, the Rocky Mountain Elk Foundation, Trout Unlimited, the Wild Sheep Foundation, and Pheasants Forever—more than I can recall actually. I've also been active in several action committees and bought items auctioned for wildlife conservation organizations.

Hunting is one of my passion sports, where I painstakingly care about wildlife when interfacing with our magnificent creation. So after committing myself to spending a month in South Africa, I wanted to learn more about the environment and wildlife that make Africa their home, beginning with Cape buffalo.

CHAPTER SIX

MEET THE DAGGA BOYS

21 So God created the great creatures of the sea and every living thing with which the water teems and that moves about in it, according to their kinds, and every winged bird according to its kind. And God saw that it was good.

—Genesis 1:21 (NIV)

Ever since the days when my dad exposed me to the great outdoors and taught me how to navigate in the wilderness, exploring our creation has permeated every aspect of my life. But there's always been a missing feature of our planet to explore: the opportunity to experience and observe the wildlife of the mysterious African continent, the prospect of photographing them, to interact with the people, their culture, and the adventure of hunting African big game.

Just the idea of harvesting big game on the African savanna has always stood out as a "must-do during my mortal life on earth" adventure I needed to check off my bucket list. The desire was fueled by a lifetime of watching Hollywood blockbusters like Tarzan movies, *The Last Safari*, *Out of Africa*, and *Hatari*. As a young boy, I imagined myself as John Wayne, strapped onto the front bumper of a Land Cruiser, lassoing a rhinoceros, or Tarzan swinging through the jungle on a vine.

The real opportunity started to present itself in 2010 when I was older, wiser, and a smidgeon more careful about how I rubbed shoulders with animals in the great outdoors. Financially, I was finally in a place where I could pull off an African hunting safari. So I began looking into what was involved with securing a hunting safari there and thought it might behoove me to engage in comprehensive homeschooling before I actually committed to such an adventure.

One day while visiting a Grand Junction, Colorado, gunsmith, I noticed from the photos covering the walls of his shop that he'd hunted in Africa. He raved about Grant Abrahamson of East Cape Safaris and told me Grant would be at a trade show in Denver in a few months and then staying with a local couple, drumming up business for his lodge. When Grant arrived, the shopkeeper introduced me to them, and they invited me to dinner.

Throughout the evening, I picked Grant's brain about all the details of his region of Africa. How does one get there? What was the weather and terrain like? How much would it cost? What animals could I expect to see, video, harvest with my bow, and could they be prepared at the lodge for dining, like kudu, gemsbuck, and eland? After wearing out his patience, I finally decided it was time. I was fifty-six years old. If I was ever going to do it, now is the time. It took a couple more years to dial in the trip, but finally, at fifty-eight years old, I was committed to going on a twenty-five-day South African archery hunting safari in July 2012.

While many hunters make annual hunting pilgrimages to South Africa, I decided that I was only doing this one time. This trip was going to be the one and only. Revolving around July Fourth, our American Independence Day, I was going to celebrate my own independence. Recently divorced, a reasonably successful businessman, father, and an active member of my church, it was my time to savor this stage of life and celebrate my new beginning. I felt I was truly living the lyrics of Garth Brooks's profound song "The River": "I will sail my vessel until the river runs dry!" This was planned to be a great expectation safari of witnessing some of the best of creation on the savanna plains of Africa—just the animals that eat green plants:

> *And to all the beasts of the earth and all the birds in the sky and all the creatures that move along the ground—everything that has the breath of life in it—I give every green plant for food. And it was so.*
>
> —Genesis 1:30 (NIV)

Departing from Colorado on June 30, 2012, I arrived at Grant's lodge in East Cape South Africa on July 1, just before midnight. The flight to the other side of the world was insanely long and took over thirty hours. Scrimping by flying economy, I didn't have a fully reclining bed as one might expect in first or business class. I flew from Denver, Colorado, to Washington, D.C., and then from Washington directly to Johannesburg, South Africa. When I arrived at Joburg, staff from East Cape Safaris picked me up, and then we drove nearly six hours by pickup truck to get to the hunting lodge. Two flights and a truck. All in all, it took two days to get there.

Traveling by myself I packed light with one Cabela duffel bag, a backpack/Catquiver III, and a locked hard bow case. I brought clothes and miscellaneous items and had a carry-on including my Leica 10X binoculars with built-in laser range finder and camera equipment.

Blown away when we pulled into Grant's private ranch, my eyes scanned the spreading layout in the moonlight and feasted on what appeared authentically right out of a movie. The lodge was elegantly erected in the middle of nowhere. The lodge included a gorgeous fireplace, a great room, and a huge dining room table with a feeling of homey comfort. The wine and food were all five star, just like a posh ski lodge. Artistically mounted animals adorned the walls, with zebra rugs on the beautiful wood floors. My room was like we'd expect to see at a hotel in Vail. There was a pool outside and sprawling African scenery in every direction as far as the eye could see, even in the star-spangled moonlight night. From the windows in my room, I could watch and hear wild animals so close we could almost touch them. It was time to crash and close my eyes lying in a comfortable bed.

Later I would learn the only Afrikaan word I'd ever know and understand: *bakkie* (pronounced "bucky" in English). It's the equivalent of an American pickup truck. Easy to remember as Bucky Badger is the mascot of my alma mater. The next morning I was formally introduced to Abrie, my professional hunter who specialized in archery and met his two African trackers who would accompany us on our hunts. Besides tracking and spotting responsibilities, they would be the ones who would take care of butchering the meat after harvesting big game animals.

My original plan was to go on a twenty-five-day safari within Grant's private ranch reserve and hunt sixteen different indigenous species of plains game animals. Most safaris don't last more than seven days, but I decided since this was going to be a once-in-a-lifetime experience, I was going to maximize the use of my time and enjoy all the experiences and mysteries the continent had to offer. I wanted to completely immerse myself in the best of Africa.

Instead of monopolizing all my time just hunting, I wanted to experience other perspectives of Africa as well. We were close to some of the best game reserves found throughout Africa, so I planned to visit Kruger and others spending days sightseeing and taking photos and videos of wildlife.

Strategically I was there during their winter—their dry season—because I was hunting with a bow. I'd be spending a considerable amount of time hunting from inside a "hide" or the African equivalent of hunting blinds. The choice was hunting all day or just mornings and afternoons.

Abrie schooled me on the behavior of the local game. Animals typically move to watering holes at different times of the day, so we had to plan our hunting around their schedule. Some came in at first light. Others wandered in later in the day. The animals somehow managed to follow an organized pecking or drinking order so they didn't conflict with each other.

Suffering from extreme jetlag, I got up late on the morning of July 2 and spent a few hours shooting my bow at a target while I recovered. Abrie showed me around the surrounding areas in his bakkie, and then I spent the rest of the day relaxing and viewing wildlife with Abrie from a hide. Throughout the day, Abrie asked me what animals I'd like to hunt while I was in Africa.

That night, we were having dinner at the big banquet table in the lodge, underneath a huge head and shoulder mount of a Cape buffalo. We were all looking at the beast when I asked, "Shouldn't I carry a big handgun like a .44 magnum?"

"Nah," Abrie said. "Hunters get into more trouble with handguns than not. It gives them a false sense of security. If you're going to carry anything, you need a high-powered rifle."

We spent the rest of the evening discussing logistics and the various game on the neighboring reserves as well. Remember, my original plan was to hunt a variety of plains game on Grant's reserve.

"What about hunting a lion? It's the ultimate archery hunt!" asked Abrie.

"No, I don't want to hunt lion, rhinoceros, elephant, or leopard."

"Well, you just eliminated four out of the Big Five. What about a Cape buffalo?"

Some spark must have piqued my interest because I briefly hesitated. I'm not sure if I was too embarrassed to decline or was hit with a momentary lapse of judgment and or unknown temptation, presumably the latter. Subliminally, a notion reminded me that this was a once-in-lifetime trip. Why not go for it all?

Later that evening, the subject of hunting Cape buffalo came up again. Abrie asked me, "I know you don't want to shoot a lion, but what about a Cape buffalo?"

Without thinking, certainly on impulse, I mentioned, "Well, I know that my seventy-two-pound Hoyt AccuTec bow generates enough energy to effectively harvest one."

Abrie knew he had me hooked. He knew he had a seasoned, competent hunter who was in great physical shape and a skilled archer. In retrospect, I suppose he was trying to ensure that I'd have a memorable trip by adding an additional element to my experience.

The next moment I was aware, he was planning a hunt for Cape buffalo.

He started calling around to the neighboring reserves, looking for Cape buffalo. It didn't take long and he found a good prospect, so he made an offer.

"I don't know if I want to do that," I said. But instead of seizing the opportunity to gracefully opt-out, an inkling inside me awoke the sleeping real estate negotiator in me. I started thinking, *Maybe I can make a better deal.*

So there I was in the middle of South Africa, wrestling with Satan's temptation, haggling over an animal the African people call Black Death. We finally inked the deal to go after a Cape buffalo the following day and planned to meet the reserve's professional hunter and his two African trackers.

Now before I go much further, let me be absolutely clear. My intent before I left home was never to hunt Cape buffalo. I'd also made a promise to my family to tone down my high adventure-seeking experiences as I grew into my so-called golden years. If I did end up hunting in Africa, I'd go after kinder, gentler game like eland and gemsbuck. I was, however, still intrigued by the African buffalo, even though I'd never hunted American buffalo.

That night in my room, I decided to dig deeper into this insidious beast of Africa. What's all the hoopla about? What makes them so dangerous? The results were staggering.

There are 297 species of mammals that make the plains and forests of South Africa their home. The astonishing beauty of zebra, kudu, and giraffe are offset by aggressive predators like lions, leopards, and, of course, the herbivore Cape buffalo comfortably defending themselves from these predators, who also roam the same territory, and feast on a variety of green plants and grasses.

After Googling "Cape buffalo" on my laptop, a long list of chilling references appeared, along with several heartwarming colloquialisms like "Black Death" and "Widow-Maker." At the top of the page, I read a short article that was quick to point out that Cape buffalo kill more than two hundred people per year, including professional hunters; that's not taking into account those who are irreparably maimed and barely escape with their lives. As I kept reading in a trance, the question struck me, *What am I getting myself into?*

Cape buffalo have been described as the most dangerous, vindictive, cunning, and aggressive animals known to man. When wounded by bullets, arrows, or other animals—including man—they're incapable of exercising discretion and possess legendary memories, exacting persistence, and vendettas until they've dispensed revenge on whoever or whatever has encroached on their space. Once provoked, they'll circle their trespassers for days, looking for opportunities to dole out retribution. They'll plan their counterattack with calculated terror, even when fleeing would seem like the most prudent action to execute.

Have you ever heard the old adage "An elephant never forgets?" Well, Cape buffalo never *forgive*. Armed with an acute sense of smell, combined with photographic memories, they've been known to wander away from threatening hunters and return *years* after they were originally confronted.

Seasoned professional hunters warn clients who hunt them, "If you're ever targeted by an African Cape buffalo and you're not near a tree, you'd better have called your estate attorney long before the hunt to get your affairs in order. You don't have long to live."

Under normal circumstances, Cape buffalo are no more dangerous than antelope or dozens of other wild African animals. Given a choice, most are happy to bask in the sun, flicking flies off each other's backs with their tails. But when provoked, they morph into lethal weapons, unlike any nightmare anyone could ever encounter.

The African Cape buffalo (Syncerus caffer) is a large African bovine, distinguished by their immense horns (some as wide as sixty inches from tip to tip), fused at their base called a boss that can grow to be fifteen inches thick. Bulls' horns take five to six years to mature, becoming as hard as a rock around age eight years old. Their horns begin growing out of the top of their head shortly after birth, angle down out to the sides, and then swoop back up. Their horns are their primary means of protection.

Savanna-type African buffalo can weigh well over two thousand pounds, stand six feet high at their shoulders, grow to eleven feet long, and have front hooves the size of small Frisbees. Their hide can be two inches thick in places, providing them with a nearly bulletproof, natural suit of armor. Overall, the African Cape buffalo is a finely tuned, well-equipped killing machine, so why on earth would I want to pursue such beast, unless tempted?

Unthreatened, African Cape buffalo walk with their heads bowed low, spending their days grazing. They thrive in a variety of sub-Saharan Africa habitats from dry grass to swamps, floodplains to mixed forests and will stay in one area until they're forced to move by, exhausting their food supply or provoked by predators. Weighing as much as they do, drinking copious amounts of water is crucial to their survival and plays an essential role in stalking them on hunts. They'll often walk as far as twelve miles just to find water.

The Cape buffalo is one of the "Big Five" game animals, along with lions, leopards, rhinoceros, and elephants. A June 30, 2008 assessment indicated the African buffalo was listed by the IUCN as LC with a declining population, and a February 24, 2018, assessment indicates NT for the species. Thus July of 2012 when I was there hunting, African Cape Buffalo were listed as Least Concern of extinction.

Besides man, their only true predators are large crocodiles and lions. Crocodiles typically target new calves and infirm buffalo that wander by themselves on the periphery of the herds, while lions will gang up in large prides and overwhelm vulnerable bulls.

The buffalo's greatest survival tool against predators like crocodiles, lions, and man is living in numbers. They graze in herds that range anywhere from fifty to more than a thousand at a time. In the dry season, they move in smaller herds from thirty to two-hundred and are made up of a number of sub-herds. As a general rule, younger male buffalo congregate together, gathering in groups called bachelor herds. Family units are made up of cows and their offspring, including the youngest bulls up to three years of age, with ten to thirty members, usually including one dominant breeding bull.

Older bulls past their prime years (called Dagga Boys by local natives) typically graze outside the periphery of the main herd. Because of their diminished numbers, they're often targets of prey—human and otherwise. This was the old rogue bull that this old rogue bull Larry would be tempted to hunt on safari.

Contrary to their male counterparts, females are famous for their altruistic behavior. At rest, they tend to move from one location to another within the herd, standing in the direction they think they'll move next. When they run out of food or grow tired of their current site, they'll collectively decide to move to new grazing grounds.

As one might expect from any collective family, they are extremely protective of one another. Whenever they're under attack or encounter unfamiliar surroundings, they'll gather around the youngest and weakest members, facing out.

Bulls between the ages of eight and fourteen are in their prime years for breeding, but only a few mature, virile bulls will manage to successfully mate with cows. Eventually, the old bulls will be systematically shunned and expelled to the periphery of the herd, making up smaller bachelor groups with others of their age, known as dagga boys to Africans.

As I'd find out from personal experience, bulls on the periphery are the most easily angered and likely to charge strangers who they think pose a threat. Intruding and encroaching on their space is not a good way to, "Meet the Dagga Boys", but they're also the bulls most professional hunters target for clients as they're at the end of their life cycle.

Hunting Cape Buffalo

The best time to hunt Cape buffalo in East Cape Africa is between June and August, during the winter dry season when the average temperature is seventy-seven degrees Fahrenheit (twenty-five degrees Celsius). January and February tend to be the hottest months when temperatures can soar past one hundred-four degrees Fahrenheit (forty degrees Celsius).

Cape buffalo tend to be more active in the morning and early afternoon. One of the best times to hunt them is during the heat of the day when they migrate to shady terrain near water.

Contrary to the popular myth, Cape buffalo do not live to kill. On any given day, they'd rather lay around basking in the sun, eating. But when provoked, they believe attacking is their best—if not only—recourse, especially if they happen to be an older and more onerous bull.

When approached by hunters, they'll initially look at them with wonder and surprise and then trot off in another direction. But if you pique their interest, they'll quickly change directions and run in your direction. That's the time to make the sign of the cross and hope there's protection from elephant guns nearby.

If we examine the long list of accidents and deaths caused by Cape buffalo, invariably, we'll find they were provoked, either directly or indirectly. Oftentimes, intruders do nothing to foment their ire. Rather, the buffalo is still harboring ill will from a previous encounter—sometimes from as long as a year ago. While we might admire a lot of their traits, forgiveness is not one of them.

The old rogue bulls that are cast out to the herd's periphery seem to relish the opportunity to settle their grievances with intruders. They're known for their intractable, irascible dispositions and deserve a wide berth. They may have been shot at by hunters, injured, or wounded in fights with other bulls in the past. Or they may have left the core of the herd because of bickering and squabbling with other bulls. But to them, all intruders look alike. It's possible that your appearance resurrects a harbored resentment that originated long ago.

One of the most common places hunters run accidentally into buffalo is in thick elephant grass or types of brush-like acacia; sometimes as high as twelve feet. While human hunters find these conditions impossible to navigate, it's prime real estate for mature bulls.

When using rifles, hunters will try to engage buffalo from 50 to 150 yards away, but it's not unusual for them to bump into them face-to-face, wandering aimlessly through the cover. Accidental encounters are responsible for the majority of inadvertent confrontations between bulls and men.

One of the worst possible adverse mishaps one can incur is to wound a buffalo. Even worse is inadvertently injuring more than one and then watching them retreat into the thick cover. When that happens, they become masters at reversing the hunter–prey relationship. Suddenly, the hunter becomes the hunted.

When wounded, the buffalo will make a hasty exit into the tall grass or brush, lay down wounded, and begin formulating their plan of attack. And there will be one. They'll wait patiently for the hunter to follow them, and when they're in proximity, they'll scramble to their feet and stand like a statue, dialing-in their final lethal charge.

While staring down a hunter, they'll swing their head back and forth and sound a series of short snorts and grunts. When he drops his head and begins to charge, you can assume that your time on this planet is highly likely to be shortened.

The challenge with hunting Cape buffalo with a bow and arrow is manifold. When hunting old dagga boys with high-powered rifles, hunters can safely drop the beast with a clean shot from over one hundred yards away. Buffalo expire from a fatal bullet relatively quickly. But with arrows, the hunter needs to sneak in as close as forty yards or less to confidently shoot and harvest a bull. Even then, if the shot placement is not precise, there's a good chance that instead of dying quickly, it could take several hours for them to expire. During this time, they can continue to move around, coming up with the most effective way to bring you down with them.

When Things Go Wrong

Under the best conditions, hunting Cape buffalo, assisted with the guidance of a professional hunter, using either a high-powered rifle or bow and arrow should be a relatively safe experience, well, as safe as pursuing an angry, resentful beast can be.

The best way to ensure a safe, calculated buffalo harvest is to follow a well-conceived plan. But that's not always possible. When facing an alarmed Cape buffalo, they hold all the cards. And they're always aces. They're used to walking for days through thick bush with limited visibility, a rare routine for most humans—even experienced hunters. But if a hunter keeps cool, is cognizant of their surroundings, and does their best to avoid alarming the bull, the chances of a humane harvest improve immensely.

Frequently, herds of wild Cape buffalo will stampede, usually when the group as a whole senses danger. If they can't determine the source or direction of the threat, they'll begin stampeding with their heads held high with no particular direction in mind. Unlike other species that follow a designated leader, each bull will follow their own plan, making it impossible to predict what they'll do next. Eventually, they'll tire, turn at a sharp angle, and take off in another direction.

Experienced buffalo hunters have learned how to anticipate running bulls. Oftentimes, they can turn the tide simply by waving their hats over their heads or by shooting the lead bull. Other times, when there is no clear designated leader, diverting the herd can be next to impossible. When this happens, it means convincing hundreds of individual bulls to change directions instead of just one—an almost impossible task.

If you're unfortunate enough to trigger the ire of a rogue bull, you have your work cut out for you. Savanna bulls are masters of their domain and have collected several well-calculated offensive strategies they've been using all their adult lives. It's one of the reasons why they're called the most dangerous animals on Earth.

On top of that is their unbounded vindictiveness. Angry Cape buffalo are known for harboring resentments and will often carry them to their grave. While elephants will often bury an intruder after they've killed it, Cape buffalo have been known to return to the scene of an attack days or weeks after they've killed their victim, to make certain it's dead. And just to make sure, they'll stomp it flat with their front hooves until they're confident they have totally eliminated the threat.

African bush legend has it that one irascible dagga boy chased a wary native up a tree and milled about the base of it for over three days. During that time, the bull taunted the stranded native by urinating on the ground and flinging putrid mud at him with his tail until he eventually got bored and wandered away.

Bow Hunting Cape Buffalo

As dangerous as gun hunting Cape buffalo is statistically, bow hunting ups the ante to a whole new level. While it's one of the most authentic, primitive (and some feel humane) forms of hunting, archery hunting is not without its risks. The beautiful moments about archery hunting are experiencing the intensity of close encounters with big game while observing them naturally. At the same time, it's sobering to be so close to potential danger.

Unlike rifle hunters using a walk-and-stalk method, bowhunters typically hunt hidden in the safety of a hide, called a blind in the United States. There are pros and cons to each method. Measuring typically eight feet by eight feet with a low ceiling and narrow slot for shooting, taking an accurate shot can be difficult to calculate from inside the confines of a hide. On the other hand, when using the walk-and-stalk method, you're at the mercy of the wind. When an angry bull picks up an upwind scent, it sets off an alarm that imminent danger is in the air.

Most hunters choose high-powered rifles as their weapons of choice—.375 and up. Assuming the hunter has aimed their sight at the bull accurately, a powerful rifle is almost certain to bring down a large bull within a short time frame. On the other hand, only a well-placed arrow can bring down a mature bull humanely and quickly. Archers need powerful tools to bring down a Cape bull as well. The best possible arrow and a bow with a 70- to 90-pound draw. But even then, you still need to successfully execute an extremely well-calculated shot.

There are relatively few lethal targets on a massive Cape buffalo. The best choices are the brain, lungs, and spine. It's virtually impossible to pierce the chest cavity on any animal from a direct, head-on charge. The charging shot is only effective for brain and spine shots with powerful elephant guns. Instead, bowhunters must wait until the bull turns to the side. The best place to stand is to the side and slightly behind the bull. But naturally, wild animals don't charge, running sideways.

Making tactics even more challenging is the Cape buffalo's natural armor. Their ribs overlap, making it difficult to shoot between them. The best technique for an archer to bring down a Cape buffalo is using a quartering away shot, placing the arrow right behind the heart as far back as the diaphragm, about a third of the way up the chest (see the heart area in the diagram above). This type of shot angle has a good chance of penetrating and slicing between the ribs, piercing the heart and lungs, leading to a quick, clean humane harvest.

Because of the way they hold their head, there is no lethal shot for a bowhunter to shoot during a head-on charge. By keeping their heads down, they shield themselves with their thick, broad "bosses" at the base of their horns and skull plate-like tank armor. An arrow is useless.

As I'd later find out, even under the best of circumstances, using the best-laid plan, there is no guaranteed way of taking a bull down with one effective shot using an arrow. They're ornery, cunning beasts who have lived their lives learning how to defend themselves in the bush. They're masters of using their surroundings to their advantage and don't want any predators moving into their space, especially a foreign man.

I wish I would have followed my own direction.

CHAPTER SEVEN

FOUR MEN AND A BAKKIE

I have fought the good fight, I have finished the race, I have kept the faith.

—Timothy 4:7 (NIV)

T he next morning, July 3rd, the smell of breakfast woke me out of a deep sleep. The meats and eggs were fresh from Grant's private animals, and everything was homecooked. We feasted until we had to leave and meet with the professional hunter from the neighbor's reserve at nine o'clock and begin our pursuit of the bull. As a rule, bowhunting guests start their days early and then drive five to ten miles on two rut lanes from the lodge to a hide somewhere on the reserve. Instead, we drove out of Grant's ranch on to an improved road leading to another private reserve about 45 minutes away, where the Cape buffalo were located.

In the bakkie with me were my trusted Hoyt AccuTec compound bow, Kevlar arrows with one-hundred-grain Thunderhead razor broadheads, and Leica ten-power binoculars. In addition were other essentials needed in the bush, stuffed inside my Catquiver III daypack, including a water bottle, an extra fleece jacket, and a hunting knife. I was set.

More importantly, I also packed into the Catquiver two items that would end up playing significant roles throughout the course of my trip. The first was my little brown Bible—the one the Gideons gave me back in 2002. At four by three inches and a half an inch thick, it has been my constant companion since the day the Gideons gave it to me and a welcome addition to what I carried onto the long flight to South Africa. Occasionally, when I'm stumped about the best course of action to take, I'll open it and immediately find the answer. Not always the one I'm looking for but the best answer nonetheless. The second item packed was my tiny green metal cross that I was given as Palanca during my first Cursillo weekend. Little did I know how important these small items would be later that day.

That Catquiver and its contents would end up saving me three times. I truly believe that I was shielded by those symbols of faith, stuffed into the back pouch of my Catquiver III daypack.

We met the professional hunter and his two trackers from the neighboring reserve as they rolled up in their bakkie. Abrie, two trackers and I were "four men and a bakkie", plus two trackers, Grant, and his son were another "four men and a bakkie", totaling 8 men in our two bakkies. All total, there were eleven, including me in the hunting party. I was the only hunter and thought *ten people protecting me should mitigate the risk of taking on the Black Death Goliath.*

We started scouting for buffalo by driving to a place where they had last seen the bull contracted to hunt the night before. When we turned the corner around some dense bush, there they were, a herd of fifty-plus magnificent Cape buffalo. I was mesmerized by their size. They were the color of gun barrel bluing and impressed me as looking like a gaggle of old-fashioned locomotives, waiting at a train station, blowing off steam. They were bigger than I expected, but unfortunately, none of them was the old rogue bull we were looking for.

The bull we were after was an old fella that had been kicked out of the herd, a *dagga boy*. The owner of the reserve wanted that specific bull harvested because he was well beyond his breeding days, near the end of his life span, and was causing trouble with the others. That fact alone should have been enough for me to raise my hand and ask, "Excuse me. Do you mind if I go back to the lodge?" Bulls of that size usually command $30,000 or more to hunt, but because this bull was being such a nuisance, we had negotiated a deal. Such a deal.

The professional hunter from the reserve looked through his binoculars and double-checked the herd and confirmed he didn't see the specific bull he was looking for. So we got back into our bakkies and started driving around the reserve he knew very well, looking for the bull. Who knows? Maybe he was hiding in the acacia brush.

After an hour of driving, we spent the next five hours of scouting on foot.

The herd was on the move, and we ended up bumping into them three different times over the course of the day. The bush was so dense in areas that we could barely see more than a couple of feet into it. I was seriously concerned, as we were on foot, about stepping around clusters of bush blindly and inadvertently bumping into the bull.

While we were walking, I noticed an old, broken-down barbed wire fence running through the property that once marked the boundary of a private cattle ranch. Once upon a time, the areas that are now hunting reserves were occupied by large sheep and cattle ranches. At the time, it was considered the highest and best use of the land. Since that time, all the domesticated animals have disappeared. I asked the group, "Hey. What about checking out this broken-down opening in the fence? Maybe he wandered in there?"

My suggestion was met with a resounding no. Oh well, it seemed like a good idea to me since I saw bull tracks that looked like bull elk tracks, only much larger.

We spent six hours from nine o'clock to three o'clock on foot and in vehicles, looking for that one bull. Occasionally, there were thick areas of bush where we had to go in and investigate on foot. Each time we did, my heart rushed up in my throat. I was worried about encountering the rogue bull and staring each other down face-to-face. When we ran into the herd for the third time, we all knew that the bull was near, but where?

Tired, thirsty, and exasperated, I reminded them of that break in the old fence. I told them I saw a solo set of large bull tracks going through the barbed wire fence. Abrie said, "No, that doesn't mean anything." So we continued looking everywhere except where I suggested. Finally, we decided to climb back in the bakkies, and the reserve's professional hunter and his two trackers said, "Well, we'll try looking for it another day. We'll call you when we find him," and they started to pack up and leave.

I said to Grant, "We still have four trackers left. Why don't you send them across the opening in the fence that I pointed out?" He finally caved in and sent them across the fence and into the dense bush. Fifteen minutes later, they found the bull, right where I thought he would be, standing alone in the acacia brush.

The next sound we heard on our radios was someone yelling in Afrikaans. They'd found the Cape buffalo, the beast we'd spent our entire day looking for. It was time to shift into the final stalk and hunt mode.

We called the reserve PH by cell phone, informing him we found the bull and to hurry back, jumped into the trucks, and drove up to where the trackers were standing. I pulled out my bow, donned my Catquiver backpack with arrows, and prepared to harvest the beast.

The bull was standing two to three hundred yards away in the bush out of sight. One of my trackers started videotaping me drawing my bow while making sure my equipment functioned properly. After a little negotiation, he agreed to be my cameraman on the stalk. It was a blistering hot afternoon, so I zipped off the lower legs of my pants and took off my shirt and then stuffed them into my daypack. We eased into the thick bush, and then I stopped when I thought I saw a big, dark object. I looked through my binoculars and zeroed in on the suspicious dark spot in the bush off to our left. Maybe that's him.

Continuing to sneak slowly, I confirmed my sighting. I mentioned to the others, "I think I see him over there", as I pointed.

They looked where I was pointing and said, "Yeah, that's him." We all conferred and agreed that he was unquestionably the rogue bull we were looking for. "Let's go over there and try to get a shot."

Directly following behind Abrie with his rifle slung over his shoulder we crept closer to Black Death. Why he wasn't poised with his rifle in the ready position like the rest of the PH's, I'll never know. My tracker behind me was filming as we snuck up on the bull. We got to within forty yards of the bull, and Abrie still had his rifle slung over his shoulder.

Thinking to myself, I thought *maybe I'd made a mistake by letting him use my second range finder, which conflicted with having his rifle ready for protection.* Abrie was using the range finder I lent him, and he agreed that the bull was no more than forty yards away. He kept motioning me to keep coming up slowly behind him. Closer, closer, closer. Then he asked me in his South African accent, "Larry, do you think you can make the shot?"

"Yeah, I can make it."

The bull was standing perpendicular to us, which is not considered an optimal position for a humane harvest. Like white-tailed deer or elk, ideally, a hunter wants to have a diagonal shot from a slight angle behind the animal, shooting the arrow through their ribs and vital organs. Our bull was almost in that position but not quite.

As you may recall, Cape buffalo have big, heavy ribs that overlap each other. They're like armor plating. So preferably, I wanted him to

113

be facing slightly away from me, maybe twenty to thirty degrees off perpendicular. I wanted to shoot a line through the back of his ribs or, even better, just behind his ribs, through the diaphragm, through the lungs, and through his heart.

So when Abrie asked me if I could make the shot, I had to qualify my response: "*I could, but not when the beast was standing with dense acacia brush between him and me.* **If the arrow deflected off the brush and merely wounded the bull, we'd be in big trouble. He'd charge us.**" So we waited patiently.

We could see him, but the brush made the shot impossible. There were branches and thorns spiking from the shafts of the brush. We continued to wait until he decided to trot off. My heart sank. We missed our opportunity. No shot.

Having come so close after all those hours searching for him, we decided to continue pursuing him on foot. We walked into the wind as he trotted off to the right. We got within ninety yards of him, and then he took off again. No, not again. It was obvious he didn't like us there. We had invaded his space, and he was giving us every opportunity to regain our sanity and go home. But we'd invested so much into pursuing him at this point we felt we couldn't quit now. I was trying to be patient, playing it safe, and honoring a humane harvest of the beast.

His next move put more distance between us as he circled around further to our right and downwind of us. I thought, *Abrie still has the bloody gun slung over his shoulder. The animal is downwind. He can hear us, smell us, and watch every movement we make.*

Our actions were not making sense to me.

Abrie continued waving to signal me to stick close to him until we got within forty yards from Black Death on our third stalk of the day. Once again, he asked me, "Larry, can you make the shot?"

"Yes, but he's still in the brush. If he walks into the opening just ahead of where he is now, I'll try a shot", I replied.

But rather than taking the two steps ahead, giving me an open window through the brush, the bull turned forty-five degrees, facing toward us. Instead of standing diagonally away from us, he swung all the way around and was facing us nearly head-on—the absolute worst position you want a bull to be when hunting them with a bow and arrow.

After what seemed like an eternity and all documented by the video camera, the bull turned a little more to his right until he was facing us directly head-on. The next sound I heard was an angry loud snort as he started charging. Then he attacked at full speed. I thought, *God, help me!* **I'm going to die today!**

The bull was charging us at more than forty miles per hour. Getting hit by Black Death at that speed is like being broadsided by a bakkie. I didn't know what Abrie or the other trackers were doing, but when he started charging, the tracker taking the live video footage dropped the camera and took off running into the wind, with the camera dangling from the harness around his neck.

Abrie scrambled to take his gun off his shoulder and fired the first shot. As he squeezed off a round, he tripped over acacia brush and fell over backward.

Unfortunately, he missed hitting and stopping the bull, but it was a blessing that the .375-caliber bullet missed me. The next resonance, after the blast of his rifle subsided, I heard was a voice speak to me. It wasn't feminine or masculine. It wasn't loud, and it wasn't quiet, but it was crystal clear. It said, "Get rid of your arrow, turn, and run as fast as you can."

I didn't argue.

My arrow was knocked to the bowstring and loaded on the arrow rest. The shooting release was wrapped around my right wrist, locked on the string, so my right hand was attached to the bowstring, while my left hand held the bow. As Black Death charged me, I did exactly what the voice said. I drew the bowstring slightly back while pulling the trigger on the release to let the arrow fall to the ground and turned the opposite direction running as fast as I could. Jessie Owens couldn't have caught me that day.

While I was running, I looked over my right shoulder and could see his horns coming up inches behind me. I thought *He's after me.* **He's got me**.

I kept running as fast as I've ever run in my life. Then suddenly, he hit me from behind with his horns wrapping around the outside of my body. He smashed against the center of my Catquiver daypack with his huge bosses in the middle of his head. The force felt like a moving train locomotive. Fortunately, my Catquiver was loaded with fleece clothing and water bottles from the others in the hunting party which shielded me from the direct impact of the bull.

The force of the charging bull never got past my little brown Bible and Cursillo cross. I had completely forgotten they were there until later when I was rummaging through my pack. When the beast hit me, my life started to replay in my mind. After the attack was over, the four professional hunters and six trackers said I was thrown fifteen to twenty feet from the impact. Landing on all fours, I wondered what happened to the Cape buffalo. Maybe I was lucky, and it was all over. Maybe Abrie did hit the goliath beast with the first shot I heard fired.

Within split seconds, the fuming bull was all over me again. Noticing the massive black beast out of my peripheral vision charging in with dust flying, I thought: **this is it...this is the end**. Simultaneously, I felt crushing pressure on my left side and shoulder. I knew it was Black Death emulating his reputation, but I was so bewildered I wasn't really comprehending the act he was committing. I thought *Black Death is committing murder*. The next moment, I heard the sound of bones crushing, and I felt bones shattering into fragments. I thought *This is it!* **I'm being crushed to death***!*

> [3]*The enemy pursues me, he crushes me to the ground; he makes me dwell in the darkness like those long dead.*
> —Psalm 143:3 (NIV)

As he attacked me from my left side, my thoughts must have been traveling at the speed of light as key waypoints of my lifetime flashed in my mind's eye. I kept thinking in an accelerated mode, *what about my kids and my grandkids?* Vividly, I remember that I wasn't so much afraid of dying as I was flooded with an overwhelming sadness and disappointment that I wasn't going to get to see my family ever again. The feeling of the end being absolutely finite and abrupt without any warning or preparation further saddened me. Amy had just delivered my new grandson Chance a month before, and I hadn't even met him. My second daughter, Martha, was pregnant and due at Christmas.

Then I was engulfed with thoughts of surrender. Because I'd already been through several surrendering experiences at Cursillo and Alpha, I was familiar with turning my life over to Jesus Christ. I remember thinking, *Now I'm surrendering not only mentally and spiritually but also physically.*

Black Death was literally trying to squeeze the life out of me. I distinctly remember committing my spirit to our Father in Heaven and was preparing to die. I clearly remember thinking, *Into your hands I commit my spirit.* I knew it was over, so I just let go and thought I was killed.

The bull hooked me under my left arm, bruising my left pectoral muscle with his horn, and flipped me into the air like a rag doll. Then I crashed onto the ground, landing on my butt, Catquiver daypack, and the heels of my boots.

They told me afterward that when the bull hit and tossed me into the air the first time, he continued to run past me, attempting to hit me but missed. Then he circled back around to attack me again.

I regained consciousness while lying on the ground, dazed and confused.

During the second contact with Black Death, Abrie fired a second shot at the bull, but I didn't hear it because I was unconscious. I realized afterward that I had blacked out from the severe trauma to my humerus and shoulder. All the audio was clearly recorded on my video camera, including the second shot that I heard for the first time, days later on the video recording.

They told me later the bull slammed into my left side and wedged his horn under my armpit, bruising the left side of my chest. This was validated by an ugly bruise on my pectoral muscle. Had his horn connected with me millimeters more toward my chest, he could have impaled my ribs, torn me in half, and ripped my heart out of my chest. Missing my vitals was way beyond a blessing.

Ironically, his horn did miss my vital organs, the same ones I was attempting to shoot in *his* chest. Thankfully, he did miss; otherwise, I would have been killed instantly.

I had no idea what happened other than I must have died. I was convinced I was killed.

When I landed on the ground after the buffalo's second attack, I sat on my butt with my heels dug into the dirt and both my arms hanging lifelessly by my side. The Catquiver daypack was propping me up—it saved me for the second time by helping break the fall. But the bull wasn't finished with me yet.

As I came to a conscious state, I noticed an incredibly bright light pouring over me. I looked up, but it didn't seem to be coming from any particular direction. It was like I was under a huge Hollywood spotlight focused on me from above, bright from every direction. It was a crystal clear blue day, as seen in the picture, without a cloud or any smoke in the sky. What was happening?

All thanks be to God the second attack was over.

As I sat there, looking down at my body, my brain spontaneously kicked into emergency room triage-mode, beginning with my legs. I thought for sure Black Death crushed them into a bloody mess of shattered pieces. But there was no blood. My legs looked fine. Then I visually examined the rest of my body. I took a deep breath, felt no pain, and my body seemed normal. I thought, *How could this be?* Remarkably, I still didn't see any blood or other signs of injury, but I knew the bull had tried to crush the life out of me.

While this was happening, I still saw the bright light over me. So I thought, *Well, this is the end. I must be dead. I just got crushed, yet it appears there are no damages. I must be in Heaven with a perfectly undamaged body.*

We hear stories about near-death experiences and bright lights, so it appeared to make sense. I had to be dead. I thought, *am I really in Heaven?*

Then I saw the dark beast again, twenty-five feet away. Black Death was dead-center in front of me, and he was not a happy camper. Apparently, he couldn't believe that he hadn't finished me off on the first or even the second charge of the attack. He was viciously stomping what was left of the arrows that fell out my Catquiver daypack, my bow, and my binoculars that had flown off my neck. He must have mistaken them for me. Maybe being an old bull, he'd lost some of his eyesight, so he was still trying to finish me off by stomping with his massive hooves. That's their standard modus operandi. They hook and gore, and then they go back and trample the life out their intruder until they're finished. Then I noticed the mountains and background of the savanna. I thought, **Maybe I'm not dead**. *It looks like I'm still in the African savanna, facing Black Death fighting for my life.*

Evidently, the goliath beast wasn't aware of where I landed. The next image I saw was him starring straight at me. He had just lifted his massive head and horns, looking up from bludgeoning my bow and arrows and stared directly at me. His flaming-red eyes bore holes through me as I sat helplessly in the dirt and gravel.

Instead of charging at me a third time, he slowly stomped toward me, swinging his head and rocking it back and forth. He continued stomping from side to side right up to me and just stared with a laser focus. I thought again, *Maybe I'm really not dead after all.* So I screamed, "Kill it!"

I'd only heard one shot so far. I thought, *What happened to the four professional hunters with high-powered rifles? Those big elephant guns? Nobody's shooting at the beast.*

So I yelled again, "Kill it!"

As the bull was slowly closing the gap, I began crab-walking backward, attempting to put as much distance between us as humanly possible. While I tried to scoot backward, I realized how badly my left arm had been shattered. My entire arm was just hanging from my shoulder by skin and muscle. I suddenly realized what I felt and heard crushing and cracking when he attacked me the second time.

As he inched up on me, the voice clearly spoke for a second time, "Stay on your back. Put your boots on the bosses between the horns and push away with your feet." I did exactly as I was told, without a second thought.

After making contact, the beast started to push his head against my boots. My measly 220 pounds were no match for his 2,000 plus. It was the equivalent of seven massive NFL linemen bulldozing me backward through the dirt.

I could hear and feel the bones grating against each other. I felt the excruciating pain of shattered bones cutting into my muscles. At the same time, the beast continued to plow me backward into the dirt. I had no idea what he was planning next. This didn't seem to be typical behavior. Then my right elbow went down into the gravel, behind me alongside the pack, gouging the flesh off, down to the bone.

After he pushed me backward several feet, I heard a loud BAM! Abrie's .375 H&H rifle went off. It hit the bull just below the right ear, shocking the beast's spine at the base of the skull. This was the third shot Abrie fired, and he finally hit with surgical precision. Hair and blood flew in all directions as his entire body shimmied from the shock of the impact. The buffalo stiffened his four legs and arched his back, jolted and stunned by the bullet energy. Then it was like the Fourth of July as shots four, five, six, and seven rang out from the other professional hunters' guns. Thankfully, Grant fired the eighth and ultimate kill shot through the shoulder into the spine that brought the beast down, slamming to the ground.

Both of us came to rest with my right boot propped up within inches of his horn, and the attack was finally over. Or was it?

I remember hearing and clearly seeing the third and fourth bullets hit the beast. I also remember seeing the fourth bullet hit the buffalo's right shoulder with blood and hair flying as the 450-grain projectile penetrated. I saw the bullet squirt out of his left shoulder, exiting through his hide and dropping to the ground, spraying blood. After the whole encounter was finally finished, I found the fourth bullet and held it in my hand. I still have it to this day.

As we heard on the video recording my tracker had taken, the shots happened within seconds. Shots three, four, five, six, and seven were followed by Grant strategically placing a shot through the beast's shoulder and into the beast's spine. He saved my life. The goliath beast was now laying on his left side with his legs still articulating walking movements. Then Abrie ran around my head and put the gun barrel between the beast's eyes and pulled the trigger for the ninth and final shot. We could hear the final gunshot blast inches from our ears. The 450-grain Barnes X bullet, with 100% weight retention, instantaneously cut through the skull plate, and smashed into the ground and gravel below after piercing the beast's brain and putting the goliath out of his misery. The entire incident took less than twenty seconds, with shots three through eight taking only eight seconds as recorded on the video clock.

Fortunately, the buffalo crashed straight to the ground, with his horn no more than twelve inches from my right boot. Not on top of me. If it had, his more than a ton would have crushed and suffocated me, even though I'd lived through the flurry of gunshots. Even together, there would have been no way all the trackers could have lifted the beast off me before I perished.

My video camera continued to run for a total of thirty seconds and then shut off automatically. There were roughly ten seconds between the ninth shot and when the tracker came up with the camera, hanging around his neck. If you look at the video carefully, you can see the bullet holes and the beast's horns. You can see me slouched over with my arm hanging down my side as I held it in traction with my right hand. Then you hear Grant say, "OK. Unload your guns."

Grant asked me, "Larry, are you all right?"

I answered calmly, "I don't think so."

Abrie wandered up and said, "Oh, Larry I think you just dislocated your shoulder. I can fix it for you."

By this time, the bright light had vanished back into the sky. Abrie told me, "Larry, I can't believe what I saw. There was a column of light over you. An angel hovered over your head and was boxing the horns of the beast."

Grant corroborated the sequence of events as he wrote to me recently: "The entire event, including the charge and eventually the shot that put the buffalo down, took less than eight seconds, even though the experience seemed much longer at the time. Because of the thick bush, clear shots at the charging buffalo were difficult. The buffalo hit Larry from behind, sending him high into the air, and upon landing, the animal overran its target. As the buffalo turned back to him, Larry raised his feet to protect himself. That's when I managed to get a clear shot to the spine of the animal with one shot from my .375 H&H, literally dropping the buffalo at Larry's feet."

Once the action had subsided, I sat motionless, propped up by my daypack. Tears were streaming down my face, not just from the attack but from knowing that the grace of God had intervened and saved my life. I was enveloped with a magnificent feeling of gratitude and thankfulness, unlike any feeling I've ever experienced before. I thanked God for saving me because I was certain I was killed.

And then the voice spoke to me a third time. "No more extreme pursuits. Focus on God and family for the rest of your life."

Once again, I wasn't in a mind-set to argue.

For the ten years leading up to the trip, I had been asking God for some type of sign or communication about what I was supposed to do with my life. I continually prayed and asked God, *Where am I going with the rest of my life? Please God, what is your will for me?*

God certainly had a powerful delivery method for a message. Obviously, the answer didn't arrive the way I expected. Nevertheless, God's instructions are indelibly etched in my mind. I'm constantly reminded of them through the never-ending pain in my left shoulder. I have to say "It's a blessed pain that hurts so good."

Hearing a voice speak to me three times was my witness, but more significant is what the 10 witnesses expressed. Grant, the professional hunters, and trackers (all ten of them) witnessed in multiple languages, "If you hadn't done *exactly* what you did, you would have been killed."

All I did was follow the voice's directions. As the crew scrambled around me to help, Abrie walked over to me and said again, "Oh, I think I can fix your shoulder. I think it's just dislocated."

"No, no. Don't touch it! I need to get to the hospital. I can feel the broken bones."

"OK, but we've got to get a picture first."

"Forget the picture. We've got to get to a hospital."

"Just wait a minute. We've got to get a picture."

The head of the buffalo was enormous. Before taking the photo, they propped the bow up against its side. There were two African trackers hiding behind the bull, holding the beast and me up. The deadweight of the beast took all ten men to heave the black mass over so it rolled enough to place the head on top of a termite hill. Then on command, managing to force a grimaced smile, Grant orchestrated the entire scene and took the picture we see in the articles published online (Google "Cape Buffalo Attack Trotter"). It was my camera from inside the Catquiver pack that survived behind the little brown Bible and cross as well. It turned out to be the one and ONLY photo, and it turned out perfect. Then I pleaded again, "We've got to get to a hospital."

By then, I was on my feet, resting my arm against my side with the assistance of my right hand holding it in a sling position so it wouldn't swing freely. If you looked closely, you could see that my humeral head was split in half. Half of it was positioned toward the front, half toward the rear. Then I begged, "Please. Please. We have to get to a hospital. My arm is starting to hurt."

"It was a close call," said Grant. "We all knew that our guardian angels looked after us on that near fateful day." Grant was focused on looking through his scope for the kill shot, so his vision was blocked, and he couldn't see the angel that Abrie witnessed.

Then the real adventure began.

CHAPTER EIGHT

THE LITTLE BROWN BIBLE AND A CROSS

⁶ Do not be anxious about anything, but in every situation, by prayer and petition, with thanksgiving, present your requests to God. ⁷ And the peace of God, which transcends all understanding, will guard your hearts and your minds in Christ Jesus.

—Philippians 4:6 (NIV)

Immediately following the attack, too dazed and confused to realize the biochemical extreme trauma numbness in my shoulder was naturally protecting me by blocking sensations from my wounds and damages, I remained in a state shock and thankfulness. However, as the reality of the battle with Black Death faded away, feelings of pain began to increase from my left arm and shoulder, rapidly intensifying and radiating over me.

Abrie drove his bakkie within a few feet of me, and I managed to shuffle over, letting the weight of my left arm hang with gravity while I continued to hold my wrist in a sling position—a field-based first-aid approach to applying traction using gravity. I climbed into the front seat, and we slowly drove away from the scene of my near-death experience. As we left, I could hear the chatter of the rest of the crew as they butchered the beast and began loading it onto a bakkie to take back to the lodge walk-in coolers.

As we very cautiously drove, I asked Abrie, "What did you mean when you said you saw an angel over my head?"

"Well Larry, I couldn't believe what I saw. There was a brilliant pillar of light, like a column coming straight down from the sky. There was an angel hovering over your head boxing the horns of the buffalo. As hard as it tried, the buffalo couldn't penetrate the light and get to you. That's what allowed me to take the perfect shot, so I pulled the trigger when the crosshairs lined up under the buffalo's ear, exactly where the bullet hole is, as I just checked it with my finger." To this day, I can still point out that bullet hole below the ear of the beast's shoulder mount.

Again, Abrie and Grant's description was repeated to me multiple times immediately following the miraculous incident and later when I returned to the lodge from the hospitals. All ten of the people who were there at the scene of the attack—the six African trackers and the four professional hunters—reiterated the same communication word for word. They witnessed, "**If I hadn't done *exactly* what I did, I would have been killed**." Again, all I did was follow the voice's directions.

We continued creeping over the savanna on the way out of the fenced area and then drove onto a rough gravel, rutted road strewn with rocks, bumps, and termite hills. Just the vibration and jarring from creeping along the road made me double over in pain. The closest medical center was the Somerset East Hospital more than five miles away across the rough savanna.

"Abrie, can you go any slower? The bumps and jostling from the road are killing me."

"I'm doing the best I can. I'm already riding the clutch."

While we drove to the hospital, Grant was trying to contact Global Rescue Services. Global Rescue is a wilderness evacuation service that could have dispatched a rescue helicopter out of Port Elizabeth. Even though I'd enrolled and paid for it before the trip, we were so far out in the bush we weren't able to reach them by cell phone.

We finally reached the small community of Somerset East. Grant had called the hospital, so the moment I walked into the emergency room, the medical staff expeditiously examined my injuries and began taking X-rays. They treated the abrasions on my forehead from the beast's horns and removed dirt and gravel from my knees and my right elbow. Upon reading the x-rays, the ER doctor administered injections for pain management.

When the ER doctor explained his assessment of my injuries to me, he said, "We know you shattered the head of your humerus, but there's nothing we can do with it here other than immobilizing it and give you morphine for pain." By this time, I could feel every micromovement of my body and could hear and feel the sensations of fractured bones grating and grinding against each other from inside my arm.

While the staff formulated a plan for the next step, I settled down in a hospital bed, replaying every detail that had happened that day. There was nothing else I could do, so I absorbed myself in continual prayer. God had saved me once. The least I could do was to continue to put my trust in God and continue following directions. What could little ole Larry Trotter expect to have control over?

Later that afternoon, they made arrangements to transport me from the Somerset East hospital to the St. George Hospital in Port Elizabeth, several hours away. After enduring a tortuous ambulance ride, accentuated by kudu and other wild animals darting across the road with brakes slamming, I arrived at St. George Hospital, where I was scheduled to see an orthopedic specialist named Dr. Bota.

By the time I arrived in Port Elizabeth on the evening of July 3, the pain was excruciating. They numbed my shoulder and immobilized it as much as possible while I met with Dr. Bota.

"Sorry, but since it's so late tonight, we're going to have to wait until morning to do the surgery. We will get an MRI first."

"Do you think you can take care of my shoulder?"

"Yes, I should be able to perform surgery and set the bones anatomically. Your MRI and surgery are scheduled first in the morning."

"Thank you, Doctor. If you run into any kind of issue at all, please let me know, and we'll try to figure out some other alternative. I appreciate you taking care of me."

He sounded confident, and I was happy that we were on the road to repairing my shoulder and arm. Doped up on painkillers, I had time to pray and think about how close I'd come to dying that afternoon as they brought me a minimal amount of food and water in preparation for surgery. I immediately faded off into a deep peaceful sleep.

Be Holy

¹³ Therefore, with minds that are alert and fully sober, set your hope on the grace to be brought to you when Jesus Christ is revealed at his coming.

—1 Peter 1:13 (NIV)

Early the next morning, they did the first of what would become a long series of MRI's over the next four months. Shortly after the MRI, Dr. Bota came into my room and said, "I'd like you to come with me." He wheeled me down the hall in my wheelchair to a large conference room with a giant screen monitor. It looked like a movie screen.

"I want to show you your shoulder."

He turned it on and told me we were looking at my MRI from the outside of my shoulder, looking in. As he focused the image, the view traveled from the surface of my skin, into the muscle, through connective tissue to the site of the shattered bones inside my left arm. I could see the entirety of my fractures. The view was like having X-ray vision, only better.

Fortunately, there weren't any open wounds associated with my injury or a compound fracture protruding through my skin. Miraculously, the horn of the Cape buffalo didn't cause much in the way of external soft tissue damage. My skin was scuffed with abrasions and torn from being launched into the air multiple times, crash-landing on the ground, and being plowed back into the gravel, but those wounds would heal in a couple of weeks.

I remember watching him focus on the humerus, looking at the jagged parts of bone inside my upper arm. Tears started trickling down my right cheek. For the first time since the attack, I was confronted with the true severity of my injuries. I was suddenly consumed with the enormity of my situation, facing a long, difficult road ahead in Africa with unknown medical and surgical facilities.

I had enough medical experience and education to know I was in big trouble. I was scared and nervous about getting an infection and more than a little concerned about the level of technology in the local health-care system. What kinds of additional risk was I facing now?

I knew South Africa was the most advanced of the fifty-four countries on the continent. The first heart transplant was done at

Groote Schuur Hospital on fifty-three-year-old Louis Washkansky on December 3, 1967, a South African grocer dying from chronic heart disease. He received the transplant from Denise Darvall, a twenty-five-year-old woman, by renowned transplant surgeon Christiaan Barnard.

"Do you see all this?" Dr. Bota asked. "Do you see all these parts here? This is a five-part fracture. Very complex. As complex as a fracture gets. Your humeral head is split in half. The humerus itself is fractured laterally across the midsection, and the greater tuberosity was fractured off the top of the humeral head, which is where the supraspinatus tendon was also detached from the bone, part of the four muscles of the rotator cuff. I'm sorry. I thought I could do this, but repairing this complex shoulder injury is beyond the scope of my expertise."

"What do we do now?

"I've already emailed your MRI to Dr. Joseph De Beer in Cape Town. You need to fly there by yourself. We'll put you in a sling, but you need to get on a plane right away. Within the next thirty minutes. Dr. De Beer wants to see you as soon as possible because he's concerned you'll lose circulation to the bone parts, and they could die. He needs to do the surgery immediately to save your shoulder."

I scrambled, making plans to get on the next airplane from Port Elizabeth to Cape Town at eleven o'clock that morning. I hired a driver, who assisted me to the airport, through security, and onto the plane. Global Rescue snapped into action and arranged for a representative to meet me at the hospital in Cape Town.

As I was waiting on the tarmac for the plane to take off, I started to recall the events of the previous day again. I was convinced that I'd died—surrendering my spirit, mind, and physical body (my entire being) completely to Jesus and His Father in Heaven. Through God's intervention, He saved me and delivered His ultimate message. We often hear about near-death experiences. This was mine, with so many feelings racing through my mind.

As I contemplated the urgency of the action I was taking and prayed deeply, I felt a peace beyond comprehension and a sense of thankfulness and gratitude of the highest emotion I've ever witnessed. All glory be to God. I made it out of the bush alive. I kept praying and praising, thanking God for not letting Black Death finish me off in the African savanna, leaving me lying crushed to death in the dirt and gravel. That would have been a senseless way to end my life. I knew there had to be a deeper spiritual purpose in my life. Now it looked like I had a second chance of living long enough to see my four children, their spouses, my grandchildren, and the rest of my family grow up over the next decades. Clearly, this dramatic miracle was my salvation.

For the first time since the attack, I was beginning to experience a measure of optimism and was so grateful that I'd lived through the worst of the nightmare. I felt God's presence and trusted that God would be at my side as I entered the pathway to recovery. I simply let go, turned my life completely over to God, and kept receiving a comforting peace amongst the turmoil.

Do Not Worry

[25] Therefore I tell you, do not worry about your life, what you will eat or drink; or about your body, what you will wear. Is not life more than food, and the body more than clothes? [26] Look at the birds of the air; they do not sow or reap or store away in barns, and yet your heavenly Father feeds them. Are you not much more valuable than they? [27] Can anyone of you by worrying add a single hour to your life?

[28] And why do you worry about clothes? See how the flowers of the field grow. They do not labor or spin. [29] Yet I tell you that not even Solomon in all his splendor was dressed like one of these. [30] If that is how God clothes the grass of the field, which is here today and tomorrow is thrown into the fire, will he not much more clothe you—you of little faith? [31] So do not worry, saying, "What shall we eat?" or "What shall we drink?" or "What shall we wear?" [32] For the pagans run after all these things, and your heavenly Father knows that you need them.

—Matthew 6:25–32 (NIV)

Once in the air, I gazed down at the continent of Africa and the Antarctic Ocean. They were so huge, and I was so tiny. Humbled by the vastness of our planet I drifted off to sleep, imagining the expanse of the universe and how truly blessed my minute being was in the midst of all I was attempting to comprehend.

After landing in Cape Town, a previously arranged driver picked me up at the airport and transported me straight to the Mediclinic Hospital—the best private hospital in Africa. I kept reminding myself that I was receiving the best care possible in Africa. I was feeling positive and trusted that God had His arms of unconditional love wrapped around me. God hadn't given up on me in fifty-eight years and reached His hand down to save me from Black Death when I should have died. My trust and faith will always be in God.

When I arrived at the Mediclinic Hospital, I checked in to let them know I had purchased medical travel insurance and that I was enrolled in the Global Rescue program. Then they escorted me up to the theater to show me where I'd be having my surgery. They don't call them operating rooms or ORs in Africa. They literally have theater seating where people can observe surgeries, so they call them theaters.

I told the attendant at the nurse's station that I was supposed to have emergency surgery immediately the following morning. She said, "Mr. Trotter, we have a room for you, but we don't know when your surgery is scheduled. You're not even on the docket. We're completely booked for the next two weeks. There's no way we can possibly operate on you tomorrow."

My heart sank. I felt like I was trudging in quicksand.

While we were talking, a distinguished gentleman with graying hair, wearing a tweed sport coat and tie, walked toward me at the nurse's station from a long hallway. He extended his hand and expressed in a noticeable gentlemanly proper English accent, "Are you Larry Trotter?"

"Yes, I am."

"I'm Dr. Joseph De Beer. Very pleased to meet you. Please come with me."

Obviously, he already knew my room number, so we walked into the room, and he asked me for the manila envelope containing my X-rays from the little hospital in Somerset East that I was holding. He said that he had already evaluated the MRI taken in Port Elizabeth.

He took out a ballpoint pen from his shirt pocket and drew a reasonable facsimile of my humerus on the back of the envelope. He said, "Here's what we know. This is a very complex five-part fracture. We're performing surgery on you immediately tomorrow morning because we're worried about the loss of blood to the bone parts. You're first in line. An anesthesiologist will come in before surgery and bring you into the theater. I don't know exactly what we're going to find until we actually get inside your shoulder and take a look at the fracture firsthand. Then I'll have to make a decision whether to try to save your bone or put in a titanium prosthetic humeral head."

"If there's any way possible to save my bone, please do."

"Of course."

He continued to describe the surgery and estimated it would take at least two and a half to three hours to perform. They were going to use all available techniques to repair my shoulder.

I asked him, "Do you mind if we pray over the surgery?"

"Absolutely, let's pray together."

So we prayed, asking our Father in Heaven to guide his surgeon's hands and be present with all the surgery team, to provide all the power of Heaven, recognizing that our Heavenly Father, is the supreme surgeon and healer. Our prayer gave peace and confirmation that I was with the right surgeon, that he was a Christian, and that he truly believed in God. For the first time since learning of the severity and complexity of my injury, I felt confident, and the Holy Spirit rained over me.

Dr. De Beer said he'd see me in the morning and then left me sitting alone in my room.

Now that the surgeon's preparations were settled, I placed a call to Fr. Brooks Keith, our Episcopal priest at the Episcopal Church of the Transfiguration in Vail. At first, he thought I was calling him to share my chronicles in Africa, but when he heard the emotion in my voice, he knew that wasn't why I called. Early in the conversation, I asked him, "Am I crazy? What's happening to me?"

"No, Larry. You've been redeemed. God saved you for a reason. What you are now is convicted. You're God's man, just like Peter, Paul, and Andrew." I continued to hang onto his words as he said,

"This isn't the life you thought you were going to have. God has something different in mind for you. Otherwise, Larry Trotter would be dead."

Later that afternoon, I reached out to my good friend and college rowing buddy, John Storck. In addition to an amazing friend, John was also my health-care power of attorney. It was imperative that I reach him.

Before I left for Africa, my personal affairs attorney, Ann Hutchison, and I got together. Interestingly, Ann is the wife of Ross Graves, another member of our 1973 boys in the boat and they were now living in Colorado. I'd met with her to get all my affairs in order in case anything happened to me during my African adventure. Thank God I did.

Among other matters, we revoked my previous personal trust I had created during my first marriage that designated where assets should go in the event of my demise and changed the health-care power of attorney from my former wife to John Storck. John was my attorney for corporate and personal affairs until he became a judge. He was the originator of my testamentary documents, including my will, my trust, and my estate planning.

When I called John, there was an eight-hour time difference. Normally, he never answers his cell phone while he's in court presiding as a judge, but he had an issue going on with one of his children, so instinct told him to answer his cell phone.

In a weakened state, I explained to John it was me, and I had nearly been killed in Africa. He immediately called a recess in court while I explained what happened. Together, we were trying to decide exactly what to do, approve Dr. DeBeer, and see if there was anything additional he could do to help from his side of the planet.

Explaining to John we were already executing plans for a shoulder specialized surgeon per Dr. Bota, I shared with John that my MRI had been forwarded to Dr. Joseph De Beer in Cape Town. We had just met this afternoon and Dr. DeBeer confirmed my surgery was on the docket for the next morning. John conducted a rapid search for the doctor, and we talked later that night. He told me he read about Dr. De Beer and that he was the number 1 orthopedic surgeon in Africa. He'd done work with the Steadman Clinic in Vail and was affiliated with the Cape Shoulder Institute.

John called another one of our rowing buddies, Dr. James R. Dyreby, who was an orthopedic surgeon and had him check out Dr. De Beer as well. I only had one left shoulder, so we weren't leaving any issues to chance. Collectively, we confirmed a level of confidence in Dr. De Beer and thought he was the best in Africa, so we agreed to follow through with the surgery.

We tried to be as diligent as possible, within a compressed timeline, in matters that were out of our hands. There was so much that was out of my control I kept praying and surrendering to God's will. As I let go and totally turned my life over to God, my reward was a sustained sense of peace that surpassed all understanding. From that point on, I made a constant effort to focus my energy positively forward instead of recalling events that happened in the past.

Later that night I managed to get the word out to my family about what had transpired over the past forty-eight hours. I left voice mail messages with my daughters and sons as well as e-mailed a few of my friends to bring them up to speed: that I was nearly killed by over a one-ton Cape buffalo.

One of my close Christian friends and accountability partners, Alan Comerer—one-half of a Christian couple I met as a fellow instructor at the Vail/Beaver Creek Ski School and a brother in Christ—told me he felt the Holy Spirit reach out to him, and he knew something traumatic happened to me on July 3, 2012, at that precise hour. He and his wife, Kathy, started praying for me immediately upon the hour of the attack of Black Death from the other side of the globe—days before I was actually in communication with anyone.

My daughter Martha e-mailed me back: "I thought you weren't going to hunt any dangerous animals? I looked up the risks you took on the Internet, and Cape buffalo kill over two hundred hunters per year, including professional hunters! Why did you do that?"

When I returned home, I had some questions to answer. I assured Martha that I had absolutely no plans to hunt Cape buffalo.

So in essence, you might say that I was destined to face Black Death without knowing it ahead of time, all the way back to 2000, when I bought my bow, twelve years before the actual encounter. To Abrie's credit, he knew my trip was going to be a once in a lifetime event. So he was simply attempting to sell me additional hunting services like hunting lions and Cape buffalo, with a bow and arrow, to ensure that I left with a memorable experience.

I did.

My family is confident now that my days of hunting dangerous game are over. When I went back to Africa in September 2019 for a two-week bush camp photo safari with my wife, Diane, my son-in-law David asked me, "Now you're not hunting, right?"

"Right. No Cape buffalo!"

It's become the running family joke.

Miraculously, with essentially no communication, my family and friends knew something bad had happened and were already praying for me. Long before I reached out to them, my family was feeling vibrations or spiritual energy and were concerned that I was severely injured on the safari as well.

Inspired, intensely motivated, and laser-focused on God and family, it was perfectly clear what my spirit heard as my true calling. God didn't request me, it was absolutely a command in no uncertain terms, how I was to live my life from that moment forward. It felt like my will had been overruled and no longer was there a choice. Executing God's command has been my absolute commitment ever since.

My surgery was scheduled for seven o'clock the next morning, the fifth of July. So there I was celebrating the Fourth of July holiday in a hospital bed, thousands of miles from my family and home in the United States. The trip was supposed to be an expression of my new independence since my divorce. This was the most dramatic miracle of my life and an unforgettable once-in-a-lifetime experience in Africa celebrating our country's declaration of independence. The elephant guns firing nine shots during Black Death's attack were the fireworks.

Recollecting where my emotional brain was, it's easy to remember thinking, *I'm in a South African hospital, the third one I've been to in the past forty-eight hours, and I'm going into surgery tomorrow morning. I thought I was crushed to death, but for the hand of God and His protection, the voice, the light, the angel, the shooting. What on earth just happened? The encounter with Black Death was all surreal! Was it all just an African nightmare that I just woke up from? But it was real! God is for real!*

Amid God, John Storck, and Dr. De Beer, I felt there couldn't be better guidance. With the desire to continue praying, I had "the little brown Bible and Cross" out, praying with God under the effects of pain medication. It didn't take long and I drifted off to sleep.

Awoken the next morning at six-thirty by a guy standing over me clutching a motorcycle helmet under his arm was an encounter of a different kind. He said he was my anesthesiologist and wanted to introduce himself before we started pre-op. Of course, I wasn't allowed to eat, so there was nothing to do for the next fifteen minutes but anticipate what I was about to experience and pray for God to keep watch over me.

The orderlies wheeled me out of my room to pre-op and then into the surgical theater. They started a countdown from ten. The next conscious time I remember was when I woke up in my room later that afternoon.

During the procedure, they moved me onto a surgical robotic chair called the beach chair. A beach scene sounded good, but instead, my arm was supported by an armrest that moved robotically per their instructions.

They performed what is humorously called a full fillet to accomplish a procedure known as an "open reduction internal fixation" utilized to reconstruct complex fractures like mine. Before they could begin reducing my broken bones to their original anatomical formation, they had to open my shoulder from the base of the collarbone to above my elbow. Then they severed the tendons in my shoulder to provide unhampered access to the damaged area, like opening a door.

My humeral head was split in half, the greater tuberosity fractured or blown off the humeral head, and the humerus shaft fractured laterally. Dr. De Beer drilled into the various bone parts and screwed rods into the bones so he could manipulate the parts until they were anatomically reduced accurately to their original location. Half of the bones had shifted anteriorly, while the other half had moved posteriorly. My shoulder was a mess.

The surgery went way beyond the anticipated time, requiring more than five and a half hours. Afterward, Dr. De Beer said that the reduction of the bone parts took ninety minutes alone, just to realign the bones and maneuver them back into place. Then they had to install a titanium fixture, drill into the bones, and position all the moving parts with the hardware before fixing them in place with titanium screws. They even had the French medical representative on hand from the company that manufactured the titanium fixture. The plate ran internally a third of the way down my humerus with eight screws securing the bones.

During the surgery, the team continually monitored my vitals and took images as their work progressed.

In the worst-case scenario, Dr. De Beer was prepared to replace the entire humeral head with a titanium prosthetic head. He had to make an on-the-spot decision whether he could save my natural bone. All factors considered, the choice is always better to save your own bone because shoulders with titanium parts have a limited lifespan. The most optimal choice was to let my body heal naturally the way God made me.

Around four o'clock that afternoon, Dr. De Beer walked into my room smiling, looking very pleased and optimistic. "It looks like you're pretty happy with the way surgery turned out," my voice calmly projected.

"Yes. The surgery went perfectly. The French representative for the fixture supplier said if it was his shoulder, he would have wanted the same surgical result."

We continued to visit a short while, and I thanked Dr. De Beer as he left to attend to his next patient. An aide brought me dinner—though I can't remember the menu. Meanwhile, all my family and American friends were celebrating with beer, Johnsonville brats, and fireworks. Shortly after e-mailing John and my family about the success of the surgery I remember having one of the best night's sleep of my life.

A remarkable phenomenon occurred after my surgeries. My soft and bone tissue started healing at an accelerated rate. They seemed to be in a miraculous period of regrowth. Even later, when I had additional surgeries with Dr. Peter J. Millett, he couldn't believe how fast my body healed. Following the Cape buffalo attack, my whole internal being shifted; my heart, soul, spirit, mind, and body changed. Whether it was the first, second, or third surgery, I healed at an astonishing rate, especially for someone my age. Both Dr. De beer and Dr. Millett commented that I was recovering faster than most people in their twenties, let alone a man of fifty-eight.

From the time of the attack, my focus remained on God's message. My thoughts and prayers weren't on anything other than getting the best medical care I could obtain and returning safely to my family. I was already looking forward to our family reunion planned for August 2012 in Wisconsin. Nothing was more important to me than being able to attend the family event and see my new grandson, my daughter who was pregnant, and the rest of my beautiful children, grandchildren, and family. I was going to do exactly what the voice commanded me in the third message: focus on God and family for the rest of my life. This was a gift I wasn't going to mess up, especially given this second chance.

During that period of healing, "the little brown Bible and a cross" continued as my constant travel companions. Whenever I had idle time, I'd read passages from my Bible and run my fingers over the cross. I'd revisit dog-eared, heavily used pages that I'd traced with my finger countless times before. With the Word and Jesus at my side, I was never alone.

Feeling confident that Dr. De Beer and his team had saved my arm and that it was going to heal properly was a good feeling and positive energy. They took fluid samples, deep tissue cultures, and surface samples to monitor my wound for infections. The plan was to place them in Petri dishes, hopefully confirming no bacterial growth while waiting fourteen days to ensure no infection was forming before I left for Colorado.

Around four o'clock in the afternoon of July 6, the day after surgery, Dr. De Beer came into my room. This time he wasn't wearing a bright, smiling face. He was very somber and concerned. Not an angry look but a frustrated, intense scowl. "You don't look so good today," I commented.

He asked, "Have you seen the X-ray the tech took at 10 am this morning?"

"Yes, I looked at the film all day after it was taken this morning. I saw eight screws, the fixture, and all the bones in place. The bone position and screws looked like what I expected to see."

"No. Sorry, the fixation failed."

"What do you mean the fixation failed? The image looks okay to me. You even said so yourself."

"That was yesterday. The purchase of some of the screws lost fixation since the surgery, and the bone parts have already shifted out of place. We double-checked the surgical film of the procedure and it appeared perfect when we finished the surgery. But now the bone parts are not anatomically correct. I'm very disappointed."

"Oh no! What do we do now?"

"Well, I'm going to have to go back in and redo the procedure. But don't worry. We won't charge you anything for another surgery."

Suddenly, my world collapsed. One moment I was on top of the universe. The next I was back under the dark shadow of the beast.

"Well, can you fix it tomorrow?"

I learned a long time ago as an entrepreneur, we don't wait for opportunities. We reach out and seize them.

"No, we can't do that. We have to wait for at least two weeks for the soft tissue to heal and make sure there's no infection. We have cultures running right now. We can't do it arthroscopically. We'll have to open your shoulder using the full fillet ORIF procedure again to make the repairs."

Overwhelmed is not a strong enough word to share what I felt. The thought of having to hang around Cape Town for fourteen days, waiting for Dr. De Beer to redo the surgery, was more than I could fathom. Then I thought, *Well, I guess that's what I'm supposed to do. There's no other recourse.*

Consistently asking God for guidance was my reinforcement to follow through with the doctor's orders and protocols. The goal was for my tissue not to get infected, so they'd be able to go back in and fix it, and then I could leave. Originally I'd planned on being in Africa for twenty-five days, so I guess time didn't really matter anyway. Even though I wanted to get back home—which, I thought, was always an option, I decided to stay because I had confidence in Dr. De Beer. We'd established a positive rapport—not always easy to find with doctors. He said he'd make sure everything was right. Why should I start mistrusting him or God now?

Blessings for Obedience

28 If you fully obey the Lord your God and carefully follow all his commands I give you today, the Lord your God will set you high above all the nations on earth. 2 All these blessings will come on you and accompany you if you obey the Lord your God:

3 You will be blessed in the city and blessed in the country.

4 The fruit of your womb will be blessed, and the crops of your land and the young of your livestock—the calves of your herds and the lambs of your flocks.

5 Your basket and your kneading trough will be blessed.

6 You will be blessed when you come in and blessed when you go out.

Deuteronomy 28:1–6 (NIV)

I asked Dr. De Beer when was the soonest he could go back in and redo the procedure. He said on the nineteenth of July. I thought, *Oh wow. What am I going to do for two weeks?*

He suggested that I stay there in Cape Town and take in the sights, but I was already paying for premium accommodations at the hunting lodge for a month, so I decided to go back to Grant's ranch and wait there. At least I could walk around and view the scenery and wildlife I came to observe.

The nurses explained the protocols for changing my bandages and pain management and put me on the schedule to come back for surgery on the morning of July 19. I flew back to Port Elizabeth, where Abrie picked me up, and we drove back to the ranch.

On the way back to the lodge in his bakkie, I started to wonder, *What am I going to do? Am I going to just hang out there, waiting for the next surgery? That doesn't seem like much fun. On the other hand, I've already paid for my room and board, incredible food, and beautiful accommodations. Maybe we can go for a ride and visit nearby Kruger National Park.*

Then Abrie shared his stroke of genius—or was it another temptation? He said he'd already taken the initiative to call Dr. De Beer and asked him, "Do you think it would be all right if I took Larry hunting while his arm is on the mend?"

So the next day, I called Dr. De Beer to confirm and asked him what he thought about me attempting to go back on safari. He said, "Sure, as long as you don't fall on your arm, reinjure it, and start hemorrhaging. You can't really hurt the bones because we have to redo the surgery anyway."

Welcome to plan B.

CHAPTER NINE

NOTHING SAYS AFRICA
LIKE A ZEBRA

Present Suffering and Future Glory

[18] I consider that our present sufferings are not worth comparing with the glory that will be revealed in us.
—Romans 8:18 (NIV)

With my entire left shoulder immobilized in a sling, Abrie cornered me and asked again, "You don't want to just sit around here for two weeks, do you? Why don't you let me take you out hunting? Maybe you could shoot my rifle using just your right arm." The gears in my head started to turn.

The next morning, Abrie took me out shooting his rifle at a target to make sure I could aim and shoot the gun using just my right arm. "What would you like to hunt?" he asked. One of the animals I wanted to hunt most was a zebra. I particularly wanted a zebra rug as a remembrance of my safari, and so did my son Matt. I'd seen them in people's homes, and they're gorgeously stunning. "Nothing says Africa like a zebra." At least to me.

When I was originally planning my trip, I wanted to hunt sixteen different plains game animals including four members of the African antelope spiral-horned species. They have majestic spiral horns that grow from the top of their heads. The largest is called an eland. They're the size of a large bull elk or bigger. They call them antelope in Africa and they weigh over one thousand pounds.

Next on the list was a kudu, the same animal that kept leaping across the road, making my earlier ambulance trip so painful when the driver had to keep stomping on the brakes. They weigh six hundred to eight hundred pounds, have long massive spiraled horns that measure more than thirty inches high. The third one was the nyala. They're the most visually striking of the spiral-horned animals. They have beautiful markings and legging colorations. Their horns are similar to kudu but not quite as tall. They typically weigh three hundred to five hundred pounds. The fourth and smallest species of the spiral-horned antelope is the beautiful bushbuck, which is similar in size to the buck whitetail deer I grew up hunting in the bush of Wisconsin. Also on my list were black-and-blue wildebeest, waterbuck, red hartebeest, zebra burchells, Cape mountain zebra, blesbok, springbok, gemsbuck, lechwe, steenbuck, and impala. Abrie thought I should be able to hunt all of those species, even with just one arm.

The following morning, we went out on the ranch and found a beautiful zebra. I propped the gun on the front corner of the bakkie and shot it with my right arm while my left arm was immobilized in the sling. We took the zebra back to the lodge and had a big dinner, celebrating the successful hunt. That night, Grant said, "We have a very special dinner for you tonight Larry. Cape buffalo fillet mignon!" It was the tenderloin of the Cape buffalo that we wrangled with on July 3. They auctioned all the meat from the buffalo to the people in Somerset East but saved the tenderloin for me. I think I ate two or three fillet mignon steaks of the beast that evening. They were absolutely delicious. While I did plan on eating what I harvested with the goal of fully experiencing the best of Africa, in my wildest dreams, I could never have anticipated my experience would end up this way.

The first day of hunting plains animals went so well we decided to continue by going after a gemsbuck. I really didn't want to hunt using a rifle, but what choice did I have? Hunting was either with a rifle or not hunt at all. Abrie also arranged to borrow a crossbow from a friend of his who was shipping his bow to us and the bow was scheduled to arrive in a day or so.

Gemsbuck was always on my list because they're a very interesting animal. Every one of them has a unique facial mask and long tall horns that can extend more than thirty-six inches above their heads. After searching for hours, we finally found a herd of gemsbuck and watched them with our binoculars.

Abrie said, "The first one in the heard looks like a good one to me." I looked them over and said, "What about the last one?"

"You're right, that's the tallest mature one." I checked the range and shot it. That evening, we had gemsbuck steak for dinner. The flavor of the meat was scrumptious.

The following day, the crossbow finally arrived, so I could return to my original plan of hunting without using rifles, which was just as well because I told Abrie, "I really don't want to shoot any more animals with a gun. It's just not what I came to do."

We sighted in the crossbow to ensure it was shooting accurately and then drove to a hide adjacent to an orange grove. The local animals love eating oranges, and there are usually dozens of loose oranges lying on the ground near the hide. When the kudu came in to eat the oranges, they put the entire fruit in their mouth and popped them like grapes. Now the challenge was to find the right one.

Abrie previously picked out what he thought would be a kudu near the end of his life span, but the kudu didn't come near enough to the hide for a shot with a bow. "Well, we'll have to come back and try hunting him again," Abrie voiced.

That night, he said he had a mature eland lined up for the next day so we'd have to plan to go after the kudu on another day.

The next morning, we were up at first daylight getting ready to head out to the hide with the intent to harvest an eland using the crossbow. After the endless grueling struggles I'd been through, I felt I was finally hunting the animals that were on my original list, taking still photos and movies. This was more like the experience I imagined, not lying in the bush crushed by Black Death. It was the type of purist approach to hunting that I preferred, complemented by time for viewing and taking pictures.

We camped like Teddy Roosevelt in a bush camp that night and were having breakfast before the eland hunt when we heard the trackers outside the compound chattering in Afrikaans with excitement. "Abrie, what's all the commotion?" I inquired.

"Well, there's a big bushbuck up there on the ridge, above us."

"That's one of the spiral-horned animals that's on my list to hunt with a bow. Can we take a look at him?"

"Sure. Let's go outside the bush camp compound."

Immediately I focused in with my binoculars. The bushbuck was an elegant spectacle. Abrie said, "The bushbuck is a Gold Medal Safari

International classed bushbuck. Furthermore, it would be a great buck to harvest because it looked like it was in its last year of life, so we wouldn't be harvesting it prematurely. Who knows? It might not even survive from predators during the winter and dry season as a solo buck."

"Can I harvest him?"

"Yeah. I'll go and get my rifle."

The buck was over 350 yards away up on a ridge, so it was too far away to shoot with the crossbow we borrowed. He was leisurely grazing as he ambled along the ridge top, but we were concerned that he might bolt, so the trackers rushed a table over and propped the rifle on top of a daypack and I assumed a sitting shooting position behind the table in a chair. Quickly, I lined up the crosshairs and touched off a moving shot dropping the buck instantly, using just my right arm. The group was ecstatic. Then the trackers incredibly ran up the very steep grade to the top of the ridge to retrieve the bushbuck and process him promptly to care for the meat and get it into the cooler immediately. Guess what's for dinner?

After they brought the bushbuck down, we all gathered around, gazing at the beauty of the animal. He was truly one of God's creatures. Who else could have created an animal so magnificent? I prayed over the buck and thanked God for the exciting African experience while reminiscing and comparing hunting bucks in Wisconsin as a youth with my dad. In the words of Teddy, when he really appreciated an experience, I said, "Bully... what a beautiful blessed morning... that was truly Bully!" That evening we dined on delectably divine bushbuck filet mignon steaks with African wine and all the trimmings. In the morning the menu was unbelievable back straps (New York strip steak) and fresh hand-picked eggs from Grant's private ranch chickens. While enjoying the flavor of the African wild game meat, I exclaimed, "Now that's what I'm talking about!"

So that made three animals I harvested that were on my list: the Cape mountain zebra, gemsbuck, and bushbuck—not including the Cape buffalo. Three of the four species I contracted to have shoulder-mounts crafted by Wildlife Artistry, a Taxidermist in South Africa, along with an elegant zebra rug and had them sent home to Colorado. They're truly authentic and memorialize the experience and the stories of the adventure.

True to walking the talk, I wanted to make the most of the zebra, so I also had pencil holders made from the hooves. I tried to use as much of the animals as possible. A rug was made out of the hide, and all the meat was consumed in Africa. The export laws state that we **can not** bring any African meat out of the country. You can eat it yourself while you're there, share it with the camp, or the outfitter can sell it. But the meat must be consumed in the African continent.

The original plan was to return with two zebra rugs, one for my son and one for me, so while at the taxidermist's shop, getting my museum-quality mounted artistry lined up, I noticed they had a beautiful zebra rug for sale from an animal that someone else had shot. For my son Matt, who always wanted one, I bought it as well. I also found a few other rugs from various animals to help me remember my African safari in my later years.

Soon after the bushbuck harvest with breakfast, we were ready for our morning eland hunt using the crossbow. From inside the hide, we started to see a few female eland wander within range. They were huge and gray with magnificent chests. Africa is the only place on Earth where we can see exotic-looking creatures like this. They were breathtaking to watch through binoculars, take videos and still photos at close range.

A few minutes later, we noticed several bulls wandering closer to our hide. We were waiting for one particular bull we'd seen off in the distance, but he never came close enough to harvest with a bow. We patiently waited and watched the magnificent bull eland for over an hour as he slowly fed away from us. Abrie said, "Let's go after him."

"Are you sure we should try stalking him? Alright then." He twisted my arm initially. At least the arm was not my wounded arm.

Reminiscent of my Cape buffalo episode, we stalked after the eland on foot, but we could never get close enough to shoot it with the crossbow. We walked over a mile and a half, and the temperature was scorching hot. Perspiration was running down my face burning my eyes with the salty sweat and pouring down the inside of my shirt both front and back while we hiked over irregular terrain through rocks, brush, and termite hills. Chasing the eland across the savanna occurred to me as not a brilliant pursuit to be attempting, given my current condition. I felt in conflict with the first part of God's command, "No more extreme pursuits," as well. I really didn't need to fall on my injured shoulder and risk a blood clot to my brain or my heart. I told

Abrie, "I think I'm done." I thought to myself, *I'm finished, no more twisting arms or temptations.*

I said to Abrie, "I don't want to hunt anymore." My arm was killing me. The hospital gave me pain medication similar to oxycodone, but I was totally against getting addicted to it, so I was only using extra-strength Tylenol. After being in health care and the assisted-living business, I knew all about oxy. Even back in the nineties, oxy was the drug of choice for anyone struggling with pain. Scores of doctors were overprescribing it to the point where it had leaked out into the black market. Addicts and thieves were breaking into pharmacies, nursing homes, assisted-living facilities, and hospitals, stealing Oxycodone, OxyContin, hydrocodone and other opioids, so they could sell them on the streets, fueling the opioid craze we're trying to overcome today.

After traipsing around in the hot sun and tripping over rocks and brush, my shoulder was absolutely throbbing and jolting my body with excruciating pain. Actually, my shoulder has never stopped hurting, since July 3, 2012. To this day, I deal with the pain every hour of every day. It's a constant reminder of God's message, the power of God, and how one split-second can change our life forever but, most importantly, my salvation in the African savanna.

After we got back to the lodge, I settled up with Grant, understanding that I had to pay for the Cape buffalo though I didn't shoot the goliath beast. I traded on the value of some of the other animals that I'd already prepaid and zeroed out the additional cost of the safari. By this time, I was into the tenth or eleventh day since I arrived back at the lodge from surgery. I still had another five days just to hang out and then fly back to Cape Town for my second surgery.

Over the next week, I was in continuous communication with my family and John Storck, getting all my affairs organized to leave. The days flew by quickly, but I always made time to take hikes around the compound. After all, this would probably be the last time I would ever set foot on African soil. I was **not** planning on ever returning. God laughed again for He had a different plan and it wasn't going to be my last time on the African continent, as seven years later my new wife convinced me to accompany her for a two-week bush camp photo safari in September 2019. Needless to say, we were very careful when twelve Dagga Boys walked down to the water hole in front of our tent to greet us 30 yards away. This time these twelve messengers together delivered a different message of peace as our experience was purely a wonderful photo safari and a sharing of mutually accepted quality time viewing the best of Africa with my new bride.

July 18, 2012, while flying back to the Mediclinic Hospital in Cape Town I was feeling great expectations anticipating the correction surgery and returning home. After arriving at the hospital, Dr. De Beer escorted me into an examination room and said, "I want to take a look at your shoulder."

I told him, "I've noticed fluid running out of the bottom of the incision."

"There is?!"

He urgently began tearing the bandage off, and a look of panic poured over his face. He started barking commands for nurses to come into the room. When he pulled the bandage off the bottom of the incision, milky fluid gushed out onto the exam table and floor. Suddenly, he shifted into emergency mode, taking fluid for cultures, rushing them to the lab, and examining my shoulder. Then he gave me the bad news.

"You have an infection confirmed under our microscope, and we've started cultures to identify the bacteria . . ."

Within seconds, I was completely deflated—again. All my hopes and dreams for a speedy surgery and a trip back home collapsed around the pile of dripping bandages littering the floor.

"Now what are we going to do?" I muttered dejectedly. "Does that mean we can't redo the surgery now?"

"We have to start loading you up with intravenous antibiotics immediately," DeBeer exclaimed.

So once again, I was back in the hospital. Instead of staring down a fuming one-ton beast, I was confronted with a lethal micro-beast so small we needed a microscope to see it.

Dr. De Beer told me, "We can't perform another surgery until the infection is gone. That could mean days or even weeks of waiting until the infection is eradicated." I moaned to myself, *This is not working out as planned. I've got to get out of here. I have to get home because right, where I live in Vail, is the Steadman Clinic—the best orthopedic surgical practice in the country, if not the world. The best surgeons and the best hospital for shoulders, knees, and hips. The best medical help is minutes from my home. **I've got to get out of here, out of Africa!** I was remembering the movie.*

I e-mailed my brother Rob and pleaded, "Rob, can you get me into Steadman Clinic?" Rob got ahold of Dr. Peter J. Millett at the clinic and explained the severity of the situation to him. Rob emailed me back and wrote, "Susan, the director of services for Dr. Millett, said to get back here as fast as you can. She'll be calling you to make the arrangements."

The next morning on the nineteenth of July, Susan called the administrator of the Mediclinic Hospital and started putting the wheels in motion. The administrator came up to me and said, "You have an urgent telephone call from the United States, the Steadman Clinic. You need to take the call."

Ironically, Susan was originally from South Africa and knew all about Cape buffalo. She couldn't believe that I was still alive. She said, "Your brother got ahold of us and explained the situation, so I spoke to Dr. Millett, and he said to get out of Africa and get back here as soon as you can! As soon as you arrive, he'll do your surgery."

The instant I put down the phone, we started working with the travel medical insurance firm I'd been dealing with during the trip to find me a way home. I told them, "I have extreme edema of my left arm, and it's turning yellow and green. I'm worried about losing my arm. There's a nasty infection in my arm, and I need to fly back home to see a special surgeon in Colorado immediately. I also need to be in first class, so I have a reclining bed and a place to rest my injured shoulder and arm lying horizontally with my arm elevated."

They called me back a few minutes later and said, "We have your request approved for a first-class flight. Your flight costs over $10,000 one way, but we'll take care of the expenses. Now that we know you're flying back for sure, we'll get you on a flight." Fortunately, I'd brought all my gear and luggage with me from the lodge. In short order, I was boarding a flight from Cape Town to Johannesburg. Once I arrived in Johannesburg, I boarded a nonstop 747 to London.

Twelve hours later, we were landing at Heathrow International Airport in London on my way back home to Colorado. Oh, how I wished I was landing there to watch the 2012 summer Olympics with all the athletes competing, including enjoying the rowing competition, rather than as a route stop on an emergency evacuation. By this time, everyone on the plane knew I was the guy who was attacked by a Cape buffalo and lived to tell the story. The pilots had feverishly worked on a way to rearrange my itinerary and come up with a shorter flight. The next regularly scheduled flight flew from London to Los Angeles and then from Los Angeles to Denver. After that, I still had a three-hour drive up to my home in Colorado. Ultimately, the pilots couldn't work out an alternative arrangement because I needed to have a reclining bed, so I had to stay on the 747, arriving in Denver on Friday afternoon, July 20.

While I was making my way back across the United States from LA, my sister-in-law, Linda, and her kids jumped into their Suburban and drove to Denver International Airport to bring me back home. We'd already made general arrangements with the Steadman Clinic for my surgery, but there was nothing available on Friday, Saturday, or Sunday, so I had to wait for an eight o'clock surgery appointment on the morning of Monday, July 23, 2012.

Part of my family were now with me, and they were thrilled to see me back home relatively safe. Even my dad made the trip from Arizona to see me. He told me it was important that he was the one to take me to the Steadman Clinic on Monday morning.

With a new concept of time, while waiting patiently, I thought what a perfect opportunity to spend the weekend with Rob, Linda, their kids, and my dad. I enjoyed long, leisurely days recovering from jetlag and hiking with my black lab Tuffy while my mind kept replaying every memory of what happened to me over the past three weeks. The replay was like a continuous loop of a nonstop surreal nightmare. Never the less, deep in my soul there was a cognizant realization the entire incident was truly a blessing in disguise, that presented itself as a true miracle and the most significant waypoint of my life; salvation. With surgery coming up, I did my best to deal with the pain, taking nothing but extra-strength Tylenol.

By the time I arrived home in Colorado, visual inspection and healing sensations exhibited that the infection was receding, so I continued hiking as my main form of exercise to keeping my blood flow at peak regenerative levels. I felt that was the best way to heal mentally and physically. The weekend slipped by quickly as I shared hours conversing with the rest of my family all over the country. My dad and brother Rob kept watching the video over and over as they observed the camera clock. Rob exclaimed, "The video shows it was only 4 seconds from the snort to the first shot fired (the beast covered 40 yards in 4 seconds from a standing position), 8 more seconds of shooting until the beast was down and 8 more seconds elapsed until the ninth and final shot." My dad stated, "You're an idiot for taking on Black Death with a bow and arrow."

My family was questioning my intentions, so I assured them that there were never any plans of going after dangerous game. Inadvertently a once in a lifetime opportunity presented itself on July 3 and I further explained the circumstances were simply a rare sequence of events that occurred as I was tempted by the devil. A dark temptation lured me in, and I was weak enough to fall for the enticement and was almost killed in the process.

My daughters said, "Thank God you're alive and you're back home safe." I made the rounds and talked to all my kids and told them that I was trying to heal so I could make the reunion in August. My children actually displayed the kindest list of questioning as to why in the world I would be tempted so easily. Father Brooks asked, "Weren't your actions like taking a knife to a gunfight or using a slingshot to kill a goliath beast?" Over time, during the first 18 months following the attack, after sharing my witness countless numbers of times, there was a full spectrum of opinions expressed by my small audiences ranging from 1-30. The most common opinion was that God saved me on purpose for a reason, that God had more plans for me in my future. The most reverent opinion included the concept of a purposeful incident and witness of a miracle that was God's plan. The whole set of events involved years of preparation and a timed sequence leading to the attack, message, and salvation. Then a period of time carrying my cross through recovery and most importantly the obligation to share the story. Basically, a continuum of opinions ranging from **Idiot to Messenger**.

On the morning of July 23, my dad drove me to the Vail Valley Medical Center for surgery. I brought along my video camera, per Dr. Millett's request, to show them exactly what happened. As soon as I walked through the doors, a huge commotion ensued. It was like the entire Steadman Clinic dropped what they were doing to attend to me. By that time, I'd become some type of minor celebrity, at least in terms of orthopedic sports injuries—if we call getting slammed around in the dirt by a one-ton buffalo sport. I was escorted into a room with Dr. Millett, head of the shoulder department, and the surgeon performing my surgery, along with four other surgeons, who were orthopedic fellows at the Steadman Clinic.

Dr. Millett said the first item he wanted to see was the video. Because he's a big game archery hunter himself, he was curious to see how the entire incident went down. They plugged the camera into the TV and played the twenty seconds of the actual attack. The final stalk video is two minutes and forty-two seconds. There are twenty minutes of us stalking the Cape buffalo, followed by the twenty-second attack specifically. The video shows the details of the entire incident.

As he watched the video, he uttered, "Oh wow. This is truly an amazing story, you are so blessed to be saved and alive. We'll help you recover. Now let's discuss your shoulder."

The next items were extremely serious as my dad sat next to me, and Peter started speaking. "Now here's what we've learned. We have calls from Dr. De Beer describing the infection in the cultures they're observing. We usually don't do surgery when there's an infection present, but we're going in anyway."

The plan sounded just like a Bruce Willis movie or an order from the White House Situation Room from the president to SEAL Team Six: "This is what we've been training for . . . We're going in! Godspeed!"

Dr. Millett continued. "We're going to go in, deal with the infection, clean you up, and take out the fixture. We're going to look at everything that's going on in there and completely reconstruct your shoulder. We're going to do the best job we can to return your shoulder to its original state."

I said, "OK. That sounds good to me."

Surgery was scheduled for ten o'clock that morning. I'd already called Father Brooks over the weekend, and he said, "Larry, before your surgery, I want you to call me," so I tried calling him but couldn't get through.

They wheeled me from my hospital room to a meeting with the anesthesiologist and to pre-op preparation. Seconds before the anesthesiologist put me under, I got a phone call from Father Brooks. A nurse handed me the phone, and he said, "Larry, this is Father Brooks. We're going to say a prayer." Just the sound of his voice brought calmness and peace to my soul. We prayed for the ultimate surgeon and healer to be there and to guide the hands of Peter my orthopedic surgeon, the entire medical team, and that everything goes according to God's plan and that nothing gets in the way of a perfect surgery and the beginning of healing. "I'll be stopping to see you tomorrow at the hospital. . . and I want to see that video."

The last-minute I remember was the orderlies wheeling me into the OR and the anesthesiologist putting me under, the same routine as the first surgery. The procedure was supposed to last approximately three and a half hours, but it ended up taking more than six. Back in my room after surgery, Dr. Millett stopped by and said, "When we got in there, unfortunately, the condition of your shoulder was worse than what I hoped it would be. The bones in the shoulder were in pretty bad shape."

Dr. Millett ended up performing a unique surgery called a reverse total shoulder reconstruction. "I do a lot of complex revisions to previous shoulder surgeries, so I do that procedure quite often," explained Dr. Millett, "but I have to admit this was my first surgery to repair the damage from an African Cape buffalo attack. You had the old hardware in there from the prior surgery, so all the tissue was badly scarred. That substantially increased the complexity of the procedure. Along with the total shoulder reconstruction, we installed a custom fixture designed for your humerus with twelve screws and a bone graft. We moved some bone around to fill in a gap in the humeral head, and we're hoping that it will all knit back together and hold."

Dr. Millett went on to describe his therapeutic plan for me. "We're putting you on a very potent intravenous antibiotic. We want to do that for three days and blast you with antibiotics. You're probably going to have more IV antibiotics afterwards until we can figure out a suitable oral medication. You're going to have to be on antibiotics for two weeks. Then we'll have to make sure there's no infection."

The unique technique of the reverse total shoulder reconstruction performed only became available in the United States in 2004, so had I been injured a decade earlier, there wouldn't have been any way to repair the severe damage from my attack. Another blessing in disguise, as the timing, fortunately, occurred when the technology and technique were available to reconstruct such an extremely complex injury.

"Larry is now skiing over one hundred days a year. He goes hunting and can use his arm for that," says Dr. Millett. "I know he's even returned to waterskiing. He told me he's even been doing some rowing, so he's had amazing results considering how bad the damage was. He could have ended up with a nonfunctional shoulder. It's a testament to his hard work with the rehabilitation and how well he's healed after surgery that he's been able to get back to all the activities he loves. He's still a relatively young guy to have something like that done. While he might need to have surgery again in the future, it probably won't be for at least another twenty years."

Mentally struggling with the known effects of oxycodone, I had to tell the Steadman Clinic staff, "I don't like taking the oxy. It just doesn't agree with me. I'd rather put up with the pain and take Tylenol." So that's exactly the pain medication I took as well as other medication to reduce swelling.

After three weeks in the African bush and thirty hours on planes returning, I was finally relaxing in the beautiful Vail Valley Medical Center. The food was great, the care was incredible, and they were killing the infection. The damage from Black Death was in check for now.

Dr. Millett visited me the next day and said, "Well, we're going to take you into X-ray and check you out." After I returned, he said, "Everything looks really good except for the one bone part that has already moved. We're afraid that it might move some more, but for now, the five bone parts and fixture are intact with the 12 screws holding everything together."

"Does that mean you're going to have to go in again?"

"We may or may not. We probably should, but we're not going to do it now. We're going to have to wait for at least a month."

With all I'd been through, I was mentally numb from the attack, surgeries, travel, waiting, and trying to stay composed as the medical staff helped me. All I could do was cling to the vine and thank God for saving me. Every time I felt pain, it reminded me that I was so close to death and blessed to be alive. I thought this would be my final surgery, and I'd be on the road to complete recovery. Like anyone else, I struggled with the news, but with the presence of Jesus and the unlimited power of our Father in Heaven, I realized I had nothing to fear. I wasn't going to let the destroyer tempt me again with any anti-Christ ploys such as fear.

⁹ But he said to me, "My grace is sufficient for you, for my power is made perfect in weakness." Therefore I will boast all the more gladly about my weaknesses, so that Christ's power may rest on me. ¹⁰ That is why, for Christ's sake, I delight in weaknesses, in insults, in hardships, in persecutions, in difficulties. For when I am weak, then I am strong.
—2 Corinthians 12:9–10 (NIV)

Two days later, I left the hospital, went back home, and started hiking every day, trying to accelerate the healing process. I even went up and hiked on Vail Pass on old Highway 6 around the same area where I felled trees in 1974 with a chainsaw. I was doing every possible healing protocol I could think of, including continued praying, all efforts to compliment executing Dr. Millett's directions and protocols with the intent of enhancing the healing process. Two weeks later, I went back and had my shoulder X-rayed, an MRI taken, and they measured the bones to make sure the bones and fixture were secure and in place.

Dr. Millett said, "I don't know what you're doing, but you are healing faster than anyone half your age. The soft tissue is already completely healed, and there doesn't appear to be any sign of infection. The bones are knitting together, and they look like they're holding in place except for that one bone that moved."

He went on to say "We discussed your case and had a consensus of the fellows: we're all in agreement that we should wait and let your shoulder heal before we go back in again. If we start doing therapy and we're not getting the proper range of motion, then we have the option of going in again and correcting that one bone part. But at least four of the pieces will be healing in the correct position."

So that was exactly what we did. I began passive physical therapy because I couldn't move my shoulder on my own volition, but I could withstand the therapist moving my arm to maintain my range of motion, particularly my external rotation.

During one of my follow-up appointments, Dr. Millett showed me the measurement from a new MRI, and the one bone part that had moved was fifty degrees off. He said, "I think if we get that piece back in place, you'll have the best possible results. Think about it." I thought *I don't think I can go through this again. The pain following surgery is such an unbearable ordeal for over two-three weeks with all the swelling during recovery.*

But that night, I weighed the relatively brief inconvenience against a life of restricted movement, called Peter in the morning, and said, "OK. I'm in. Let's get the best possible results we can."

He said, "Great. I have a lot of commitments scheduled at the moment, and I'm traveling, but I'll come in specially to do just your surgery when I return on Saturday, October 6th." Feeling extremely blessed to have the best shoulder specialist in the world coming in to do my surgery on his day off, lead to an emotional sequence of prayers of thankfulness. Peter is an ultimate example of being the hands and feet of Jesus, right here on Earth, right now.

"I'll be there," I promised.

Over the next two weeks, I went down to Grand Junction to visit my friend Alan, who shared with me that he knew I had a traumatic event in Africa at the exact time the incident occurred. We visited the desert and even took my boat out on Lake Powell. We caught up on old times and enjoyed an abbreviated vacation, the one we'd planned to take before I left for Africa at the end of June.

On the way to the lake, we dropped off my black Labrador, Tuffy, at a kennel in Fruita. On the fifth of October, as we were getting ready to leave the lake, I called the kennel and told them I was on my way to pick up Tuffy. They said, "Oh Larry, I'm so sorry, I have some terrible news. Tuffy died last night." I thought, *Really? Already burdened with too much to think about, I could only pray and get through my surgery the next day.*

Returning to Vail on the evening of the 5th, I was ready for the surgery the next morning Saturday, October 6. Peter performed my surgery on his day off, and we were becoming good friends by then, but more notably I learned he was a brother in Christ. Absolutely, without a doubt, I can truly state that Peter is an instrument of God.

With all attention and focus on surgery, I never even had time to mourn the passing of Tuffy, my eleven-year-old friend, and constant companion. Father Brooks called again and prayed for a successful surgery—number 3. He reminded me, "Larry, very few people get a message like this. You're a big guy with a big personality, and you needed a big metamorphosis. God felt like you needed a substantial life change. God has a plan and a purpose for you."

During the surgery, they broke free the one obstinate bone part and repositioned it into the appropriate anatomically correct position. The surgery went much faster this time. Instead of having five moving parts to deal with, they only had one. They were able to secure the one bone piece in place against the other bone mass that was already healing with the new fixture.

After the surgery, we repeated the same post-surgery protocol as before. To this day, I can show you the three scars from the surgeons' scalpels forming a Grand Canyon scar running down the front side of my arm. It's a lifetime reminder of my brush with death, the twenty-second miracle, and ultimately my salvation. But for the hand of God, I wouldn't be sharing this story now.

After examining another set of X-rays following the third surgery, the surgeons started cheering from down the hall. Dr. Millett came in with the fellows and said, "Congratulations, Larry! The bones have not moved!" They were able to get all the bones in place as anatomically correct as possible. All five bone parts were finally secure. Once again, God reached out to perform another miracle. The pattern was becoming obvious, it was a "String of Miracles!"

On October 16, ten days after my surgery, examining more X-rays and another MRI, Dr. Millett measured all the bone parts and confirmed that the bone structure looked good; the same results were found in my follow-up appointment in November as well. All examinations looked normal and indicated that I was truly healing and on **the** final road to recovery. My constant pain continued to remind me of the importance to offer great thanks to God for carrying me through such a test of my faith, and just like rowing the final five hundred meters, I dissociated the pain from my mind; my spirit was leading with God's help.

> [7] *The Lord is my strength and my shield;*
> *my heart trusts in him, and he helps me.*
> *My heart leaps for joy, and with my song, I praise him.*
> —Psalm 28:7 (NIV)

After several weeks of passive physical therapy, I got the OK to begin active physical therapy and strength training on December 1. I was excited to get back to normal life and was looking forward to the upcoming ski season.

Reflecting back to August, after my second surgery, I attended the family reunion in Wisconsin wearing a sling. In the family photo, I was sitting with my kids, my two grandkids, my sons-in-law, and my new grandson, Chance. We were finally together. I was able to get back and be with my whole family. The only two reminders of the events gone by were my ever-present sling and the ever-present pain, which had become insignificant in the overall paradigm of my second chance at life.

Doing exactly what God commanded me to do after the Cape buffalo attack: I was spending time with my family, my priest, and my church: the body of Christ. I was already on the board of directors or vestry, the finance committee, and the diocese secretariat of Cursillo, but I wasn't leaving anything to chance. I became more active than I already was and focused on God and what I could give back to humanity.

During the winter of 2012–2013, I registered to become a mountaintop minister. Through sermons, I witnessed this true story of God's intervention in my life from the top of Vail Mountain. I looked for new and exciting ways to give back to the church. I offered the Cape buffalo mount for an online auction and asked for a minimum bid of $25,000. A total of 100 percent of the proceeds would go to the church. Unfortunately, it hasn't sold yet, but the mount is still available if you'd like to buy Black Death, a central figure of this incredible story. Of course, thee absolute central main character of this string of miracles is GOD. If this book creates a stir and helps sell the goliath beast, then 100 percent of the proceeds will go back to God and His church. I wasn't going to offer it for less because the value, without the witness aspect, is well over $30,000. I'm hoping we can still raise a substantial amount that will go to the church as a token of gratitude toward our mission to be Jesus's hands and feet here on Earth.

The Wisconsin reunion in August was a fabulous opportunity to focus on my family. Since my return from Africa, I've tried to dedicate my time to my family and to travel annually to California and Texas to visit my daughters, who have children of their own. During 2012, my daughter Martha was getting bigger by the day. Her baby was supposed to be born on Christmas Day, but Preston waited and was born on New Year's Eve.

During the trip to the family reunion in Wisconsin, I went back to Green Lake and Ripon, where I'd built my first house and assisted-living facility. I visited one of my best friends, Dr. Randy Zieth. He and I have water and snow skied together for over thirty-five years. He was tremendously supportive of me while I was in the divorce process with my first wife in 2010. He is a brother in Christ who prayed with me through my life messes, including the near-death experience. Randy is one of my accountability partners and a wonderful doctor.

I also went to Video Age Productions to look into making a DVD from the video recording of my attack. It's the same video I share with people today. I did **not** publish the DVD or post it on YouTube because I felt I had been called to share this witness in more intimate settings as a testament that God is for real, God's alive and proactive today. Otherwise, I wouldn't be here. There's no other explanation as to why I survived. I've only shared this private DVD with friends and fellow church members so far, until the publication of this book {see Copyright page in front of book for ordering Live Video of **"STALK and ATTACK"**}.

Since then, everyone has urged me to write a book about the miracles I've witnessed over my lifetime. So here is the witness of miracles and savanna salvation to share with you, your loved ones, family and friends.

CHAPTER TEN

ON EARTH AS IT IS IN HEAVEN

¹⁹ Again I say to you that if two of you agree on earth concerning anything that they ask, it will be done for them by My Father in heaven. ²⁰ For where two or three are gathered together in My name, I am there in the midst of them.
—Matthew 18:19–20 (NKJV)

When Father Brooks officiated our wedding on April 15, 2019, he said, "Sometimes you get angels in a moment of crisis. Other times you get an angel that's a little more comfortable with being in for the long term. Diane's every bit a messenger from God to Larry as were those messengers during the attack."

After all I've toiled through, truly my marriage to Diane is indeed a message from God: that a way of life is possible to live as it will be in the Kingdom of Heaven while we're dwelling here on Earth. After all, isn't that what God wants for us? "Thy Kingdom come, Thy Will be done, on Earth as it is in Heaven." But whether we discipline ourselves to fully live in a heavenly manner while still on planet Earth really has to do with developing and sharing the proper perspective with ourselves and others.

These thoughts on perspective bring to mind the poem "Blind Men and an Elephant" by John Godfrey Saxe. Paraphrased, it goes like this:

A group of blind men heard that a strange animal, called an elephant, had been brought to the town, but none of them were aware of its shape and form. Out of curiosity, they said: "We must inspect and know it by touch, of which we are capable." So, they sought it out, and when they found it they groped about it. In the case of the first person, whose hand landed on the trunk, said "This being is like a thick snake." For another one whose hand reached its ear, it seemed like a kind of fan. As for another person, whose hand was upon its leg, said, the elephant is a pillar-like a tree-trunk. The blind man who placed his hand upon its side said the elephant, "is a wall." Another who felt its tail described it as a rope. The last felt its tusk, stating the elephant is that which is hard, smooth, and like a spear.

Each of the six blind men came away from essentially the same experience but with their own unique perspective. Each of us has the power to do that, to live the type of life we want for ourselves, family, and friends, viewing the world with a more comprehensibly positive outlook.

One of the simplest and best ways to ensure a positive perspective is by modeling our life around the simple acronym JOY. If we simply put **J**esus first, **O**thers second, and **Y**ourself last, then we can build a mindful platform upon which living our lives can be built. On the other hand, if we focus on ourselves first, we run the risk of closing our minds off from God's will and forgetting about the others in our lives.

Life events (some good, some not so good) are constantly being thrown at us. But we can deny their successful outcome if we put ourselves first. Our lives go out of focus. We see the world from an inaccurate perception or, worse, a negative perspective. An accurate perception of our life on Earth is blurred.

Perspective is about putting the white marble in first, others next, and then adding ourselves to the top of the pile. Another acronym I frequently share is FROG. It stands for "**F**ully **R**ely **O**n **G**od." If we surrender our lives to God while still here on Earth, we'll derive an abundance of love, peace, and joy from living with a proper perspective. If we put the great commandment first, to love God with all our heart and soul and mind, to love our neighbors as ourselves and we can accept that God always unconditionally loves us, then we'll be accepting and actually living the will of God. As the African savanna miracle turned out, that was the principal message I received during the Cape buffalo attack, to focus on God and family for the rest of my life.

If we focus on ourselves and all the issues and temptations of the world, we lose sight of the Kingdom of God and what Heaven is all about. We allow ourselves to get caught up in a world of pain and life's obstacles, obstacles that keep us from knocking on the door of our Father in Heaven and praying with God as He guides us through life events including miracles.

There was a twelve-year period when I continually asked God for guidance about my purpose and mission in life. What was God's will for me? I never heard an immediate answer from God—or at least I didn't think I did. Where was God's answer to my prayers? Then I started shifting from *my* will to *God's* will. That's when God started answering my prayers, and my ideals started to change. I looked at life from a different perspective, with a different vision, a different mission. Looking through God's eyes, my paradigm shifted, and the scales came off my eyes.

> Jesus told us that it's OK to knock on Heaven's door. He said, *Ask, Seek, Knock*

> *⁷ Ask and it will be given to you; seek and you will find; knock and the door will be opened to you. ⁸ For everyone who asks receives; the one who seeks finds; and to the one who knocks, the door will be opened.*
>
> —Matthew 7:7–8 (NIV)

It's not until we decide to live our lives with the proper perspective that God allows us to experience Heaven on Earth. But what is Heaven? Is it a time, a place, or a mystery? The description of Heaven is very vivid in the book of Revelation:

> *³ And I heard a loud voice from the throne saying, "Look! God's dwelling place is now among the people, and he will dwell with them. They will be his people, and God himself will be with them and be their God. ⁴ 'He will wipe every tear from their eyes. There will be no more death' or mourning or crying or pain, for the old order of things has passed away."*
>
> —Revelation 21:3–4 (NIV)

The boy who died and came back from Heaven in the book *Heaven Is For Real* shared his experiences with his parents after he returned to Earth. Heaven is not a place where we'll need our bodies or other tangible possessions. He said it's beyond comprehension and beauty. The love he experienced was beyond comprehension. After I read the book, it all started to make sense to me.

Revelation 22:1–5 describes Heaven as an abundant place where the pain, suffering, and hardships we experience on Earth cease to be:

Eden Restored

> **22** *¹ Then the angel showed me the river of the water of life, as clear as crystal, flowing from the throne of God and of the Lamb ² down the middle of the great street of the city. On each side of the river stood the tree of life, bearing twelve crops of fruit, yielding its fruit every month. And the leaves of the tree are for the healing of the nations. ³ No longer will there be any curse. The throne of God and of the Lamb will be in the city, and his servants will serve him. ⁴ They will see his face, and his name will be on their foreheads. ⁵ There will be no more night. They will not need the light of a lamp or the light of the sun, for the Lord God will give them light. And they will reign forever and ever.*

According to the book of Revelation, Heaven is a place where Jesus sits at the right hand of God and holy men in white sing with all the angels and archangels of Heaven. At our worship services at church here on Earth, specifically during the Eucharist, when we receive communion, I always feel like we're receiving a glimpse of what it will be like when we'll be in Heaven at the banquet table with Jesus, and we'll break bread and share wine. We will be part of Jesus, the branches attached to the vine. The beautiful reality is that we can be in Christ and He in us, right here, right now. Engraved inside my bride's and my wedding rings are the words from John 15:5 (NIV):

> *I am the vine; you are the branches. {If you remain in me and I in you}, you will bear much fruit; apart from me you can do nothing.*

That's a perspective we can live with here and now. We do not need to wait for our spirit to pass to Heaven. We are focused on living this way now, even though I freely admit that I still have flaws. It's the perspective that my bride and I vowed to live every day, though we occasionally stumble and fall because we are mortal beings. We can fall skiing, hiking, or walking down steps, but we get up again. With perseverance, we stumble and fall less frequently. All thanks be to God, Jesus is still working on us all. We still can be God's masterpieces; we're just unfinished, with plenty of molding by Jesus's hands remaining. But we've also come a long way. What a glorious aspiration in life, to focus on walking in the ways of Jesus, trying to emulate Him, accepting and following God's Word that He brought to us over two thousand years ago and He continues to share with us now, today, while we are here, still on Earth.

Are all the milestones that have occurred throughout history been accidents, or is there a purpose behind them? Earlier, I spoke about Rick Warren's book beautifully describing that we are here for a reason, for a purpose-driven life. I spoke about the following perspective of purpose— the five SHIPS: WorSHIP first, followed by FellowSHIP with other worshippers and followers of Jesus, learning and disciplining ourselves to be disciples of Jesus or DiscipleSHIP, StewardSHIP or ministering to the needs of our fellow man, and ApostleSHIP or being sent to share the good news that Jesus is alive today, for real and proactively exists today among our broken and fallen world. We need Him now more than ever as we observe this imperfect world before us.

We live on a planet with so much grandeur and beauty, all glory be to God. Unfortunately, as God's son taught us, in this world, there will be trouble. By ourselves, life often seems like we are riddled with conflict and a seemingly bipolar society as well as horrific, challenging, life-threatening battles. But if we're focused on God along with brothers and sisters in Christ in a collective perspective, praying together, we'll find comfort and peace while living a more positive life with a capacity to deal with whatever life throws at us:

> *33 I have told you these things, so that in me you may have peace. In this world you will have trouble. But take heart! I have overcome the world.*
>
> —John 16:33 (NIV)

When people worship together in fellowship, walking as disciples, ministering to one another, and sharing what they've learned and experienced, they can take comfort in being proactive rather than reactive, taking action like Jesus would do. The whole concept is called koinonia and is the Greek word for deep fellowship, where Christ is in us, and we are in Christ. "In Christ" appears many times in the New Testament.

It's the concept of piety. It means if we are in Christ, Christ is in us. God is always reaching out to us. But are we reaching back to God? Jesus wants to be in us, in the same vacuum that everyone tries to fill with worldly possessions and vices. If we let Him in, we all can be brothers and sisters in Christ. He is in us, and we are in Him. When we have that kind of perspective, the reality of discovering Heaven on Earth becomes authentic.

I spoke earlier about how we exist as vessels of the Holy Spirit. If we believe and open up our souls, the Holy Spirit will come in. And there is even hope for skeptical people, people with doubt. The book of John witnesses doubting Thomas:

> *Now Thomas (also known as Didymus), one of the Twelve,*
> *was not with the disciples when Jesus came. So the other*
> *disciples told him, "We have seen the Lord!"*
> *But he said to them, "Unless I see the nail marks in his hands and put my*
> *finger where the nails were, and put my hand into his side, I will not believe."*
> *A week later his disciples were in the house again, and Thomas*
> *was with them. Though the doors were locked, Jesus came and*
> *stood among them and said, "Peace be with you!" Then he said*
> *to Thomas, "Put your finger here; see my hands. Reach out your*
> *hand and put it into my side. Stop doubting and believe."*
>
> *Thomas said to him, "My Lord and my God!"*
> *Then Jesus told him, "Because you have seen me, you have believed;*
> *blessed are those who have not seen and yet have believed."*
> —John 20:24–29 (NIV)

I believe the story about the little boy who went to Heaven. I can believe that Jesus's eyes are green just as he described. After reading the book, I did a little research of my own and learned that green is the rarest of genetic eye coloration. Of course, a tiny portion of the people on Earth have green eyes, but according to the little boy, God also possessed amazing energy. He described the transfiguration, shared in scripture where he became a shining light.

After the boy returned home, his father asked him an endless list of questions. He was intrigued about Pappy, his father, who had passed away years earlier, so he asked the boy, "Did you see anybody like Pappy?"

"Yes. I sat on Pappy's lap."

"Well, how was he?"

"He was awesome. He was really glad to see me there."

So the father pulled a picture of Pappy out and asked him, "Is this who you saw?"

"No. That's not who I saw."

"Well, that's Pappy."

"I know, but that's not the man I saw."

"Well, what did he look like?"

"He looked a lot younger than that."

So he went up into the attic and dug around a box with all his old photographs. He found a picture of Pappy but in his mid-twenties and in his prime. He went back downstairs to his son and asked him once again, "You said you were with Pappy, right?"

"Yeah. He was so awesome."

"Did he look like this?"

"Yeah. That's Pappy. That's who I saw."

What the little boy saw was a much younger version of his grandfather. What a heavenly awareness; our energy and image will be in our prime, not the image of an old, frail, elderly person. Can we only imagine? Everyone in Heaven is in their prime!

The boy said Heaven was beautiful. It was the best we see on Earth and more, magnified an infinite number of times.

There are a lot of books that describe near-death experiences and their impressions of Heaven. One of the consistent threads throughout the encounters is the presence of light. Often, people venture toward the light but are turned away because ultimately, it's just not their time. They're only there for a short visit. There have been glimpses of Heaven by people who have had horrible accidents, illnesses, and physical traumas—each of them, their own Cape buffalo. They all report seeing very similar phenomena. How can that be unless there's truth to so many witnesses?

Why can't we experience the Kingdom of Heaven on Earth as Jesus asked us to pray in the Lord's Prayer? The answer is, of course, we can. We already have an amazing planet here. If we're prudent stewards and take care of our environment, we can hope Earth is here for future generations to enjoy.

The real question is, where are we going to be for eternity? And we do not know when this mortal life on Earth ends. Jesus taught us that He is coming back:

> *And if I go and prepare a place for you, I will come back and take you to be with me that you also may be where I am.*
> —John 14:3 (NIV)

> [7] *"Look, he is coming with the clouds,"*
> *and "every eye will see him,*
> *even those who pierced him";*
> *and all peoples on earth "will mourn because of him."*
> *So shall it be! Amen.*
> —Revelation 1:7 (NIV)

If we live in the Kingdom of Heaven now, we should be prepared. Jesus speaks about being the bridegroom and all of us the bride in the parable of the Ten Virgins:

> *At that time the kingdom of heaven will be like ten virgins who took their lamps and went out to meet the bridegroom. Five of them were foolish and five were wise. The foolish ones took their lamps but did not take any oil with them. The wise ones, however, took oil in jars along with their lamps. The bridegroom was a long time in coming, and they all became drowsy and fell asleep.*
> *At midnight the cry rang out: "Here's the bridegroom! Come out to meet him!" Then all the virgins woke up and trimmed their lamps. The foolish ones said to the wise, "Give us some of your oil; our lamps are going out."*
>
> *"No," they replied, "there may not be enough for both us and you. Instead, go to those who sell oil and buy some for yourselves." But while they were on their way to buy the oil,*

the bridegroom arrived. The virgins who were ready went in with him to the wedding banquet. And the door was shut.
Later the others also came. "Lord, Lord," they said, "open the door for us!" But he replied, "Truly I tell you, I don't know you." Therefore keep watch, because you do not know the day or the hour.

—Matthew 25:1–13

According to Revelation, the nonbelievers will perish with the anti-Christ as they plummet into an abyss while the believers will be taken up by Jesus Christ. If that's true, what space do we want to occupy? Where do we want our spirits to dwell for eternity?

What oftentimes erodes our chances for spending eternity with Jesus in Heaven is getting wound up on ourselves and the minute-by-minute rush through life on Earth, darting from one event to the next, attempting to fill our voids with worthless worldly possessions, trying to get ahead, or hiding from it all with vices of many sorts.

2 Do not conform to the pattern of this world, but be transformed by the renewing of your mind. Then you will be able to test and approve what God's will is—his good, pleasing and perfect will.

—Romans 12:2 (NIV)

So can we have Heaven on Earth? Why not? The Lord's Prayer Jesus taught us: God's will be done, "On Earth as It Is in Heaven."

After six and a half decades of witnessing miracles, it amazes me that they continue to occur. We just can't make these witnesses up. We can't deny they exist. Whenever I knock on God's door and ask, praying with our Father in Heaven, the most amazing miracles happen. We can all hopefully find peace knowing that Heaven doesn't only exist eternally at the end of our lives on Earth, but by living the ways of God's Kingdom in Heaven now, here on Earth, we can live God's will, "On Earth as It Is in Heaven." We can welcome miracles into our lives if we ask, seek, and knock.

That's why after seven years of vacillating from one thought process to another while discerning God's will, God called me to the perspective that I needed to share the miracles and experiences that have happened to me with you. I prayed often, asking myself, should

I keep these life events to myself, or should I share them with others? I was finally at a place where I knew what my motive was: following God's will, not mine.

At the beginning of my professional life, after graduating from college, I acknowledged that God existed, but I felt that my accomplishments had more to do with what I did. If it was going to be, it was up to me. Spiritually, I was still an infant up until 2002 when I really began reading and embracing the Bible, the Word of God. I've made a lot of mistakes. I still don't live every facet of my life as well as I'd like to. But as I matured spiritually, I began to experience breakthroughs and transformations. Like the metamorphosis of a butterfly, I went from an egg to a caterpillar, from a caterpillar to a chrysalis, from a chrysalis to a butterfly. The same transformation happened with my spirituality. Sometimes the miracles happened in an instant. Sometimes they took months or years, even decades.

As my perception of my maturity became more obvious and I stepped through various milestones and waypoints, I began to realize that I could do considerably more with God's help than I could by myself. With God's help, I accomplished the dreams and goals that surprised and amazed me.

Do Everything Without Grumbling

12 Therefore, my dear friends, as you have always obeyed—not only in my presence but now much more in my absence—continue to work out your salvation with fear and trembling, 13 for it is God who works in you to will and to act in order to fulfill his good purpose.
—Philippians 2:12–13 (NIV)

When my mother plopped me down in Sunday school each week, she did the best she could, hoping that at least some of the teachings would stick. Like many youngsters, it simply isn't a time for deep understanding until we experience life by living through a maturity continuum. But at least she helped plant seeds. Sometimes at a young age, that's all we can hope for. Fortunately, it's never too late. I've witnessed spiritual development with family members, friends, and relatives while praying they would expand their narrow perspective of the world. To a perspective more consistent with the Kingdom of

God, without all our worldly distractions, to the ultimate place of peace and understanding. We're all given numerous opportunities to change. For those who are spiritually obstinate, change sometimes takes a Cape buffalo when nothing else works.

My family had a Cape buffalo event long before mine, on May 11, 2006. In the middle of the night, my twenty-seven-year-old daughter Amy in California had a grand mal seizure. She was also six months pregnant with her first child. Her husband, Aaron, thought she was dying. They rushed her to the hospital where he worked in Nuclear Medicine, and the hospital went into full alert medical investigation.

Living in Wisconsin, we didn't know any details about her medical situation until we got a call from Aaron that she was lying in the hospital. We waited all day for news. The emotional stress was unbearable from waiting, trying to cling to the vine with as much patience as we could discipline ourselves. Being hundreds of miles away, we were beside ourselves about both our daughter and our new unborn grandchild. At eleven o'clock that night, we finally got a call from Aaron. He could barely speak and get words out of his mouth. We were all overcome with emotion. He managed to speak awkwardly and explain that when he performed her MRI and CT scans, they found a two-and-a-half-centimeter mass that was growing on the right side of her brain.

We immediately snapped into action, searching for available airline tickets so my wife could fly to California the next morning. Unfortunately, I had to stay back and hold down the fort. We were ministering to the elderly in my assisted-living facilities and we both couldn't simultaneously walk away from them. They needed to be cared for twenty-four hours a day, seven days a week.

My youngest son, Mike, was staying with us on a break from college, so he was available to man the computers, searching for an airline ticket. In the meantime, I walked downstairs, out the door, and started circling the trout pond we had in our backyard. I was circling and praying. Circling and praying. Eventually, my son came down and said he'd found an airline ticket, so I went back inside after praying for at least a half-hour, maybe forty-five minutes.

> [13] *I can do all this through him who gives me strength.*
> —Philippians 4:13 (NIV)

I knocked on Heaven's door. I asked our Father in Heaven to take over. This was a challenge far greater than any of us could handle on our own. I surrendered my spirit to God and then walked upstairs with my son Mike and learned that my wife, Nancy, had booked a flight out of Milwaukee at six o'clock the following morning.

Only hours after the first seizure, Amy had two more grand mal seizures. By the time Nancy arrived, the staff had her seizures under control with medication. Both Amy and the baby were resting comfortably—well, as comfortably as they could be after experiencing three medical emergencies in rapid succession. She said that each grand mal seizure was like running a marathon, so she felt like she'd run three marathons in less than twenty-four hours.

Simply put, I kept praying continually. Aaron's imaging department performed MRIs daily. They were trying to figure out what it was—this two-and-a-half-centimeter mass on the right side of her brain. The waiting was painfully excruciating. I prayed to God for enough patience to help our family make it through each day. What else could we do? Talking to Amy each day, as well as Aaron and receiving updates from Nancy, we managed to endure each 24 hour period of time as the days passed.

Days kept slipping by slowly. It seemed like it took forever. At that point in time, my worldly plate was full. But when Amy was rushed to the hospital, I just tipped it upside down. I realized that none of the stuff I had going on in my life mattered. The only treasure that mattered and what my entire focus was on at that moment in time, was what was happening with Amy. We were all under a Cape buffalo attack, but this attack went on for weeks instead of ending in twenty seconds.

After two weeks of MRIs, they concluded that the mass had stopped growing. It first presented itself during her pregnancy and kept growing until it manifested into seizures. Then for two weeks, it mysteriously stopped growing. At the end of the first two weeks, it started to shrink. Amy went from getting weekly to monthly MRIs. The mass was not growing.

On August 10, 2006, Amy gave birth to granddaughter Peyton on St. Laurence Day, the day commemorating the saint's death in AD 256, where he was burned at the stake by Julius Caesar for harboring the treasures of their church and distributing them back to the people. The spelling coincidence and birth date were unreal. God taught us all patience as we didn't receive a confirmation regarding the type of mass she had until Christmas Eve. A year later, she went to another neurology center for a second opinion. Doctors could not explain how the mass grew to a size that presented seizures during pregnancy, ceased growing, and then shrank. I knew there was only one explanation, and it didn't come from man. At the time of Peyton's second birthday, the neuro-specialists still couldn't explain Amy's miracle, and the mass hasn't changed since. I truly believe that God wrapped healing energy around it and contained it. That was over fourteen years ago, and Amy is the epitome of spiritual, mental, and physical health, all thanks and glory be to God.

After this Cape Buffalo incident, Peyton turned out to be healthy and beautiful in so many ways. Last fall at thirteen years old, she competed in a cross-country race, winning first place at a regional meet. She's also a straight-A student in school. She's matured into quite an accomplished young lady, certainly a candidate for some type of medical practice. All my grandchildren are exceptionally talented gifts from God. All glory be to God.

Before Amy's miracle, she was a beautiful, healthy woman and a devoted Christian, just as she is today. Throughout the episode, she was clearly a messenger from God. She kept telling everyone not to worry because God had her situation under control. God had her in His hands.

Because so many people were interested in Amy's progress, we posted updates on "Caring Bridge," a website for people struggling with health-care crises.

Back when I was waiting for news about Amy's recovery, I continued knocking on Heaven's door. I called my best friends and Christian brothers and sisters in Christ. Each of them went back to their churches and prayer groups requested prayers and involvement. People of all faiths and clergy were praying for her. Even people who had never met her now knew Amy. Eventually, people all over the world started knitting prayer shawls.

All the local churches in Amy's area started praying, followed by churches across the state. Then multiple denominations started praying. When our local Episcopal Church started praying, our praying spread to the Episcopal Church of the United States of America. Amy went to a small parochial school in the little town of Princeton, Wisconsin, so the Roman Catholic Church started praying.

People praying all over the world went viral and was all documented on Caring Bridge.

Not only did Amy influence everyone she knew, but she was also truly a messenger of our Heavenly Father. I've shared her Cape Buffalo story with countless others. On Christmas Eve 2006, over seven months after her seizures presented the mass, I received a call from Amy. She said the mass hadn't grown, and the brain and cancer specialists officially ruled out the mass being malignant cancer. The awesome news was the best Christmas gift ever!

Isn't it interesting that human nature is such that we still need these kinds of messages to capture our attention and become aware? We'd think that people would tire of asking, "How can God do that or allow this to happen?" But Amy's incident was one instance in millions where occurrences happen for a purpose —perhaps to encourage other people's faith and provide hope in their own lives.

We've all heard it asked many times, "If God is so loving and caring, why does God create or allow so many disasters in life?" Could we possibly be misinterpreting them, not understanding that we need these types of events in our lives to get our attention and to provide a nudge in the right direction? As painful as life events are to understand for people who are directly affected, these types of events are exactly the type of takeaways we get when we go through the Alpha program.

There is a short booklet written by Nicky Gumble that answers most of the difficult questions people ask about life events. If we adopt the perspective that life events are God's will and have a purpose, then this explanation can provide at least minimal solace when they occur. If not for us, perhaps it will for others. Sometimes it takes decades to figure out why and what God's overall plan really means.

There's a fascinating parallel between maintaining our spiritual perspective and Harry Lodge's book, *Younger Next Year*. In the book, he claims we can feel and look fifty well into our eighties and beyond. Our health is within our control. It's a matter of the lifestyle we choose to practice during our time here on Earth. One of the biggest points he makes relates to getting an appropriate amount of exercise.

Thousands of years ago, we didn't need expensive gym memberships. If we wanted some food to eat, we had to grow it, hunt it, and gather our food. Entire families were active together all day long.

Today people don't eat nutritiously or get nearly enough physical exercise. We just go to the grocery store, after sitting all day at work, to pick up manufactured convenient products for dinner. In addition to offering themselves as life-sustaining activities, here are some types of sports we can enjoy like skiing on a mountain or lake, hiking, biking, swimming, rowing, paddling, and the list goes on simply because they're fun, emotionally stimulating, and exercise. There are ways of stimulating or tricking our brain into thinking we are on a safari, walking across an African savanna to bring back a kudu for supper.

As Christians, we have the liberty to exercise our own free will as well as God's. How we blend those together is a perspective we create ourselves. We can have a physical lifestyle of excellent health. I know many skiers who have skied well into their nineties, including Vail's first ski school director, Morrie Sheppard. He literally skied his last year on Earth at age ninety-five. A tremendous man and a beautiful soul. I was honored to spend time with him over the years. How did they do that? By putting God first in their life, others next, followed by themselves. They were lucky enough to find their passions early in life and found a way for them to peacefully coexist along with the responsibilities of raising families.

Not only do we have control over our bodies, but we also have control over our spirituality, our emotions, and our intellect. If our spiritual life continues to mature, how beautiful is that? On the other hand, we can't isolate physical health from spiritual health.

Beloved, I pray that all may go well with you and that you may be in good health, as it goes well with your soul.
—3 John 2 (EVS)

Life can be fruitless to be pious while letting our physical being go. I truly believe that it is spirit, mind, and body. They're all part of the equation. I will never forget our rowing coach, Doug Neil, explaining to us that the spirit leads the mind, and the mind leads the body. It seems too easy, but living with discipline in all facets of our being is the key.

Also essential to our personal development and feeling younger next year are relationships with people. I don't believe we can be a well-read, spiritually sound, perfect physical specimen, and isolate ourselves on an island. There needs to be balance and fellowship within our lives.

Following my highest priority connection with God (and perhaps because of it), my primary passion sport has always been skiing. Today I'm in harmony with my bride, whose passion sport is also skiing. We ski 120 days a year at Vail. I continue to share my passion for skiing by teaching private advanced lessons on Vail Mountain and still have instructors who want me to help them improve their skiing.

In the summer, we water-ski over 60 days. In the course of 1 year, Diane and I ski 180 days. While enjoying a wonderful form of physical exercise, skiing also stimulates the emotional part of our brain, which might be just as important. I believe living our passions stimulate our spirituality as well. Whether waterskiing on a clear Wisconsin lake or skiing waist-deep powder in the Colorado Rockies, we bolster our emotional brain and connection with God through the visual, audio, and kinesthetic sensations of gracefully gliding over God's greatest environs on Earth.

Like me, my new bride has a passion for being in touch with God's creation. She's been to Africa six times. She persuaded me to go back to Africa in September 2019 after almost being killed there in 2012. For our official honeymoon, we went on a bush camp safari. We were staying in very nice tents in the middle of nowhere, near the animals' watering holes. We loved the setting, shared our commonalities, and loved encountering the wildlife together.

I've always enjoyed experiencing different environs firsthand all over the world from mountains in Alaska and British Columbia to Austria and France. I can never experience enough of them. Although some people know me for my hunting, that's never been my primary attraction to the wilderness. I enjoy just being out among the animals in their natural habitat, although I have to admit that we do enjoy wild game and delight in eating wild game that hasn't been processed and sold in a grocery store. We love the flavor and healthy nutrition of eating natural grass-fed hoofed animals as well as birds of the air.

Even after all the life events that have occurred, I still enjoy rowing, whether it's on a lake, a river, or even on an indoor ergometer. I typically row all summer in my single shell. I'll row the new technology eights, fours, and quads if they're available. That just doesn't go away. And when I do, it's déjà vu all over again. The passion is reignited, and I'm back at the National Championships and Henley Royal Regatta.

One of the worst ways to live is to exist without passion. How many times have we seen people retire without anything to do, only to pass away several months later? Some people have nothing in life they're passionate about. I don't necessarily find fault with that if there are circumstances out of someone's control. Not everyone is fortunate enough to go to college and find their dream job. For many people, all they've ever done is work at jobs they despised, merely to support their family. A month after they retire, they're gone. Another sad incident happens when people die a month after their spouse passes. There's even a name for it. It's called the widowhood effect. But for most of us who still can make personal choices, I believe it's critical that we find passions in life we love in connection with God, whether it's a person, place, or passion activity. The best-case scenario is all of the above.

The Need for Self-Discipline

> [24] *Do you not know that in a race all the runners run, but only one gets the prize? Run in such a way as to get the prize.* [25] *Everyone who competes in the games goes into strict training. They do it to get a crown that will not last, but we do it to get a crown that will last forever.* [26] *Therefore I do not run like someone running aimlessly; I do not fight like a boxer beating the air.* [27] *No, I strike a blow to my body and make it my slave so that after I have preached to others, I myself will not be disqualified for the prize.*
> —1 Corinthians 9:24–27 (NIV)

We can have the JOY of Heaven on Earth if we put **J**esus first, **O**thers next, and live **Y**our passions. First, we need to realize what's available to us through our relationships with Jesus, family, friends, and communities. This Earth has so much to offer and for us to experience. I feel tremendously blessed to be in a marriage now that I know will last beyond our adventures on Earth.

I'm never going to argue with the voice that saved my life in Africa. I am going to focus on God and family for the rest of my life. As simple as that sounds, it represents a huge responsibility. Fortunately, I'd already started. I was already engaged in following the command to some degree before the attack, but now I'm practicing it with my utmost dedication for His Highest.

All my grandchildren love to ski in one form or another, and they're already involved in the type of progression we'd expect, coming from the Trotter family. Topics during short discussions while riding up chairlifts, are sharing our spirituality and our life stories with one another. My granddaughter, Martha's eldest, Ellianna is a budding artist. At three years old, she drew her image of me with the Cape buffalo towering over me with the angel suspended overhead in a pillar of light, reaching down from Heaven. The drawing is known as "Papa's Cape Buffalo Attack." Nobody told her how to draw it. She'd certainly never been to Africa. But she said, "God told me how to draw it." It's framed in the center of the kitchen at our lake house in Wisconsin. Now at ten years old, Ellianna has completed her second rendering of the same scene. She's at the top in her class in academics and athletics. She's a beautiful exemplary elder sister for her three brothers, all beautiful blessings from God. I've shared the following miracle of her mother, Martha, my second sweetheart of a daughter, with others as well.

Martha and her husband wanted more children after Ellianna but couldn't get pregnant. They went to the best fertility specialists they could find and took every test known to man. Eventually, they found out that Martha had a syndrome called polycystic ovarian syndrome (PCOS), which for most people would mean they couldn't have children. At best, Martha could produce one healthy egg per year. Looking at her, you'd never guess that she was working through some form of medical malady. She was an amazing athlete in high school, won every award she could win in conferences, established school records, followed by the same performances in college. Unfortunately, success on the basketball court, track, or academics has nothing to do with conceiving a family.

So how was she going to have more children while besieged with PCOS? She and her husband, David, began praying. I was praying, and the entire family was praying. Then a miracle occurred: she got pregnant on Easter Sunday 2012. The due date was Christmas Day, but Preston took his time and was born on New Year's Eve, the year of the Cape buffalo attack. That was the grandchild whom I didn't think

I was ever going to see while sprawled out in the dirt, thinking Black Death was attempting to finish me off. Preston was another miracle.

It truly was another miracle. What else would you call it when every specialist in the field of fertility told us that it was highly unlikely Martha would conceive another child and that she was fortunate to have one child, let alone two? They did feel already gifted from God with the birth of their daughter, Ellianna, and son, Preston, yet they prayed to have a full family like ours. They prayed to have another child. After months of intense praying, against all odds, she got pregnant again. Gavin was born on June 14, 2015. I received the word when I was on a canoe trip in the Quetico Provincial Park in Ontario, Canada, with Mark Munsen, a good ole Eagle Scout friend of mine. We were in the middle of nowhere for ten days, sixty air miles from the nearest road. Two hard days of paddling and portaging in, followed by two hard days out. Fortunately, he brought along a Garmin InReach satellite phone that was connected to the Iridium satellite phone system, so we could send and receive text and e-mail messages announcing Gavin's birth. Gavin was another miracle.

Just when you think the three miracles of three children is amazing, I have to share with you the miracle of abundance. Yes, we can have the abundance of joy, love, and peace Jesus promises right here on Earth. Two years later, Martha and David and our family had our prayers answered with another healthy baby boy, Gabriel. Another miracle and named after the Arch-Angel Gabriel who announced to Mary that she was going to bare the birth of the Christ child, the savior of the world. All glory be to God; a full house!

Those canoe trips themselves were sacred. Dozens of times I immersed myself in the spectacular wilderness of lakes and rivers in the middle of June, year after year, to feel closer to God, to be with Jesus, and to feel the Holy Spirit cloaking me and whoever I was with. Every person who went with me felt the same energy.

On a particular canoe trip, I was with Big Lou Schueller, another one of my old rowing buddies from the University of Wisconsin. He brought along his daughter Brook as well as a friend, Mark. On the way in with Mark in my bow, we hit bad weather that became a serious obstacle, but using my map and compass, I found our way to where we needed to go in the middle of the Quetico Provincial Park. Somewhere along the route, we lost Lou and Brook for the entire week, leaving Mark and me on our own.

While paddling in, Mark heard me speak about creation, a little about my faith, and how glorious it was to be alive and immersed in some of the best environs of our planet. After we set up camp, I pulled out my little brown Bible and sat there in the wilderness, reading in peace. Mark said, "You seem like a man of faith. Do you mind if I ask you about some issues I'm facing? My marriage isn't going well. My wife's talking about getting divorced." He went on to ask me questions about conflict, so I turned to Matthew 18:15–22 and read it to him:

Dealing with a Sinning Brother

15 Moreover if your brother sins against you, go and tell him his fault between you and him alone. If he hears you, you have gained your brother. 16 But if he will not hear, take with you one or two more, that "by the mouth of two or three witnesses every word may be established." 17 And if he refuses to hear them, tell it to the church. But if he refuses even to hear the church, let him be to you like a heathen and a tax collector.

18 Assuredly, I say to you, whatever you bind on earth will be bound in heaven, and whatever you loose on earth will be loosed in heaven.

19 Again I say to you that if two of you agree on earth concerning anything that they ask, it will be done for them by My Father in heaven. 20 For where two or three are gathered together in My name, I am there in the midst of them.

The Parable of the Unforgiving Servant

21 Then Peter came to Him and said, "Lord, how often shall my brother sin against me, and I forgive him? Up to seven times?"

22 Jesus said to him, "I do not say to you, up to seven times, but up to seventy times seven."

I gave it to him, and he read it. So he asked if I had any more passages to read.

For most of the week, my little brown Bible and I became Mark's best friends as he devoured the New Testament—specifically the passages I had already marked. Like myself facing years of a marital mess, he was in the midst of turmoil, trying to figure out life and his relationship with his wife.

As he read the passages, he asked me for my interpretation of them. I'd usually explain with points like "The first time I read those verses back in 2002, here's what I thought. But here's what it means to me today." He kept the Bible for the rest of the trip. He did give it back at the end of the canoe trip.

When we were setting up our tent on the last night paddling out of the park, I said, "Let's just use one tent. We don't need to get all our gear out." So I pulled my tent out and put it up with the mosquito screen still zipped tight. My eyes were astonished as I called out to Mark, "Hey, you have to come over here and look at this. Do you remember when we talked about FROG? Fully Rely On God? Look at that." There was the most iridescent and purest green frog sitting inside the tent. Mark and I looked at each other and thought, *Oooh . . . what's that mean?* How did it get in a sealed tent? We looked at each other and both thought it had to be a sign from God.

After we got back from our canoe trip, Lou told me that Mark was never the same. Do we call that a sign, a miracle, or was it just a frog? For us, it was transformational for Mark and a chance for me to share the Word of God with another person struggling with his faith.

On another canoe outing, I went tripping (canoeist lingo) for a men's retreat, a total of five of us all members from our local Episcopal Church. As it turned out, four of them had to leave early, so I decided to paddle solo, which would allow me to stay longer by myself. We had a wonderful time eating wild, native walleyes by the pound, just enjoying God's country. Finally, we got to a point where they looped back to where we started, and I went on for a few extra days of fishing.

From that point on, no matter what direction I paddled or what time of day it was, the wind blew from behind me. There were times when I felt Jesus present in the bow. The trip was during a time when I was trying to figure out where my marriage was really going, where my life was going. It was at a hard, difficult period of my life. I asked Jesus to be with me, to come into me, move within my inner spirit, touch my soul, create a new being, renew my heart. From that point on, I continually felt Jesus's presence and had a glorious time on the lakes and in the forests of Ontario, Canada.

On the way out, a hot gale force wind came out of the southwest, blowing thirty to forty miles an hour. It was superheated air blasting at more than ninety-five degrees Fahrenheit. I knew from experience that a torrential rainstorm was on the way, and I needed to get to a certain place to be safe, so I shifted into overdrive and paddled with a mission to beat out the storm. On my GPS, it indicated that I was paddling at over four and a half miles an hour solo, with a fully loaded canoe. Finally, I got to the site where I needed to camp, just ahead of the dark clouds and impending storm.

Getting out of the canoe and moving quickly, the first detail was to look for a place to store my paddles. I thought I'll put them between two particular trees. This looks like a safe spot. Then a voice said,

"Don't put them there. Put them over here." I didn't debate, simply followed the voice's directions.

Then I grabbed my two packs including my tent and thought, *Here's a good spot to pitch my tent.* Once again, the voice said, "Don't place your tent there. Pitch it over here." So, okay no argument, that's where I pitched my tent.

Finally, I went back and carried my canoe onto the shore and then to a nice open spot. A third time, the voice said, "Don't put your canoe there. Put it over here."

I didn't think much about the voice at the time, but an energy or guardian angel's voice was communicating directions to me. I thought, *Where did that come from?* After pitching my tent and making a quick supper, I slid into my tent just before a howling wind and storm started to blow across my campsite.

Totally exhausted from paddling at race speed to get to that campsite, I quickly crashed and fell off to sleep. Throughout the night, there were periods of time when loud noises awoke me with the blasting sound of wind banging branches, trees snapping and crashing to the ground, as the lightning and rain passed overhead. Praying for God's protection, I was praising God and at complete peace through the storm.

When I poked my head out of the tent the next morning, I looked around and thought, *Wow. That's really amazing. Is this real?* A huge tree snapped off by the wind fell exactly where I was originally going to put my tent. Yet I was safe. Next I thought, *I'd better go check my canoe.* Another tree lay across the spot where I was originally going to put my canoe, yet in the place where I ended up storing it, my canoe was unscathed. Last, I found my paddles. They too were untouched, but where I was going to put them was another fallen tree. It would have easily snapped my paddles like twigs. In all three cases, had I not heeded to the voice I heard, I could have been seriously injured and stranded in the wilderness for days or killed. Since then, I've taken people back there and showed them the spot where I was a breath away from losing my life.

More recently, Diane nearly lost her life on a motor scooter just months after we were married. The throttle jammed into the go position, launching her between two steel signposts, and catapulted her into the bank of a ditch on the backside of a concrete aqueduct. Instead of being killed, fracturing her neck, or being paralyzed, she came away with a fractured collarbone, rotator cuff tear, bruised ribs, and a sore kneecap.

These are a few incidents, examples of miracles or divine intervention that happen along the path of life and become the fabric of our lives. How do we reconcile them? Do we recognize them for what they are or simply deny that they even happened? Were they by accident or coincidence? Or are they actually miracles to a degree or another?

My Cape buffalo attack was over in twenty seconds. But buffalo attacks don't always happen quickly. In the case of both of my daughters' situations, their Cape buffalo stories extended weeks, months, and years over time.

What happens to us isn't usually on our schedule. It's God's time and God's will. It's God teaching us. If we have an open heart and spirit, then perhaps we can recognize that there are miracles today. We can realize that angels aren't just for the tops of Christmas trees. Maybe we can realize that God speaks to us when we least expect. It might happen after we've been praying in solitude. It might happen after we've prayed with other brothers or sisters in Christ. Never the less, I believe it's important to share our stories with others. Perhaps if fifty thousand people read this book, there will be fifty thousand new stories circulating that will help others deal with their Cape buffalo attacks.

Can we have Heaven on Earth? Are miracles for real?

After witnessing miracles my entire lifetime, I could go on for hours about experiences that have happened to me. From more incidents while canoeing in the wilderness to other adventures. From basic daily living to both of my parents' passing on to Heaven. They're all amazing stories and stand on their own, but I don't want to belabor the point.

One outcome of this book I'd like to see during my lifetime is more evidence that none of us are alone with our stories, regardless of what form our Cape buffalo attacks emerge. If we can just be open and simply share our experiences and witnesses with one another, the sharing may help us confirm with each other the presence of God's miracles and may further prove that we can live like the Kingdom is here now, for all of us to experience Heaven on Earth.

That is my global prayer, Amen.

CHAPTER ELEVEN

WHY SO LONG?

Patience in Suffering

> [7] *Be patient, then, brothers and sisters, until the Lord's coming. See how the farmer waits for the land to yield its valuable crop, patiently waiting for the autumn and spring rains.* [8] *You too, be patient and stand firm, because the Lord's coming is near.*
>
> —James 5:7–8 (NIV)

Less than three months following my third and final surgery, I was slowly inching my way back into normal life. Literally inches and degrees of range of motion measured by physical therapists. At that time, my goals were simple: to return to all activities of daily living, continue my active participation with my church and family, and be able to teach skiing the winter season of 2012-13. I had a lot of work ahead of me.

In November 2012, I returned to passive physical therapy, with an emphasis on returning to the normal range of motion of my shoulder, an issue I still struggle with to this day, eight years after the attack. Every month my shoulder's range of motion slowly but continually improves. I also heeded Dr. Harry Lodge's suggestions from his book *Younger Next Year* by sustaining my aerobic exercise 6 days per week for 45-60 minutes, plus maintaining my passion sport activities. With daily physical activity, I was able to trigger my biochemistry and systems by elevating circulation and core temperature that's been shown to enhance daily positive cell growth. Now more than ever, I was motivated to apply my body's natural healing capability of recovering from my injuries and surgeries. The pain was excruciating. But it was what I had to live through—just like rowing through the last one hundred meters at the Henley Royal Regatta.

My next hurdle was passing the ski school fitness test. At the time, all new and returning ski instructors were required to pass a standard battery of physical fitness tests that emphasized balance and range of motion as well as upper and lower body strength. Fortunately, because of my aggressive regimen following surgery, I passed with flying colors and was cleared to teach skiing that year.

Even before the ski season started, I had a private request lesson scheduled for Saturday, December 22, so that became the proverbial "carrot at the end of the stick" and continued to motivate my recovery during times when I would have rather stretched out on the sofa, taking a nap. As soon as the mountain opened for the season, I got back on the snow as I usually do, getting the summer kinks out and recovering my rhythm of movement.

Unlike many other people recovering from catastrophic injuries, I wasn't concerned about getting back on the snow. I hadn't injured myself skiing, so "getting back on the saddle" wasn't an issue with me. Following Dr. Millett's instructions to a tee, I never missed my daily morning walks, rowing on my ergometer, and physical therapy appointments. By the time I was skiing with my first ski lesson of the season, I was probably in better shape than most others who hadn't gone through what I did on July 3. Remarkably, I managed to ski through the entire 2012–2013 season without falling once, even teaching advanced lessons in the back bowls with deep powder.

When I first started skiing again, I found that if I held my left hand and arm in a relaxed, stable skiing position, using good technique, I could ski through the day with relatively little pain. I couldn't raise my arm above my shoulder, but I could lightly touch my pole to the snow, avoiding sudden jarring movements, which is what good skiing technique is anyway.

Fortunately, the movements I made on skis were habits I was intimately comfortable with and had done my entire life. Over the years of skiing, teaching, and examining other instructors, I had my skiing stance and movement patterns tuned toward skiing ultra-safe.

Mentally and spiritually, I was absorbed in a state of gratitude. I had a lot to be thankful for. First, I was happy to be alive. I was grateful that I wasn't paralyzed, forced to live out the rest of my days in a wheelchair, or a nursing home bed. I was happy that I could use my arm again, and I was delighted to be able to ski and teach.

That gratitude continued nonstop, through the entire first year of my recovery and I recovered to within 90 percent of my original physical condition and flexibility. The following summer, I even went back to waterskiing in Wisconsin. Ironically, that turned out to be more nerve-wracking than the possibility of falling on my shoulder in deep snow. How would my shoulder hold up while being yanked out of the water behind a powerful ski boat? My first venture was with my ski buddy Randy Zieth. I started the way I always did, by standing in water up to the middle of my thigh and then step up and go. Another miracle. I was able to water ski like the good old days again. It was remarkable how smoothly my passion sports were coming back and building my confidence.

Throughout the entire process, all I could do was count my blessings for being alive and able to recover. Feeling called, I asked, "What can I do to start giving back again?" It was such a gift just to be alive and get back to a normal lifestyle.

> [20] *always giving thanks to God the Father for everything, in the name of our Lord Jesus Christ.*
> —Ephesians 5:20 (NIV)

Unlike other victims of catastrophic airplane and automobile crashes or victims of traumatic life-changing events, I didn't experience much in the way of negative feelings, depression, or post-traumatic stress disorder. I guess I was so busy with rehabilitation from the surgeries, battling an infection by a micro-beast, and returning to normal life, there just wasn't any room to feel sorry for myself or feel any more fear beyond what I'd already experienced facing Black Death. As a matter of fact, after being attacked by a monstrous beast, I don't think I will fear or be afraid of anything again. There were no distractions to tempt me from giving God my absolute best.

On the other hand, the image of the goliath beast charging at me was most certainly indelibly etched in my mind. To this day, I can recall the details and share my emotions and feelings I felt at the near-death scene, millisecond by millisecond. Yet it doesn't haunt me. I'm not plagued with nightmares like soldiers returning from combat. It's simply part of my life story now.

As I continued focusing on God, my spirituality, and family, I persevered following the straight and narrow pathway less traveled. It was so amazing that I was able to journey out of such a dark place and enter the light. By all opinions, I should have been killed. I planned flights to be with my family in the fall and stayed with both my daughters, one in California and one in Texas. For the first time in many years, I could spend a couple of weeks with each of them and my grandkids because nothing was going to stop me from sharing time with my family, certainly not hunting. Life with my family was a sacred and blessed time.

During this season of my life, I was in constant communication with Father Brooks and after our Sunday morning worship service I would get on the Gondola One out of Vail Village and ski up to officiate the Vail outdoor worship service as a mountaintop minister during the winters following my African savanna salvation. Every Sunday at 12:30 p.m., you'd find me standing at the top of the back bowls, next to Two Elk restaurant, gazing across to the Holy Cross Wilderness at Mount of the Holy Cross, never losing connection with the One who gave His life on the cross for all of us.

The sermons I shared were about a man I knew very well who went through a grisly experience with Black Death, captured in vivid detail. The man went to hell and back, was blessed to witness his own miraculous near-death experience, given a clear message from God, and experienced salvation. The audience was riveted, on the edge of their seats. Several minutes before closing, I confessed that the man was me. And stated, **but for the hand of God, I wouldn't be here telling this story**.

After I finished sharing my witness, people of all ages—from their early twenties to late seventies—approached me in tears, praising God and wanting to know where my stories were online so they could share them with their family and friends back home. Those sermons became the nucleus for this book.

Before the mountaintop services, I had no idea the kind of influence my witness might have on other people's lives. I simply accepted God's will and call to share my witness with anyone willing to listen. I continued to share my experiences with other groups in the valley during the spring and summer. One of the most rewarding moments was the opportunity to share my witness after church over coffee in a more informal setting, where people gathered in fellowship.

By that time, I had told the story so many times the chronology of events would flow out on autopilot. Recalling the end of July 2012, I remember my brother in Christ, Hank, remarked during the week following my first surgery in Vail, "I'm going to call the *Vail Daily*. They should write a story about this." They did.

The next week, I met with Randy Wyrick at the *Vail Daily*. I shared the story with him and gave him a copy of the DVD I had professionally made. That spurred the first of two *Vail Daily* stories about Black Death. The first one was titled "A Miracle among Us" on August 2, 2012, complete with the picture Grant took of me leaning behind the Cape buffalo with two African trackers holding me and the beast upright. The second one was published on the first anniversary of my attack titled "Vail Valley Man Auctioning Mount of Cape Buffalo That Almost Killed Him" on August 16, 2013. They were also published in the *Denver Post* and their website as "Gypsum Man on Safari Survives Attack by African Cape Buffalo," on August 2, 2012, where the story went viral. Dr. Peter Millett also published two articles, "Larry Trotter's One-Year Recovery After Cape Buffalo Attack," as well as an article on the medical and surgical facts of the story on the Steadman Clinic website. The stories were spreading like wildfire.

After I told the initial story, our church continued sponsoring different events and asked me to share my experience about that sacred day with a Dagga Boy. I told the story dozens of times a week for about five years, including on Cursillo weekends. To this day, I've told the story so many times my wife, Diane, asks permission to leave the room whenever I start. She's heard it enough. On the other hand, she's also the first one to point out that I must have been saved for her, that if it weren't for the miracle of God's hand saving my life, we would not be enjoying life together as bride and groom.

After volunteering for five years with the mountaintop ministry, I tried to make contact with Abrie and e-mailed Grant. I wanted each of them to reiterate and corroborate what they told me they saw on that fateful day on July 3, 2012. I saw the light from my perspective, but naturally, I couldn't see what they saw from there vantage place or the six trackers and the other professional hunters. Grant lost track of Abrie. Rumor has it that he injured his back and had to have surgery and a long recovery period. He may not even be a professional hunter anymore.

However, I did keep in contact with Grant. For two years, he confirmed via the internet, that he did indeed witness the same spectacle and would be happy to write his accounting of the incident. After recounting the story hundreds of times and being published on the Internet, I thought it would be prudent to have endorsements by the other eyewitnesses at the scene of the attack. It's a unique situation where there were eleven people—including myself—telling the same story, detail by detail. Of course, we also have the original video of the incident recorded and available with this book.

Not until the last few years did I genuinely feel like my story was worth sharing on a broader scale beyond my circle of friends and fellow worshippers at church. Sharing my witness began to feel like it may be of value to people who didn't know me, and that it may be fascinating for them to read. My biggest concern always was whether my book would become just another one of the other massive numbers of books published each year, collecting dust on someone's bookshelf and not really be read in its entirety. Wondering and praying for over seven years, I continually asked God if my lifetime of witnesses and the message of my salvation experience was worthy of publishing in the name of our awesome God and of interest to a global audience?

One of the points that became obvious to me was that everyone has their own Cape buffalo story. So that became the goal for this book: to make this common thread our mutual connection while providing the impetus to get other people talking about and sharing their Cape buffalo stories, reaffirming with others that God is alive. God is real and proactive in all our lives today.

> 23 *"Am I only a God nearby,"*
> *declares the Lord,*
> *"and not a God far away?*
> 24 *Who can hide in secret places*
> *so that I cannot see them?"*
> *declares the Lord.*
> *"Do not I fill heaven and earth?"*
> *declares the Lord.*
>
> —Jeremiah 23:23–24 (NIV)

Confirmations of the commonality of mutual Cape buffalo stories fueled by me sharing my story, kept appearing with different people from all walks of life, in different places, and in different venues. They originated as visitors attending our church services who then took the witness to their churches. They, in turn, took it to spiritual gatherings like Cursillo, where it was brought back to even more churches all over the country. Father Brooks shared with me that he was getting calls from the National Episcopal Church in New York: "Do you know you have this guy Larry Trotter that we're reading about from your congregation?" The story was spreading in every direction. It was multiplying on its own with absolutely no help on my part. Through word of mouth, my story manifested. Online, the story went viral and was tweeted beyond anything imaginable. I had never looked at a tweet before someone pointed it out to me. From celebrities to the general public were tweeting about the man attacked by Black Death. Nonhunters tweeted that they'd rather the man died instead of the buffalo, and Bruce Willis defended me. The energy was truly unbelievable. The story was published by many major newspapers across the United States and around the world back to Africa. A God wave was swelling across the planet and gaining amplitude.

The story and the process took time to mature at its own rate. At the same time, my spirituality was continuing to mature. I was not only becoming a better person because of the miracle and my recovery, but I was also becoming a better parent, grandparent, friend, and partner with my wife, Diane. We spent years talking about what I should do about this story, this witness of God's reality. Should I keep the witness to myself? Or if we did share it, how would I ensure that it not become sensationalized and too much about me instead of God being the main character: to spread the good news that God is all around us all the time and available to help everyone with their Cape buffalo if we let God into our lives?

If there's going to be a financial benefit from this book, it's all going directly back to God. The one and only financial benefactor of this book will be God. A total of 100 percent of the royalties will be sent to the church, to help spread the good news and be the hands and feet of Jesus here on Earth today.

For people looking for another message from this book, it's simple: you can't make this stuff up. Not even Hollywood could dream up a story like this. Like other intriguing survival stories, my story is real and true. The miracle of my recovery and metamorphosis is real. And my story is not the only one. Similar miracles are happening every day. We just aren't aware of them unless we agree to share them with others.

As it turns out, with time the content of this book had to evolve on its own. Finally, it was simply time to write the book. There was a point when publishing the witness might have been premature, a point where it might have only reached a limited number of people. But through the course of my sermons and sharing it with others, it took on a life of its own. At the same time, my life on Earth is finite, so if I'm going to share this witness with others, I need to share it with people now, before I won't be in a position to share the witness accurately. I finally reached a point where it needed to be shared more than being kept hidden. So now whenever I share my story and people come up to me and say, "You know, you should do more with this story. You should write a book or something," I can tell them, "*Seeing the Light through Black Death — Salvation in the African savanna,* has been published."

CHAPTER TWELVE

EPILOGUE

Luke 10:25-27 New International Version (NIV)

The Parable of the Good Samaritan

^{25} On one occasion an expert in the law stood up to test Jesus. "Teacher," he asked, "what must I do to inherit eternal life?"

^{26} "What is written in the Law?" he replied. "How do you read it?"

^{27} He answered, "'Love the Lord your God with all your heart and with all your soul and with all your strength and with all your mind'; and, 'Love your neighbor as yourself.'"

—Luke 10:25–27 (NIV)

For most of my young adult life, I felt that if I was to make anything of my life, it was all up to me. "If it is to be, it is up to me" was my battle cry. If I planned my life well, there was nothing I couldn't achieve, given good health, energy, and sweat. After all, I had a track record to prove it. What could possibly stand in the way?

Genius is one percent inspiration and ninety-nine percent perspiration.

—Thomas Edison

Like many of us, my spirit needed time to truly understand it's place here on Earth, not as a mortal with the goal of serving myself, but as a witness of God's miracles and the wonderful blessings He can provide if we let God's will be executed. My life wasn't up to me or luck. My life actually was all about living God's will, receiving and appreciating God's blessings.

As life moved on, some of the details began to get interesting. Some of my businesses were, shall we say, "less successful than I expected," and I struggled with family relationships. I began to feel like maybe I wasn't quite as indestructible as I originally thought. Nevertheless, I still enjoyed enough positive life experiences to make me think that I could be a success. I was attempting to live life to its fullest.

As I slowly began to embrace Jesus and include Him in my life, I struggled with the difference between God's will, divine intervention, miracles, grace, and my own free will. How much success could I accept as a result of hard work? How much success is a gift from God?

We can look at our lives as if nothing is a miracle or as if everything is a miracle. I preferred the second, and I slowly warmed up to the idea that I couldn't take credit for the successes in my life.

According to the *Merriam-Webster Dictionary*, divine intervention is defined as *a divinely natural phenomenon experienced humanly as the fulfillment of spiritual law.* At the time, the definition wasn't much to go on, but I was willing and open to accept help.

More simply stated, I believe divine intervention is when God steps in and changes the outcome of a situation. It's another way of defining miracles. People point to divine intervention when there's no other explanation than the hand of God intervening in an outcome that includes miraculous healing, people being put in the right place at the right time, and circumstances that protected someone from falling into harm's way.

Since then, I've learned that virtually all our life occurrences and events we experience during our lives here on Earth are the result of God's will for us. God ordains His plan and already knows the outcome long before we do.

Praise and Prayer[7] I will tell of the kindnesses of the Lord,
the deeds for which he is to be praised,
according to all the Lord has done for us—
yes, the many good things
he has done for Israel,
according to his compassion and many kindnesses.
[8] He said, "Surely they are my people,
children who will be true to me";
and so he became their Savior.

> [9] In all their distress he too was distressed,
> and the angel of his presence saved them.
> In his love and mercy he redeemed them;
> he lifted them up and carried them
> all the days of old.—Isaiah 63:7–9 (NIV)

My life never presented a concept where God wants us to languish during our time on Earth. God still expects us to live our lives using as much free will as we can muster. Furthermore, God has shown me His presence and always offers proactive help in everything we do, whether it's struggling with a life-threatening disease or waiting for a message of God's will on how to live our lives. We're never walking this journey alone. If I have times of struggle now, it's the small annoying issues that pop up living everyday life, but refinement never comes easy. Many times, I've felt Jesus walking or paddling right alongside me, leading me, encouraging me, and carrying me. I wouldn't be alive to share any of these thoughts, witnesses, experiences, or stories with anyone or to write this book but for the hand of God on July 3, 2012, at three-thirty in the afternoon. The only way I've managed to survive the most difficult situations in my life was by clinging to the vine.

It is my belief we can agree that living as an imperfect mortal human is okay. To have feelings, to have emotions, and being ourselves as we express our free will. But I've learned the hard way, that what action we choose upon feeling our emotions is what really counts. We are free to choose how we're going to respond to one stimulus or another. More often than we probably want, or at least that I want, our response may not be presented in respectable ways. But if we pause and ask the Holy Spirit for guidance, our actions can bear witness to those who observe us and need our positive example, by living and acting as exemplary witnesses. We can be good or bad examples for our children, grandchildren, and all the people we engage, as we live our lives. It's a matter of being proactive or reactive:

> [6] *Do not be anxious about anything, but in every situation, by prayer and petition, with thanksgiving, present your requests to God.* [7] *And the peace of God, which transcends all understanding, will guard your hearts and your minds in Christ Jesus.*
>
> —Philippians 4:6–7 (NIV)

Looking toward the future, my goal is to continue working as hard as I can to walk in the ways of Jesus, trying to fulfill my discipleship, trying to become a better man, husband, father, grandfather, friend, brother in Christ. I know the opportunities are there because grandchild number 11 was just born and number 12 is on his way. Between my wife and I, we have seven children and let's not forget all their spouses.

When I was attacked by the Cape buffalo, it shattered not only my left arm and shoulder but also confidence in myself. Months later, Fr. Brooks Keith said, "There's a biblical irony to me that Larry was injured on the first day of his trip. In my experience, when God teaches man lessons, God is not subtle. In this case, the timing of that attack and the fact that he was standing there with a bow and arrow when his tracker threw down the camera, ran for his life, and others of the ten protecting him watched from the sideline tell me everything about the gospel. Everything about Christian faith is present in Larry's story: pride, hubris, expectations, and intervention to save Larry's life for a reason."

Black Death clearly got my attention and convinced me that I'm not always the one in charge. I may think I am, but trials like the attack are not-so-subtle reminders that there's more to living life than following our own limited plans. We are really all servants of God and each other. Aren't we all better people if we focus on walking in God's ways rather than trying to make it on our own?

Ten years before I was sprawled out on the African savanna ground, I had subtly begun welcoming Christ into my life. I had become active in the Episcopal Church in Wisconsin and where I live in Vail, Colorado. I attended numerous spiritual enrichment venues, including Alpha and Cursillo weekends, and stretched my hand out to fellow Christians. After years of contemplating the Word of God, I finally began to understand the idea that there was room for God in my life.

My Christian retreat weekends planted the seeds for spiritual growth, just as Matthew wrote about the mustard seed in the New Testament:

The Parables of the Mustard Seed and the Yeast

³¹ He told them another parable: "The kingdom of heaven is like a mustard seed, which a man took and planted in his field. ³² Though it is the smallest of all seeds, yet when it grows, it is the largest of garden plants and becomes a tree, so that the birds come and perch in its branches."

—Matthew 13:31–32 (NIV)

The parable of the mustard seed was written during the early days of the church when it began to experience explosive growth. It represented then (just as it does now) comfort knowing that a life with Christ can provide believers with an abundance of hope, joy, love, and peace. At the same time, it reminds us that we still need to practice what Jesus came to teach us through His Word. One of my favorite prayers is from the *Book of Common Prayer*:

Blessed Lord, who caused all holy Scriptures to be written for our learning: Grant us so to hear them, read, mark, learn and inwardly digest them, that we may embrace and ever hold fast the blessed hope of everlasting life, which you have given us in our Savior Jesus Christ; who lives and reigns with you and the Holy Spirit, one God, forever and ever. Amen.

Once the seed has been planted, there's no limit to what we can achieve if we allow God to work in our lives. But for that to happen, it's essential that we become open, willing vessels, capable of receiving God's messages and understanding His will. Oftentimes, it's a matter of perspective. How can we best serve Jesus, others, and yourself—JOY?

Matthew wrote about the importance of perspective and how true light can't be hidden. While standing on a hill, he observed bright lights:

¹⁵ Neither do people light a lamp and put it under a bowl. Instead, they put it on its stand, and it gives light to everyone in the house. ¹⁶ In the same way, let your light shine before others, that they may see your good deeds and glorify your Father in heaven.

—Matthew 5:15–16 (NIV)

When Jesus preached the eight Beatitudes during the Sermon on the Mount, He delivered a message of peace, humility, charity, and brotherly love as part of transforming the inner person. Jesus promised us, by His death on the cross, His grace and forgiveness of our sins for our **salvation** with eternal life, if we believe in Him and keep the faith to strive to live His way of life. The Beatitudes provide us with a way of life here on Earth as we work our way through the trials and tribulations of this imperfect world:

> *³ Blessed are the poor in spirit,*
> *for theirs is the kingdom of heaven.*
> *⁴ Blessed are those who mourn,*
> *for they will be comforted.*
> *⁵ Blessed are the meek,*
> *for they will inherit the earth.*
> *⁶ Blessed are those who hunger and thirst for righteousness,*
> *for they will be filled.*
> *⁷ Blessed are the merciful,*
> *for they will be shown mercy.*
> *⁸ Blessed are the pure in heart,*
> *for they will see God.*
> *⁹ Blessed are the peacemakers,*
> *for they will be called children of God.*
> *¹⁰ Blessed are those who are persecuted because of righteousness,*
> *for theirs is the kingdom of heaven.*
> *¹¹ Blessed are you when people insult you, persecute you and*
> *falsely say all kinds of evil against you because of me.*
> —Matthew 5:3–11 (NIV)

Earlier in the book, I spoke about the value of including accountability partners in our lives. While we can enjoy life with Christ by ourselves, partnering with others is a significantly better way of inviting God into our life.

> *¹⁸ Assuredly, I say to you, whatever you bind on earth will*
> *be bound in heaven, and whatever you loose on earth will be*
> *loosed in heaven.*
> *¹⁹ Again I say to you that if two of you agree on earth*
> *concerning anything that they ask, it will be done for them by*

My Father in heaven. ²⁰ For where two or three are gathered together in My name, I am there in the midst of them.
—Matthew 18:18–20 (NKJV)

Accountability partners—hopefully including your spouse, family members, and a few of your best friends—can be wonderful resources for enhancing your time here on Earth. Accountability partners DO have to be human beings (not buildings or stuff), God's children, Jesus's sisters and brothers, the branches of the Vine. By participating with a church of our choice—which, of course, is the body of Christ—we can experience the wonderful companionship and fellowship of a broader Christian community. Life is simply too difficult to try to survive alone.

Long before I was intimately introduced to the Word of God, my dad brought home a program from work called Change Your Weaknesses to Strengths. Since then, a lot of people have laid claim to them, but ultimately, they all offer the same points:

- Identify your weaknesses
- Every weakness has a corresponding strength
- Get advice
- Hire skill development
- Get good enough
- Seek to help others

For some reason, it stuck with me. I thought if we know what our weaknesses are, then we can change them to strengths if we're willing to work at it. I know that I still have work to do in many areas of my life. Here is a checklist of nine attributes or fruits of our spirit we can review to assess our strengths and weaknesses, found in Paul's letter to the Galatians:

²² But the fruit of the Spirit is love, joy, peace, forbearance, kindness, goodness, faithfulness, ²³ gentlenesses, and self-control. Against such things, there is no law. ²⁴ Those who belong to Christ Jesus have crucified the flesh with its passions and desires. ²⁵ *Since we live by the Spirit, let us keep in step with the Spirit.* ²⁶ *Let us not become conceited, provoking, and envying each other.*

—Galatians 5:22–26 (NIV)

Regardless of how successful we are, anybody who is open and has an accurate perception of themselves will realize there's usually plenty of opportunities for improvement in how we live. Consistent over six and a half decades, I've learned no matter how well we might perform specific facets of our life, there's always someone who can do it better. This is both humbling in a positive way and an opportunity to realize there is a community of people willing to share life and bond in unity.

Life and skiing pair perfectly together, and skiing has always been a life sport for me, a lifelong learning process, and a life teaching opportunity. Skiing is much more than just making our way down an incline. Skiing can teach us a lot about life. From little incidents like when we fall down, we simply get back up, brush the snow off, and continue on our way to understanding the interrelationships among the forces, physics, and the environment (our creation) and our spirit, mind, and bodies (our being). The complexity of this passion sport is best shared with family and friends. It's a common way of also sharing a spiritual life with sisters and brothers in Christ and embracing the feeling of the peace that surpasses all understanding. Sharing skiing is truly a gift from God.

I believe passion activities or sports are pathways to staying healthier and even younger in mind, body, and spirit. Experiencing the grandeur of mountains exposes us to locations with some of the most beautiful displays of creation, reinforcing where we came from. I believe ultimately, growth in any aspect of our lives has its foundation in spiritual growth and development. May we all find our mustard seed and nurture the glorious unfolding of a taste of Heaven during our lifetimes here on Earth as we approach an eternity of peace beyond human comprehension in the realm of the Kingdom of Heaven.

This was never meant to be a book about hunting. Nor is it an advertisement for or against the commercial business of African hunting. But for people who are hunters, perhaps it will serve as an entertaining adventure, beyond just hunting and harvesting animals. More importantly, I hope it reaches out and stimulates active communication among people of all perspectives, interests, and pursuits of happiness.

What I've learned from my experiences is that everyone has a Cape buffalo story. When people read about my story in the newspaper, or they hear me tell it during one of my sermons, it suddenly shifts from being *my* story to *theirs*. They start telling everyone else about their Cape buffalo stories. Just by listening to others, we find a way to take the load off their shoulders, give the burden to Jesus, and begin a healing process. They instantly feel our support and understand that there's no reason to trudge through life alone, especially now that everyone on Earth has experienced the global Covid-19 viral attack. I further pray that this book will contribute to everyone's post-pandemic healing.

As I've already touched on, it took seven years from July of 2012 to July of 2019 to discern the call to write to you these 12 chapters. Accepting writing this book occurred in August of 2019 when a final sign became apparent after praying for months on how to pay for the publishing process of this book. It was August 2019 when my prayers were answered with someone who owed me $10,000, sent me a check in the mail repaying the note with interest. I never expected to be repaid, but there was the seed funds of $13,500 delivered to start the publishing process. Then, in November of 2019, another person who owed me $16,500 sent a check paid in full through the US Postal Service, reconfirming the first sign of providence answering my prayers. Another miracle!!! All thanks be to God! Amen! Amen! And Amen!

The first crude draft of the manuscript was completed by Christmas 2019. After Christmas, I researched, audited, edited, rewrote, and refined the manuscript with the power of the Holy Spirit. And then the global Pandemic hit Vail, Eagle County, Colorado and all North American Vail Resorts ski areas closed March 14, 2020. Eagle County, mid-March 2020, had the highest per capita incidence of Covid-19 in the United States of America. Diane and I evacuated to Boulder, CO for two months of quarantine. Can we imagine how

Saint Paul must have felt writing to the Philippians while in a Roman prison. Though certainly not in prison, I felt isolated. The pandemic period was a perfect time to connect with our Father in Heaven, His Son and the Holy Spirit. There was no doubt the Holy Spirit was present and commanded my full attention editing, rewriting, and the finishing of this book truly was a blessed Covid-19 Pandemic project. On May 17, 2020, we drove to our Lake Cabin in northern Wisconsin where quarantine is the normal natural way of life in some of the best of creation, on still waters.

July 31, 2020, I felt, with God's help, I finished the final edited manuscript after 75 rewrites. My prayer to everyone who reads this book is that the twelve chapters or messengers reach everyone and touches everyone with healing power to recover from this global Pandemic mess. Clearly this book of miracles is no accident.

One of the reasons for me being reluctant about writing this book initially was that I didn't want it to be an autobiography. I didn't want it to be about me but rather all about God as I've experienced God over my lifetime. At most, I want to be merely the messenger and the witness, witnessing God's involvement in my life. I would like it to be about sharing God's will.

After over seven years of contemplation, I finally felt called to publicly share my gratitude and thankfulness to God for saving my physical and spiritual life. I needed to give back part of me to God. I couldn't just hide a lifetime of miracles. I couldn't ignore God's message. My soul ached and my inner being didn't feel right with all the life events that I've been through, to simply squirrel away my experiences as secrets to myself. If this book can be a global message, I hope it can be a catalyst for people to share a God wave of Cape buffalo stories and minister to one another and serve God through active stewardship.

I'd like to encourage all of us to pursue passionate lives of purpose and not be afraid to share them with others. Granted, life's not always perfect. There are always plenty of challenges. But there's value in sharing the good news of clinging to the vine and rejoicing in how God's hand is pulling us all through life.

Hopefully, I'm not at the end of the road yet, for I understand that I still have a long way to go with Jesus as He finishes sculpting me. Over my sixty-six years on Earth, one of the most significant points I've learned is that God is always present. God's been here all along the way, whether I recognized it. As I continue my journey, it's become clearer, so clear that I couldn't continue keeping my witness to myself. The voice has called me to share how a lifetime of experiences, miracles, and the grace of God endures as the Holy Spirit never stops counseling. To witness hearing the Word of our Father in heaven. To witness seeing and hearing Jesus speak. The voice has called us all to better understand the Word of God, by Seeing the Light through Black Death and by sharing my experience of Salvation in the African savanna.

> *The people living in darkness*
> *have seen a great light;*
> *on those living in the land of the shadow of death*
> *a light has dawned.*
>
> —Matthew 4:16 (NIV)

Now my battle cry is as clear as the lyrics from Michael W. Smith's song "Fight My Battles": "This is how I fight my battles. It may look like I'm surrounded, but I'm surrounded by you" In the background someone wails - "Jesus"!

My point is, after witnessing a lifetime of miracles, there is no doubt whatsoever, in my mind and soul, that God is for real, alive, and proactive today!

As the Reverend Brooks Keith has reiterated,

> *God doesn't deal with people in small ways. This is a big story for a big guy. Larry didn't need a subtle message. Some people do. Larry didn't get that. He's a walking miracle and testimony as well.*

QUOTED SCRIPTURES AND PRAYERS IN ALPHABETICAL ORDER

Acts 10:12–15 (NIV) (pages 79)	Acts 10:12–15 (NIV)
	It contained all kinds of four-footed animals, as well as reptiles and birds. Then a voice told him, "Get up, Peter. Kill and eat."
	"Surely not, Lord!" Peter replied. "I have never eaten anything impure or unclean."
	The voice spoke to him a second time, "Do not call anything impure that God has made clean.
Book of Common Prayer/Episcopal Church, a Collect of the Day {a prayer} (page 193)	Blessed Lord, who caused all holy Scriptures to be written for our learning: Grant us so to hear them, read, mark, learn and inwardly digest them, that we may embrace and ever hold fast the blessed hope of everlasting life, which you have given us in our Savior Jesus Christ; who lives and reigns with you and the Holy Spirit, one God, forever and ever. Amen.

1 Corinthians 9:24–27 (NIV) (page 173)	1 Corinthians 9:24–27 (NIV) The Need for Self-Discipline 24 Do you not know that in a race all the runners run, but only one gets the prize? Run in such a way as to get the prize. 25 Everyone who competes in the games goes into strict training. They do it to get a crown that will not last, but we do it to get a crown that will last forever. 26 Therefore I do not run like someone running aimlessly; I do not fight like a boxer beating the air. 27 No, I strike a blow to my body and make it my slave so that after I have preached to others, I myself will not be disqualified for the prize.
1 Corinthians 10:13 (NIV) (page 25)	1 Corinthians 10:13 (NIV) 13 No temptation has overtaken you except what is common to mankind. And God is faithful; he will not let you be tempted beyond what you can bear. But when you are tempted, he will also provide a way out so that you can endure it.
1 Corinthians 10:31 (NIV) (page 51)	1 Corinthians 10:31 (NIV) 31 So whether you eat or drink or whatever you do, do it all for the glory of God.
2 Corinthians 12:9–10 (NIV) (pages 151-152)	2 Corinthians 12:9–10 (NIV) 9 But he said to me, "My grace is sufficient for you, for my power is made perfect in weakness." Therefore I will boast all the more gladly about my weaknesses, so that Christ's power may rest on me. 10 That is why, for Christ's sake, I delight in weaknesses, in insults, in hardships, in persecutions, in difficulties. For when I am weak, then I am strong.

Deuteronomy 28:1–6 (NIV) (page 137)	Deuteronomy 28:1–6 (NIV) Blessings for Obedience **28** ¹If you fully obey the Lord your God and carefully follow all his commands I give you today, the Lord your God will set you high above all the nations on earth. ² All these blessings will come on you and accompany you if you obey the Lord your God: ³ You will be blessed in the city and blessed in the country. ⁴ The fruit of your womb will be blessed, and the crops of your land and the young of your livestock—the calves of your herds and the lambs of your flocks. ⁵ Your basket and your kneading trough will be blessed. ⁶ You will be blessed when you come in and blessed when you go out.
Ephesians 3:16–19 (NIV) (page 68)	Ephesians 3:16–19 (NIV) ¹⁶ I pray that out of his glorious riches he may strengthen you with power through his Spirit in your inner being, ¹⁷ so that Christ may dwell in your hearts through faith. And I pray that you, being rooted and established in love, ¹⁸ may have power, together with all the Lord's holy people, to grasp how wide and long and high and deep is the love of Christ, ¹⁹ and to know this love that surpasses knowledge—that you may be filled to the measure of all the fullness of God.
Ephesians 5:20 (NIV) (page 183)	Ephesians 5:20 (NIV) ²⁰ always giving thanks to God the Father for everything, in the name of our Lord Jesus Christ.

Galatians 5:22–26 (NIV) (page 195-196)	Galatians 5:22–26 (NIV) But the fruit of the Spirit is love, joy, peace, forbearance, kindness, goodness, faithfulness, gentleness, and self-control. Against such things, there is no law. Those who belong to Christ Jesus have crucified the flesh with its passions and desires. Since we live by the Spirit, let us keep in step with the Spirit. Let us not become conceited, provoking, and envying each other.
Genesis 1:21 (NIV) (page 97)	Genesis 1:21 (NIV) 21 So God created the great creatures of the sea and every living thing with which the water teems and that moves about in it, according to their kinds, and every winged bird according to its kind. And God saw that it was good.
Genesis 1:30 (NIV) (page 98)	Genesis 1:30 (NIV) And to all the beasts of the earth and all the birds in the sky and all the creatures that move along the ground—everything that has the breath of life in it—I give every green plant for food." And it was so.
Habakkuk 2:3 (ESV) (page 45)	Habakkuk 2:3 (ESV) For still the vision awaits its appointed time; it hastens to the end—it will not lie. If it seems slow, wait for it; it will surely come; it will not delay.
Isaiah 41:10 (NIV) (page 18)	Isaiah 41:10 (NIV) 10 So do not fear, for I am with you; do not be dismayed, for I am your God. I will strengthen you and help you; I will uphold you with my righteous right hand.

Isaiah 63:7–9 (NIV) (pages 190-191)	Isaiah 63:7–9 (NIV) Praise and Prayer 7 I will tell of the kindnesses of the Lord, the deeds for which he is to be praised, according to all the Lord has done for us— yes, the many good things he has done for Israel, according to his compassion and many kindnesses. 8 He said, "Surely they are my people, children who will be true to me"; and so he became their Savior. 9 In all their distress he too was distressed, and the angel of his presence saved them. In his love and mercy he redeemed them; he lifted them up and carried them all the days of old.
James 5:7–8 (NIV) (page 181)	James 5:7–8 (NIV) Patience in Suffering 7 Be patient, then, brothers and sisters, until the Lord's coming. See how the farmer waits for the land to yield its valuable crop, patiently waiting for the autumn and spring rains. 8 You too, be patient and stand firm, because the Lord's coming is near.

Jeremiah 23:23–24 (NIV) (page 186)	Jeremiah 23:23–24 (NIV) 23 "Am I only a God nearby," declares the Lord, "and not a God far away? 24 Who can hide in secret places so that I cannot see them?" declares the Lord. "Do not I fill heaven and earth?" declares the Lord.
Jeremiah 29:11 (NIV) (page 9)	Jeremiah 29:11 (NIV) 11 "For I know the plans I have for you," declares the Lord, "plans to prosper you and not to harm you, plans to give you hope and a future."
John 6:35 (NIV) (page 55)	John 6:35 (NIV) 35 Then Jesus declared, "I am the bread of life. Whoever comes to me will never go hungry, and whoever believes in me will never be thirsty."
3 John 2 (EVS) (page 171)	3 John 2 (EVS) Beloved, I pray that all may go well with you and that you may be in good health, as it goes well with your soul.
John 14:3 (NIV) (page 164)	John 14:3 (NIV) And if I go and prepare a place for you, I will come back and take you to be with me that you also may be where I am.
John 15:5 (NIV) (page 1)	John 15:5 (NIV) I am the vine; you are the branches. If you remain in me and I in you, you will bear much fruit; apart from me you can do nothing.

John 16:33 (NIV) (page 161)	John 16:33 (NIV) 33 "I have told you these things, so that in me you may have peace. In this world you will have trouble. But take heart! I have overcome the world."
John 20:24–31 (NIV) (pages 28-29, 162)	John 20:24–31 (NIV) Now Thomas (also known as Didymus), one of the Twelve, was not with the disciples when Jesus came. So the other disciples told him, "We have seen the Lord!" But he said to them, "Unless I see the nail marks in his hands and put my finger where the nails were, and put my hand into his side, I will not believe." A week later his disciples were in the house again, and Thomas was with them. Though the doors were locked, Jesus came and stood among them and said, "Peace be with you!" Then he said to Thomas, "Put your finger here; see my hands. Reach out your hand and put it into my side. Stop doubting and believe." Thomas said to him, "My Lord and my God!" Then Jesus told him, "Because you have seen me, you have believed; blessed are those who have not seen and yet have believed."

Luke 10:25–37 (NIV) (page 189)	Luke 10:25–27 (NIV) The Parable of the Good Samaritan [25] On one occasion an expert in the law stood up to test Jesus. "Teacher," he asked, "what must I do to inherit eternal life?" [26] "What is written in the Law?" he replied. "How do you read it?" [27] He answered, "'Love the Lord your God with all your heart and with all your soul and with all your strength and with all your mind'; and, 'Love your neighbor as yourself.'"
Malachi 3:10–11 (NIV) (page 70)	Malachi 3:10–11 (NIV) [10] "Bring the whole tithe into the storehouse, that there may be food in my house. Test me in this," says the Lord Almighty, "and see if I will not throw open the floodgates of heaven and pour out so much blessing that there will not be room enough to store it. [11] I will prevent pests from devouring your crops, and the vines in your fields will not drop their fruit before it is ripe," says the Lord Almighty.
Mark 12:41–44 (NIV) (page 70)	Mark 12:41–44 (NIV) Jesus sat down opposite the place where the offerings were put and watched the crowd putting their money into the temple treasury. Many rich people threw in large amounts. But a poor widow came and put in two very small copper coins, worth only a few cents. Calling his disciples to him, Jesus said, "Truly I tell you, this poor widow has put more into the treasury than all the others. They all gave out of their wealth; but she, out of her poverty, put in everything—all she had to live on."

Matthew 4:16 (NIV) (page 199)	**Matthew 4:16 (NIV)** ¹⁶ the people living in darkness have seen a great light; on those living in the land of the shadow of death a light has dawned.
Matthew 5:3–11 (NIV) (page 194)	**Matthew 5:3–11 (NIV)** ³ "Blessed are the poor in spirit, for theirs is the kingdom of heaven. ⁴ Blessed are those who mourn, for they will be comforted. ⁵ Blessed are the meek, for they will inherit the earth. ⁶ Blessed are those who hunger and thirst for righteousness, for they will be filled. ⁷ Blessed are the merciful, for they will be shown mercy. ⁸ Blessed are the pure in heart, for they will see God. ⁹ Blessed are the peacemakers, for they will be called children of God. ¹⁰ Blessed are those who are persecuted because of righteousness, for theirs is the kingdom of heaven. ¹¹ Blessed are you when people insult you, persecute you and falsely say all kinds of evil against you because of me.

Matthew 5:15–16 (NIV) (193)	Matthew 5:15–16 (NIV) 15 Neither do people light a lamp and put it under a bowl. Instead, they put it on its stand, and it gives light to everyone in the house. 16 In the same way, let your light shine before others, that they may see your good deeds and glorify your Father in heaven.
Matthew 6:8–13 (NKJV) (page 69)	Matthew 6:8–13 (NKJV) 8 Therefore do not be like them. For your Father knows the things you have need of before you ask Him. 9 In this manner, therefore, pray: Our Father in heaven, Hallowed be Your name. 10 Your kingdom come. Your will be done On earth as *it is* in heaven. 11 Give us this day our daily bread. 12 And forgive us our debts, As we forgive our debtors. 13 And do not lead us into temptation, But deliver us from the evil one. For Yours is the kingdom and the power and the glory forever. Amen.
Matthew 6:19–21 (NIV) (page 71)	Matthew 6:19–21(NIV) Treasures in Heaven 19 Do not store up for yourselves treasures on earth, where moths and vermin destroy, and where thieves break in and steal. 20 But store up for yourselves treasures in heaven, where moths and vermin do not destroy, and where thieves do not break in and steal. 21 For where your treasure is, there your heart will be also.

Matthew 6:24 (NIV) (page 71)	Matthew 6:24 (NIV) [24] No one can serve two masters. Either you will hate the one and love the other, or you will be devoted to the one and despise the other. You cannot serve both God and money.
Matthew 6:25–32 (NIV) (page 128)	Matthew 6:25–32 (NIV) Do Not Worry [25] Therefore I tell you, do not worry about your life, what you will eat or drink; or about your body, what you will wear. Is not life more than food, and the body more than clothes? [26] Look at the birds of the air; they do not sow or reap or store away in barns, and yet your heavenly Father feeds them. Are you not much more valuable than they? [27] Can anyone of you by worrying add a single hour to your life? [28] And why do you worry about clothes? See how the flowers of the field grow. They do not labor or spin. [29] Yet I tell you that not even Solomon in all his splendor was dressed like one of these. [30] If that is how God clothes the grass of the field, which is here today and tomorrow is thrown into the fire, will he not much more clothe you—you of little faith? [31] So do not worry, saying, "What shall we eat?" or "What shall we drink?" or "What shall we wear?" [32] For the pagans run after all these things, and your heavenly Father knows that you need them.
Matthew 7:7–8 (NIV) (page 159)	Matthew 7:7–8 (NIV) Ask, Seek, Knock [7] Ask and it will be given to you; seek and you will find; knock and the door will be opened to you. [8] For everyone who asks receives; the one who seeks finds; and to the one who knocks, the door will be opened.

Matthew 13:31–32 (NIV) (page 193)	Matthew 13:31–32 (NIV) The Parables of the Mustard Seed and the Yeast **31** He told them another parable: "The kingdom of heaven is like a mustard seed, which a man took and planted in his field. **32** Though it is the smallest of all seeds, yet when it grows, it is the largest of garden plants and becomes a tree, so that the birds come and perch in its branches."
Matthew 18:15–22 (NKJV) (pages 31-32, 58-59, 157, 194-195)	Matthew 18:15–22 (NKJV) Dealing with a Sinning Brother **15** Moreover if your brother sins against you, go and tell him his fault between you and him alone. If he hears you, you have gained your brother. **16** But if he will not hear, take with you one or two more, that "by the mouth of two or three witnesses every word may be established." **17** And if he refuses to hear them, tell *it* to the church. But if he refuses even to hear the church, let him be to you like a heathen and a tax collector. **18** Assuredly, I say to you, whatever you bind on earth will be bound in heaven, and whatever you loose on earth will be loosed in heaven. **19** Again I say to you that if two of you agree on earth concerning anything that they ask, it will be done for them by My Father in heaven. **20** For where two or three are gathered together in My name, I am there in the midst of them. The Parable of the Unforgiving Servant **21** Then Peter came to Him and said, "Lord, how often shall my brother sin against me, and I forgive him? Up to seven times?" **22** Jesus said to him, "I do not say to you, up to seven times, but up to seventy times seven."

Matthew 19:23–24 (NIV) (page 71)	Matthew 19:23–24 (NIV) [23] Then Jesus said to his disciples, "Truly I tell you, it is hard for someone who is rich to enter the kingdom of heaven. [24] Again I tell you, it is easier for a camel to go through the eye of a needle than for someone who is rich to enter the kingdom of God."
Matthew 25:1–13 (NIV) (pages 164-165)	Matthew 25:1–13 (NIV) At that time the kingdom of heaven will be like ten virgins who took their lamps and went out to meet the bridegroom. Five of them were foolish and five were wise. The foolish ones took their lamps but did not take any oil with them. The wise ones, however, took oil in jars along with their lamps. The bridegroom was a long time in coming, and they all became drowsy and fell asleep. At midnight the cry rang out: "Here's the bridegroom! Come out to meet him!" Then all the virgins woke up and trimmed their lamps. The foolish ones said to the wise, "Give us some of your oil; our lamps are going out." "No," they replied, "there may not be enough for both us and you. Instead, go to those who sell oil and buy some for yourselves." But while they were on their way to buy the oil, the bridegroom arrived. The virgins who were ready went in with him to the wedding banquet. And the door was shut. Later the others also came. "Lord, Lord," they said, "open the door for us!" But he replied, "Truly I tell you, I don't know you." Therefore keep watch, because you do not know the day or the hour.

1 Peter 1:13 (NIV) (page 126)	1 Peter 1:13 (NIV) Be Holy [13] Therefore, with minds that are alert and fully sober, set your hope on the grace to be brought to you when Jesus Christ is revealed at his coming.
1 Peter 4:12–14 (NIV) (page 57)	1 Peter 4:12–14 (NIV) Suffering for Being a Christian [12] Dear friends, do not be surprised at the fiery ordeal that has come on you to test you, as though something strange were happening to you. [13] But rejoice inasmuch as you participate in the sufferings of Christ, so that you may be overjoyed when his glory is revealed. [14] If you are insulted because of the name of Christ, you are blessed, for the Spirit of glory and of God rests on you.
Philippians 2:12–13 (NIV) (pages 1, 166)	Philippians 2:12–13 (NIV) Do Everything Without Grumbling [12] Therefore, my dear friends, as you have always obeyed—not only in my presence but now much more in my absence—continue to work out your salvation with fear and trembling, [13] for it is God who works in you to will and to act in order to fulfill his good purpose.
Philippians 4:6–7 (NIV) (pages 123, 191)	Philippians 4:6–7 (NIV) [6] Do not be anxious about anything, but in every situation, by prayer and petition, with thanksgiving, present your requests to God. [7] And the peace of God, which transcends all understanding, will guard your hearts and your minds in Christ Jesus.
Philippians 4:13 (NIV) (page 167)	Philippians 4:13 (NIV) [13] I can do all this through him who gives me strength.

Proverbs 3:5–6 (NIV) (page 34)	Proverbs 3:5–6 (NIV) ⁵ Trust in the Lord with all your heart and lean not on your own understanding; ⁶ in all your ways submit to him, and he will make your paths straight.
Proverbs 16:3 (NIV) (page 53)	Proverbs 16:3 (NIV) ³ Commit to the Lord whatever you do, and he will establish your plans.
Psalm 28:7 (NIV) (page 154)	Psalm 28:7 (NIV) ⁷ The Lord is my strength and my shield; my heart trusts in him, and he helps me. My heart leaps for joy, and with my song I praise him.
Psalm 44:21 (NIV) (page 75)	Psalm 44:21 (NIV) ²¹ would not God have discovered it, since he knows the secrets of the heart?
Psalm 127:3–5 (NIV) (page 7)	Psalm 127:3–5 (NIV) ³ Children are a heritage from the Lord, offspring a reward from him. ⁴ Like arrows in the hands of a warrior are children born in one's youth. ⁵ Blessed is the man whose quiver is full of them. They will not be put to shame when they contend with their opponents in court.

Psalm 143:3 (NIV) (page 116)	Psalm 143:3 (NIV) ³ The enemy pursues me, he crushes me to the ground; he makes me dwell in the darkness like those long dead.
Revelation 1:7 (NIV) (page 164)	Revelation 1:7 (NIV) ⁷ "Look, he is coming with the clouds," and "every eye will see him, even those who pierced him"; and all peoples on earth "will mourn because of him." So shall it be! Amen.
Revelation 21:3–4 (NIV) (page 159)	Revelation 21:3–4 (NIV) ³ And I heard a loud voice from the throne saying, "Look! God's dwelling place is now among the people, and he will dwell with them. They will be his people, and God himself will be with them and be their God. ⁴ 'He will wipe every tear from their eyes. There will be no more death' or mourning or crying or pain, for the old order of things has passed away."

Revelation 22:1–5 (NIV) (page 160)	Revelation 22:1–5 (NIV) Eden Restored **22** ¹Then the angel showed me the river of the water of life, as clear as crystal, flowing from the throne of God and of the Lamb ² down the middle of the great street of the city. On each side of the river stood the tree of life, bearing twelve crops of fruit, yielding its fruit every month. And the leaves of the tree are for the healing of the nations. ³ No longer will there be any curse. The throne of God and of the Lamb will be in the city, and his servants will serve him. ⁴ They will see his face, and his name will be on their foreheads. ⁵ There will be no more night. They will not need the light of a lamp or the light of the sun, for the Lord God will give them light. And they will reign forever and ever.
Romans 12:2 (NIV) (page 165)	Romans 12:2 (NIV) ² Do not conform to the pattern of this world, but be transformed by the renewing of your mind. Then you will be able to test and approve what God's will is—his good, pleasing, and perfect will.
Romans 8:18 (NIV) (page 139)	Romans 8:18 (NIV) Present Suffering and Future Glory ¹⁸ I consider that our present sufferings are not worth comparing with the glory that will be revealed in us.
2 Timothy 4:7 (NIV) (page 110)	2 Timothy 4:7 (NIV) ⁷ I have fought the good fight, I have finished the race, I have kept the faith.

ABOUT THE AUTHOR

Laurence W. Trotter II is a retired businessman who, along with his wife, Diane, split their time between Colorado and Wisconsin.

Larry and Diane spend a substantial amount of time with their immediate family of children and grandchildren as well as relatives, who live across the country, following the message from God he received on July 3, 2012: "Focus on God and family for the rest of your life."

Larry and Diane continue mission work around the world and are active in their church.

INDEX

Index

Symbols

kudu 98, 125, 140, 141

L

Lake Mendota 16, 18
Lake Onondaga 18
Lake Powell 153
Lake Quinsigamond 18
Laura Hillebrand 66
Laurence Whittemore Trotter 8
lechwe 140
Led Zeppelin 68
Lee Strobel 29, 35
leopard 83, 100
Lifest 67
Lincoln Memorial 43
lion 81, 83, 89, 90, 91, 94, 100, 101
Lords prayer 69
Los Angeles 147
Louie Zamperini 66
Lou Schuler 175
Lutherans 61

M

Margaret Millar 63
Mark 17, 73
Mark Huggenvik xi, 17, 67, 73
Mark Munsen 175
Martha 27, 37, 132, 148, 155, 174
Martin Luther King, Jr. Memorial 43
Matthew 12, 13, 37, 57, 63, 69, 71
Mediclinic Hospital 129, 146
Menasha Corporation 39
Methodists 61
Michael Joncas 64
Michael W. Smith 67
Mike Porter 52
MIT 18, 19
Morrie Sheppard 171
Mother Emily 73
mountain top minister 155
Mount Morris 49
Mount of the Holy Cross 52, 184
MRI 152, 154
Mule Deer Foundation 95

Mule Deer Unlimited 85

N

Nancy 47, 54, 168
Naomi Rose 90
National Audubon Society 84
National Ski Patrol 48, 49
National Wildlife Federation 84
National Wild Turkey Federation 85
New International Version 56
New Revised Standard Version 56
Newsboys 66
New Testament 7, 12, 13, 28, 37, 56,
  57, 58
Nicky Gumbel 29
Nordic Mountain 49, 50
nyala 98, 140

O

Old Testament 56
On Eagles Wings 64
Open Reduction Internal Fixation
  ORIF 134
Oshkosh 67
Oxford 21
oxycodone 144, 151

P

Pacific Twelve 22
Palanca 62
passive physical therapy 152, 155
Pat Edwards 15
Paul Testwuide 48
PCOS 174
Penn State 19
People for the Ethical Treatment of
  Animals 84
PETA 84
Peter Millett 185
Peyton 168, 169
Pheasants Forever 85, 95
Philmont Hymn 64
PhilMont Scout Ranch 63
poachers 90, 93

Printed in the United States
by Baker & Taylor Publisher Services